Neil Woodward.

The Tyndale New Testament Commentaries

General Editor:
THE REV. CANON LEON MORRIS, M.Sc., M.Th., Ph.D.

GALATIANS

To
my brothers and sisters
in the Church
of South-East Asia

THE LETTER OF PAUL TO THE GALATIANS

AN INTRODUCTION AND COMMENTARY

by

THE REV. CANON R. A. COLE, M.Th., Ph.D.
Church Missionary Society of Australia
Lecturer, Trinity Theological College, Singapore

Inter-Varsity Press
Leicester, England

William B. Eerdmans Publishing Company
Grand Rapids, Michigan

Inter-Varsity Press
38 De Montfort Street, Leicester LE1 7GP, England

Wm. B. Eerdmans Publishing Company
255 Jefferson S.E., Grand Rapids, MI 49503

Published and sold only in the USA and Canada by Wm. B. Eerdmans Publishing Co.

©R. A. Cole 1989

1st edition 1965
2nd edition 1989

Reprinted 1994

Unless otherwise stated, quotations from the Bible are taken from the Revised
Standard Version, copyrighted 1946, 1952, © 1971, 1973 by the Division of Christian
Education, National Council of the Churches of Christ in the USA, and used by
permission.

British Library Cataloguing in Publication Data

Cole. Alan, *1923–*
  The letter of Paul to the Galatians. 2nd ed.
  Bible. N.T. Galatians. Critical studies
  I. Title.   II. Series
  227′.406

  IVP ISBN 0-85111-878-X

Library of Congress Cataloging-in-Publication Data

Cole, R. A. (R. Alan), 1923-
  The letter of Paul to the Galatians : an introduction and
  commentary / by R. A. Cole. — 2nd ed.
  p.   cm. — (The Tyndale New Testament commentaries : 9)
  1. Bible. N.T. Galatians—Commentaries. I. Title. II. Series.
  BS2685.3.C62 1989
  227′.407—dc20   89-27537
                                                CIP

  Eerdmans ISBN 0-8028-0478-0

Set in Palatino
Typeset in Great Britain by Parker Typesetting Service, Leicester
Printed in USA by Eerdmans Printing Company, Grand Rapids, Michigan

*Inter-Varsity Press is the book-publishing division of the Universities and Colleges Christian
Fellowship (formerly the Inter-Varsity Fellowship), a student movement linking Christian
Unions in universities and colleges throughout the United Kingdom and the Republic of Ireland,
and a member movement of the International Fellowship of Evangelical Students. For information
about local and national activities write to UCCF, 38 De Montfort Street, Leicester LE1 7GP.*

GENERAL PREFACE

The original *Tyndale Commentaries* aimed at providing help for the general reader of the Bible. They concentrated on the meaning of the text without going into scholarly technicalities. They sought to avoid 'the extremes of being unduly technical or unhelpfully brief'. Most who have used the books agree that there has been a fair measure of success in reaching that aim.

Times, however, change. A series that has served so well for so long is perhaps not quite as relevant as when it was first launched. New knowledge has come to light. The discussion of critical questions has moved on. Bible-reading habits have changed. When the original series was commenced it could be presumed that most readers used the Authorized Version and one could make one's comments accordingly, but this situation no longer obtains.

The decision to revise and up-date the whole series was not reached lightly, but in the end it was thought that this is what is required in the present situation. There are new needs, and they will be better served by new books or by a thorough up-dating of the old books. The aims of the original series remain. The new commentaries are neither minuscule nor unduly long. They are exegetical rather than homiletic. They do not discuss all the critical questions, but none is written without an awareness of the problems that engage the attention of New Testament scholars. Where it is felt that formal consideration should be given to such questions, they are discussed in the Introduction and sometimes in Additional Notes.

But the main thrust of these commentaries is not critical. These books are written to help the non-technical reader to understand the Bible better. They do not presume a knowledge of Greek, and all Greek words discussed are transliterated; but the authors have the Greek text before them and their comments are made on the basis of the originals. The authors are free to choose their own modern translation, but are asked to bear in mind the variety of translations in current use.

The new series of *Tyndale Commentaries* goes forth, as the former series did, in the hope that God will graciously use these books to help the general reader to understand as fully and clearly as possible the meaning of the New Testament.

LEON MORRIS

CONTENTS

AUTHOR'S PREFACE TO THE FIRST EDITION

The Epistle to the Galatians is spiritual dynamite, and it is therefore almost impossible to handle it without explosions. It has often been so in the history of the Church. The great spiritual awakening of Martin Luther came as he expounded and studied this Epistle, while it was a sermon on Galatians that brought peace of heart to John Wesley. Small wonder that both of these men dearly loved the book; it spoke directly from Paul's experience to their own. But this letter is not one with a message simply for those of centuries earlier than ours, nor is it an Epistle that can be read in comfortable detachment without personal involvement. At every point it challenges our present-day shallow, easy acceptances and provokes our opposition. It was a controversial letter; and it is vain to expect any commentator, however humble, to avoid controversy when expounding it – especially when the issues are just as alive today. The only danger is that we may try to use God's Word as a 'big stick' wherewith to belabour our theological opponents instead of allowing the exegesis to search our own hearts and condemn our own cherished presuppositions.

What, then, is the Epistle to the Galatians? It is a statement of Paul's gospel, which is also that of the Church universal. It is an *apologia pro vita sua* by the prince of apostles. So far, so good; but already we may be on dangerous ground. For Paul was a man whose 'orders' were not accepted by many of his fellow-countrymen. His claim to apostleship they regarded as unwarranted. More; in its refusal to allow salvation to depend on anything save the work done for helpless man by God almighty, and enjoyed by a faith which is itself the gift of God, it is a cry for Christian freedom. True, this condemns those who make salvation depend on forms and ceremonies as well as on faith in Christ (for the crime of the Judaizers was not that they substituted something for Christ's work, but that they tried to add something to it). But it equally condemns those earnest Christians who subconsciously make salvation depend, not only on faith in Christ, but also on the observance of negative moral laws ('There are three things I will not do . . .', in the words of the old negro spiritual). Which of us can throw the first stone?

Furthermore, at the risk of being accused of an anachronism, it could be said that Galatians is a passionate appeal for Inter-Communion. The table-fellowship for which Paul fought at Antioch was certainly not restricted to the Lord's Table, but it is hard to see how it could have failed to include it. On a matter like this, it is painfully easy to allow our own pet theological or ecclesiastical prejudices to blind our eyes; but Paul's reaction is obvious. He cannot conceive the possibility of two groups of Christians in one place who refuse to eat with each other because of theological scruples (for we wrong the Judaizers if we fail to realize that, whatever we may think about the 'play-acting' of Peter and Barnabas, this was a real theological scruple with them).

Again, there seems to be here a recognition that it is possible for the Church of God to be one without being uniform in custom, habit, or sphere. Paul never seems to have compelled the Gentile churches to act like Jews; indeed, this is precisely the charge that he brings against the erring Peter. Now those of us with a 'Reformed' background find this congenial and easy to understand. But it remains equally true that he does not expect Jewish churches to act like Gentile believers; he never says that it is wrong for them to be circumcised, or to keep the law, or to observe the festivals. All he insists is that these things have nothing to do with the gift of salvation. Not only so, but here is also a glad recognition of differences of sphere appointed by God: Paul is to go to the Gentiles; James and the rest are to work among the Jews.

This involves full mutual recognition, which is symbolized, not by any supplemental ordination, but by the offering of the 'right hand of fellowship'. Mutual trust, mutual acceptance, mutual recognition: was this a slender platform on which to work? Yet it was on such a basis that the whole Mediterranean basin was won for Christ.

These are hard sayings for all of us; and who can hear them? Yet, if this is indeed the message of Galatians for today, surely we neglect it at our peril.

R.A.C.

PREFACE TO THE SECOND EDITION

The literature on Galatians, which aroused such attention in the heady days of the Reformation, is immense. It would be pretentious, in a work of this limited size, to attempt to refer to all the commentators of the past. Any modern commentator on this letter is only a dwarf on the shoulders of giants, and happy is the one who has absorbed, sometimes unconsciously or even at second hand, the quintessence of the wisdom of the past.

I have refrained from quoting Luther and Calvin, or later giants like Ramsay and Lightfoot: but I would not wish that to be taken as a failure to acknowledge their worth. Among modern commentators, particular tribute must be paid to Burton (ICC), with his careful and exact linguistic approach, although this now needs to be modified in some areas because of further linguistic evidence. Bruce (NIGNTC) is, as always, careful and erudite, a mine of information, with many historical, linguistic and theological gems especially in his footnotes. Ridderbos (NICNT) is solid and theological, in the 'reformed' pattern, although somewhat succinct. Guthrie (NCBC) is painstaking and thorough, with a particularly good introduction. Cousar (Interpretation Series) has many penetrating insights. But the prince of them all is Betz (Hermeneia Series), and on him I have drawn particularly heavily, especially for his keen theological interpretations, and his suggestions as to the factors that left the Galatians particularly open to new false teaching.

Other commentators will be mentioned by name for specific points as they occur, but most, for obvious and praiseworthy reasons, tend to repeat one another over much of the area, and there is nothing therefore to be gained by simply piling up names.

The text chosen as basis for this revision of my commentary is the RSV. The source of other translations is noted in brackets immediately after the quotation. Throughout the Commentary, I have also included my own paraphrase of the text of Galatians, usually section by section, and this is printed within single quotation marks.

It is a joy to write this Second Edition from the midst of an Asian Church, facing many of the same problems as the Galatians. It is my humble hope that readers will find its relevance to their own situation too.

R.A.C.

CHIEF ABBREVIATIONS

Abbott-Smith G. Abbott-Smith, *A Manual Greek Lexicon of the New Testament* (Edinburgh: T. & T. Clark, 1960 edition).

AV Authorized Version (King James' Version), 1611.

BAGD *A Greek-English Lexicon of the New Testament and Other Early Christian Literature,* ed. by William F. Arndt and F. Wilbur Gingrich, a translation and adaptation of Walter Bauer, *Grieschich-Deutsches Wörterbuch;* second edition revised and augmented by F. Wilbur Gingrich and Frederick W. Danker (Chicago: University of Chicago Press, 1979).

BDF F. Blass, A. Debrunner and R. W. Funk, *A Greek Grammar of the New Testament and Other Early Christian Literature* (Chicago: University of Chicago Press, 1961).

Betz H. D. Betz, *Galatians: a Commentary on Paul's Letter to the Churches in Galatia,* Hermeneia Series (Philadelphia: Fortress Press, 1979).

Bruce F. F. Bruce, *The Epistle to the Galatians: A Commentary on the Greek Text,* NIGNTC (Exeter: Paternoster Press, 1982).

Burton E. de Witt Burton, *The Epistle to the Galatians,* ICC (Edinburgh: T. & T. Clark, 1921).

Cousar Charles B. Cousar, *Galatians, a Bible Commentary for Teaching and Preaching,* Interpretation Series (Atlanta: John Knox Press, 1982).

Daube	D. Daube, *The New Testament and Rabbinic Judaism* (London: Athlone Press, 1956).
Davies	W. D. Davies, *Paul and Rabbinic Judaism* (London: SPCK, ²1955).
Ellis	E. E. Ellis, *Paul's Use of the Old Testament* (Edinburgh: Oliver & Boyd, 1957).
ET	English translation.
GNB	Good News Bible, 1976.
Guthrie	Donald Guthrie, *Galatians*, NCBC (Grand Rapids: Eerdmans, and Basingstoke: Marshall, Morgan and Stott, 1982).
IBD	*The Illustrated Bible Dictionary*, 3 vols. (Leicester: Inter-Varsity Press, 1980).
ICC	The International Critical Commentary.
IDB	*The Interpreter's Dictionary of the Bible*, 4 vols. (Nashville: Abingdon Press, 1979).
IDBS	Supplementary volume to *The Interpreter's Dictionary of the Bible* (Nashville: Abingdon Press, 1979).
JB	The Jerusalem Bible, 1985.
Judge	E. A. Judge, *The Social Pattern of the Christian Groups in the First Century* (London: Tyndale Press, 1960).
Lightfoot	J. B. Lightfoot, *The Epistle to the Galatians* (London: Macmillan, 1900).
Luther	Martin Luther, *A Commentary on St Paul's Epistle to the Galatians* (Grand Rapids: Baker Book House, 1979 [reprint of 1575 English edition]).
LXX	The Septuagint (pre-Christian Greek version of the Old Testament).
Marshall	I. Howard Marshall, *Acts: An Introduction and Commentary*, TNTC (Leicester: Inter-Varsity Press, 1980).
mg.	margin.
MM	J. H. Moulton and G. Milligan, *The Vocabulary of the Greek New Testament Illustrated from the Papyri* (Grand Rapids: Eerdmans, 1980 edition).
Moffatt	J. Moffatt, *A New Translation of the Bible*, 1926.
MT	The Masoretic Text of the Hebrew Old Testament.

Munck	J. Munck, *Paul and the Salvation of Mankind* (ET, London: SCM, and Richmond: John Knox Press, 1959).
NCBC	The New Century Bible Commentary.
NEB	The New English Bible: Old Testament, 1970; New Testament, ²1970).
NICNT	The New International Commentary on the New Testament.
NIGNTC	The New International Greek New Testament Commentary.
NIV	The New International Version, 1973, 1978, 1984.
O'Brien	P. T. O'Brien, *Colossians and Philemon*, Word Bible Commentary (Waco: Word Publishing 1987).
Ridderbos	Herman N. Ridderbos, *The Epistle of Paul to the Churches of Galatia*, NICNT (Grand Rapids: Eerdmans, 1953).
Ropes	J. H. Ropes, *The Singular Problem of the Epistle to the Galatians*, Harvard Theological Studies (Cambridge, Mass.; Harvard University Press, 1929).
RSV	The Revised Standard Version: Old Testament, 1952; New Testament, ²1971.
TDNT	*A Theological Dictionary of the New Testament*, ed. by Gerhard Kittel and Gerhard Friedrich, a translation by Geoffrey W. Bromiley of *Theologisches Wörterbuch zum neuen Testament*, 10 vols. (Grand Rapids: Eerdmans, 1964–76).
TNTC	Tyndale New Testament Commentary.
UBS	United Bible Societies.

INTRODUCTION

Before we approach the exegesis of Galatians, there are three basic questions which we should ask, with some other minor questions which arise from them. The first is: Who were the Galatians to whom the letter was written? The second is: When was the letter written? The third is: Why was the letter written? Fortunately, there is no need to ask a fourth question: By whom was the letter written? Even extreme critics agree that it was written by the apostle Paul; indeed Galatians, along with Romans, Corinthians and Philippians, is sometimes used as a yardstick by which to judge the authenticity of other letters.

Basically, all of these questions must be answered from the evidence of the letter itself, with some help from Acts, and occasional assistance from other Pauline letters, notably the Corinthian letters and the letter to the Romans, though sometimes these other sources solve one problem at the expense of creating another.

Nevertheless, any problems thus created are minor, and the main answer seems clear in each case. In fact, it would not be unfair to say that some at least of the problems are of our own making, for the questions have at times been made unnecessarily complicated by a reluctance to accept simple solutions that will satisfy the available evidence.

Some theories propounded as explanations in the last thirty years have been so artificial and convoluted that they are unlikely to be correct. While it is a basic rule of textual criticism that 'the more difficult the reading, the more likely it is to be correct', this is not necessarily true in more general study of the New Testament. Several such theories will therefore be mentioned briefly in this commentary, but not seriously argued since (with all due deference to their learned proponents) they do not seem to merit it, especially not in a work of this size. Those who are curious are referred to lengthier commentaries for discussions, after which they can make their own judgments.

A further point to be made is that, while the three questions mentioned above are both interesting and relevant, it is not necessary to solve them completely before one can read and appreciate the message of the letter. Indeed, it might be fair to say that solution of the first two problems should hardly affect exegesis, particularly because exegesis should never be based on an unproven hypothesis, however likely that hypothesis may be.

The third question, on the other hand, is very important and must be solved basically by referring to the letter itself. Interest in the first two questions, and therefore space and attention given to them, is by no means as great in modern commentaries as it was in earlier works. The third however, with its associated questions, remains just as absorbing a topic today. This modern neglect may be because it is realized that the hypothetical answers to the first two questions do not basically alter the exegesis of this letter. On the other hand, it may simply be the recognition that absolute certainty on these two questions is impossible on the limited evidence that we have, and no new relevant evidence is likely to emerge. In short, all that can be said has been said already, and said often. This shift of interest to the third question will also be reflected in the present commentary.

I. WHO WERE THE GALATIANS?

To whom was this letter sent? There are basically only two possibilities. The letter could have been sent to the ethnic Galatians, three Celtic tribes akin to the Gauls, who had invaded and subsequently occupied central Asia Minor in the third century before Christ, as the 'North Galatian' theory of its destination asserts. The other possibility is that the letter in fact was written to the racially mixed inhabitants of the Roman province of Galatia, and that the name 'Galatians' was simply used as a handy common term to cover them all, as the 'South Galatian' theory asserts. For, if this was so, then the letter was almost certainly sent to the Christian churches of the non-Celtic south, of whose evangelization we read in Acts 14.

Much here depends first on the linguistic usage of Paul when describing or identifying an area, secondly on the composition of the Roman province of Galatia at various times, and thirdly on the probable extent of Paul's evangelistic journeys in that part of Asia Minor, to judge from the New Testament evidence. Can we then, on the basis of these, maintain the so-called 'North Galatian' position?

Despite much discussion on the subject (for which see larger commentaries), it now seems fairly well established that Paul in his letters (though not necessarily Luke in Acts) usually employed the title of the Roman province to describe an area and its inhabitants, rather than using ethnic or linguistic titles which might be more exact. This, if accepted, would support the view that, for Paul, 'Galatians' simply means 'inhabitants of the Roman province of Galatia'. It is therefore important to consider the composition of the province at various times.

The province of Galatia took its origin from the Celtic kingdom of King Amyntas, who willed it to Rome, but which, at its height, covered a much larger area between the Black Sea and the Mediterranean, always including but not limited to the central area inhabited by the three Celtic tribes. In the time of Paul, after several modifications of frontiers, the province still included large sections of Lycaonia, Pisidia and Phrygia, and was certainly not restricted to the old Celtic heartland. Even there, the Celts seem to have settled as overlords of an original Phrygian population so that the inhabitants were not monochromely Celtic. Although centuries later some certainly still spoke a Celtic language akin to Gaulish (according to Jerome), yet the city dwellers of the area at least were so Hellenized that they were usually known as 'Gallograeci', or 'Hellenized Gauls'.

At first sight, this question of the racial origins of the recipients of the letter might not seem important, but, in past generations, some commentators (even the great Lightfoot) leaned heavily on supposed 'Celtic' characteristics of the recipients to explain the problems which led to the writing of Paul's letter, and thus to establish its destination. This however is sentimental rather than scientific exegesis. The Corinthian Christians, as it has been well remarked, show many of the same characteristics as these 'Galatians', whoever they were, and no scholar has ever tried to prove that the Corinthians were Celts. In short, we are dealing here not with racial characteristics, but simply with the characteristics of 'natural man' and 'natural woman': that is what gives to the letter its universal application and contemporary value. We cannot therefore solve the problem of the destination of the letter in this way, by isolating the racial characteristics, real or imaginary, of its recipients.

Does the history of Paul's evangelistic travels in the general area assist us to pin-point the identity of the churches in question? So far from admitting the point that, if the letter is written to the inhabitants of the Roman province of Galatia in general, it could cover the northern Celts as well as other inhabitants in the south, many commentators have tried to settle the question summarily by claiming that Paul did not and could not have evangelized the northern area at all. In this case, of course, any other argument for a North Galatian destination would fall to the ground completely, for Paul seems clearly to be writing to his own converts. In all fairness, the letter itself gives us no direct clue as to the geographic area of Paul's evangelism. The only two possible references in Acts to evangelism in the north are vague, although Acts 16:6 and 18:23 could perhaps be stretched to cover evangelism and pastoral care by Paul in this area. However, in either instance it would have involved a break with what seems to have been Paul's general strategy of initial evangelism of the main cities of a district, and would also have involved considerable deviation from the most direct routes across Asia Minor, which he usually followed. Recent research on the system of Roman roads in Asia Minor has confirmed that communication (and therefore travel) in this northern area was much more difficult than in the south.

Other than these two passages, there is no reference in Acts either to any evangelism in the northern area or even to the subsequent existence of churches there. This does not of course make the existence of such churches impossible: the 'silences of Acts' on other matters are well known and recognized. But when this silence is taken along with the fact that no North Galatian churches are mentioned elsewhere in the New Testament, and that even the 'delegates' from Galatia, Gaius and Timothy, who accompanied Paul on his financial mission to Jerusalem, seem to have come from the south of the Roman province (Acts 20:4), it becomes almost conclusive.

True, Lightfoot made great efforts to establish from inscriptional evidence the existence of an early Celtic church, complete with its early martyrs, in Ancyra (modern Ankara), one of the original three Celtic cities, but he has not usually convinced other scholars. Even if there had been such a church, in a large centre like Ancyra, it would have been so Hellenized in thinking and outlook that it would hardly have differed from any other Hellenized city church of the eastern Mediterranean. Celtic gods would long ago have taken Greek names, as older Lycaonian gods had done further south (Acts 14:12), and the resultant pagan syncretism would have been the same whether in the north or the south of the area. An original Celtic background would therefore have had little bearing on the main question of the destination of the letter, as determined by the supposed racial characteristics of its recipients, which is Lightfoot's argument: still more basically, if no such churches existed at the time, no letter would be directed to the area.

It is unconvincing to argue that Jewish influence, clearly a major factor among the 'Galatians', would have been as likely in the north as in the south. While perhaps not so numerous, there were certainly Jewish colonists in the larger northern cities, as shown by the tombstones discovered there, though, because of the difficulty of communication, these colonies were not so closely linked with Jerusalem and the mainstream of Jewish life as those further south were. That in itself, combined with the difficulties both of terrain and communication, would make pursuit of Paul by his opponents, the Judaizers, very unlikely in this northern area. If this is so, then the problem that gave rise to the letter could not have arisen there.

Lastly, it is sometimes argued that the supposed reference to the initial evangelism of the 'Galatians' as being due to Paul's illness (4:13 – an uncertain interpretation) proves that the evangelism must have taken place in the 'healthier' area of the bleak northern plateau rather than in the southern area, with its supposedly 'malarial' climate. This is again in the area of speculation, not scholarship: would a sick man (if this is the correct interpretation of the passage) have deliberately tackled the rigours of the far harsher northern climate?

It is of course quite possible that Paul did evangelize the northern area, but, if so, we certainly cannot prove it from the evidence of Scripture, whether of Acts or the Pauline letters. The earliest patristic commentaries believed that this evangelism had taken place, but this is no proof. By their day, the older Roman province had shrunk once again to the original Celtic area in the north, with a few minor additions, so naturally they understood the name 'Galatians' in terms of the linguistic usage of their own day and took it to mean 'ethnic Galatians', living in the north, to whom they assumed that the letter had been sent.

To argue, with some advocates of the North Galatian theory, that to use the term 'Galatians' to describe Phrygians or Lycaonians would have been regarded by them as insulting is unfounded. The 'Galatian' was never a comic figure to the ancient world in the way that, say, the 'Phrygian' was, nor did the name in itself mean, as sometimes claimed, 'country bumpkin'. Besides, what other single collective term could Paul have used to cover the different groups, and what more appropriate term than one taken directly from the name of the province? It does not therefore seem that the term 'Galatians' can be limited to the Celtic inhabitants of the north, while it may possibly include them, if indeed there were churches among them at the time.

Let us now turn to the South Galatian theory, which seems both simple and neat, and certainly fits such evidence as we have. Again, this does not necessarily prove it to be correct, but it certainly gives it probability. This theory assumes that the 'Galatians' addressed in the letter are those groups in the south of the Roman province who had been evangelized by Paul and Barnabas on their first missionary journey (Acts 13 and 14), and revisited by Paul and Silas on their second missionary journey

(Acts 15:36 – 16:6). The 'Galatians' would then be the converts of Derbe, Lystra, Iconium, 'Pisidian' Antioch, and doubtless other small places whose names are unrecorded. We know the fact of their evangelization from the New Testament; we know of Jewish opposition (Acts 13:50; 14:19); and many other small details in the Galatian letter could be very well explained against this known background.

The triple mention of Barnabas in the letter (2:1, 9, 13) might confirm a southern destination, since Barnabas would have been well known to the southern Galatians (Acts 14:12), but quite unknown to the northern Galatians. If Paul did indeed evangelize North Galatia at the later date suggested, then Barnabas had long ceased to be his travel companion (Acts 15:39), in favour of Silas and Timothy (Acts 15:40; 16:3): why then mention him here? Admittedly, Paul also mentions Titus in the letter (2:1), one certainly unknown to the South Galatians: but there is a special reason in the context for this mention. In addition, it is only fair to say that Barnabas is also mentioned in 1 Corinthians 9:6, although there is no biblical evidence to show that he had ever visited Corinth.

Other supporting points in favour of a South Galatian destination could be made, although they are certainly not decisive, but merely makeweights. For instance, the reference to the reception of Paul by the Galatians as 'an angel of God' (4:14) might possibly be a reference to the way in which he had been hailed at Lystra as Hermes, messenger of the gods (Acts 14:12). However, it has been pointed out that this 'angelic' identification was not sustained by the Lycaonians for very long (Acts 14:19), so that perhaps we should not build too much upon it.

Of course, opponents of the South Galatian theory will simply say that this argument from Acts is an example of 'drunkard's search'. If a drunkard has lost a coin on a dark street with only one light, he will search for it beneath the light, not because the coin is more likely to be there rather than elsewhere, but simply because it is the only place where he can see to search for it. In fairness, we must acknowledge the validity of this attack, but say in reply that, if the letter is not written to this particular known group of Christians in the south, then we can know nothing of its possible recipients, for we are completely ignorant

23

of conditions in North Galatia and its assumed churches.

It will be noticed that, in these arguments, both sides build heavily on the historicity of the travel account in Acts, even allowing for selectivity in the narrative, and the possible omission of much material considered by Luke as irrelevant to his main purpose. While a number of modern commentators on Acts (unlike Haenchen) have returned to a high view of its historical reliability (see Marshall), and while this is certainly the position of the present author, it is not strictly necessary to the argument here, except that, if we reject the evidence of Acts, we have no evidence whatsoever on either side as to the foundation of these churches. All would become pure speculation, and, while this may be legitimate, it is certainly not profitable, for one cannot base a logical argument upon pure speculation. The question of the historicity of the account in Acts becomes more directly relevant when considering the relative chronology of Paul's various visits to Jerusalem, as recorded in Acts and Galatians respectively.

If then we return to the original question, 'Who were the Galatians?', we can only say that they were inhabitants of part or parts of the Roman province of Galatia, possibly including the Hellenized Gauls of the north, and certainly including the Hellenized Lycaonians and others of the south. It seems impossible that Paul would have written a letter directed to 'the Galatians' in general which excluded this latter group, particularly in view of his very close and early relations with them (Acts 13 and 14).

To put the matter in another way, it would be strange if we had a Pauline letter addressed to a group of otherwise unknown Christians in the north of the province, where Paul could have spent little time and about whom the book of Acts is strangely silent, but no letter to a familiar group in the south, of which we know much. Again, this is not a compelling argument, but it certainly increases the probability. All the rest of the 'Pauline' letters are written to churches whose early relationships with Paul are clearly spelled out in Acts: witness Thessalonians, Corinthians, Philippians and the 'Asian' letters. Romans is not an exception, for even Rome finds mention in Acts as an intended place of visit, if not of initial evangelism by Paul (Acts

28:16). It would be indeed strange if the Galatians were the only exception to this general rule.

II. WHY WAS THE LETTER WRITTEN?

The simple answer to this question is that the letter was written because of some serious problems that had arisen in Galatia. Paul never wrote letters without good reason, or, if he did, none such have survived. Normally, his letters were written either in reply to questions received from a church (1 Cor. 7:1), or to disquieting news that he has heard about a church (1 Cor. 1:11), or both. Even a letter like Romans, which at first sight seems to be of a more 'casual' nature, on closer examination proves to be not only an exposition of the gospel, but also a treatment of certain well-defined problems, of the existence of which at Rome Paul either knew or guessed (*e.g.* Ro. 14:1–9)

Therefore, we are really asking: what was the problem in Galatia? That it was a serious problem, we can tell from the abruptness with which Paul introduced the matter, without his usual opening section of tactful commendation of the local church (Gal. 1:6; contrast 1 Cor. 1:1–9). The problem seems to have been some new line of teaching, probably introduced soon after Paul's departure (1:6), by an unnamed person (1:9) or persons (1:7).

Whatever its proponents believed or claimed, Paul utterly denies to this new teaching the title of a gospel (1:6): to him, it is only a distortion of Christ's true gospel (1:7). It certainly involved the acceptance of circumcision as a necessity for salvation (5:2). Whatever its proponents may have initially said, this acceptance of circumcision involved in Paul's eyes the obligation to keep the whole of the law of Moses (5:3). It is indeed very likely that the new missionaries themselves actually preached this total obligation, but there is no direct evidence in Galatians as to this, apart from a reference (4:10) to the new observance of 'days, and months, and seasons, and years' by the Galatian converts. These words, virtually a quotation from Genesis 1:14, are probably best taken as referring to Jewish festivals, but see the Commentary at 4:10 for alternate possible explanations of a more general nature.

Worse still, to Paul at least, this obligation to keep the whole law implied that salvation was to be attained by obedience to the law, not, as he had initially preached to them, by simple faith in Christ (3:2). That was what made it 'no gospel', an utter apostasy from Christ (5:4). To Paul, this move was therefore an abandonment of Christian liberty in exchange for the old slavery under the law from which they had just escaped (5:1), and a rejection of the gift of the 'Spirit of freedom' which to him was the fulfilment of the great promise made by God to Abraham (3:14).

It was therefore to Paul just as complete an apostasy as that faced by the writer of Hebrews (Heb. 6:4–6), and, as such, its proponents came under a similar solemn curse (1:8 and Heb. 6:8). Admittedly, in the letter to the Hebrews it was a case of open abandonment by the converts of their new-found Christianity in favour of their old Judaism: but Paul seems to have seen the Galatian declension as being just as serious, since it made obedience to the law just as essential to salvation as trust in the crucified Messiah.

To Paul, it was unbelievable that such foolishness could have occurred so quickly (1:6): he cannot understand it. It was as though advanced scholars were deliberately returning to the kindergarten ABC, to the elementary lessons which no doubt once had their rightful place, but had long ago been superseded in God's plan ('weak and beggarly elemental spirits', 4:9). Whatever may be said about his later letters (see O'Brien on Col. 2:8), Paul does not seem to be referring here to 'elemental powers', much less to forces of evil, as the cause of their trouble or the object of their worship. It is the immaturity and futility of these observances to which Paul draws attention in this context. Indeed, he wonders if all his toil in evangelism of the Galatians had been for nothing after all (4:11).

Paul is so indignant and the matter is so urgent that we cannot expect a detailed account in the letter itself of the teaching brought by these new and unidentified missionaries. After all, both he and the Galatians knew well what the teaching was: why should he expand it? It is however fairly clear even from the limited evidence within the letter that the teachers were not simply Jewish missionaries, whether orthodox or sectarian, seeking to win Gentile Christian converts to the faith of Judaism, although, if some of the Galatian converts to Christianity had previously been Jewish proselytes, as in Acts 13:43, such an attempt at re-conversion would have been understandable. It is also most unlikely, as some have speculated, that they were simply local Gentiles who were attracted to Jewish forms of Christianity, or even that they were Jewish sectarians, tinged with Gnosticism, philosophic speculation and magical practices. Ephesians and Colossians know such groups, but not Galatians. Rather, they were Jewish Christians who were insisting on circumcision, and probably also full observance of the law of Moses, on the part of Gentile Christians, as essential for salvation.

That was the point at issue: Jewish Christians might still continue to circumcise their children, and presumably might also teach them to keep the law, without compromising the gospel. According to Acts 21:21, although Paul was accused of opposing these general practices among Jewish Christians, he in fact did not. Indeed, when in a Jewish environment, he observed the precepts of the law himself (1 Cor. 9:20 and Acts 21:26), and of course he himself had been circumcised, and he had indeed circumcised Timothy (Acts 16:3).

If all this is so, the teachers must have been the group often called by the handy, if coined, modern name of 'Judaizers'. Paul himself only uses the verb, not the noun (2:14), and he uses it in the slightly different sense of 'behave like a Jew'. Paul cannot be referring in Galatians to Jewish teachers attempting to proselytize Gentile Christian converts to Judaism, for that would have involved the complete rejection of Christ and his cross: and this the new teachers did not apparently do. Instead, according to Paul, they robbed the cross of all its importance (2:21), and removed its shame as a 'stumbling block' (5:11). Paul accuses them bluntly of doing this simply to avoid Jewish persecution (6:12). They may have been Jewish Christians desperately trying to accommodate Christianity to Judaism, as doubtless many did in early days, when, before the final breach with Temple and synagogue (beginning with Acts 8:1), Christianity was still regarded by many Jews as a Jewish sect (Acts 28:22). No doubt this pressure for accommodation of Christianity to Judaism increased as the cataclysm of 70 AD grew steadily nearer, and national feelings mounted higher. But by religion these teachers were Christians, not Jews: that was what aroused Paul's anger.

Can we find any other hints in Galatians that help us to pin-point the identity of the teachers? From the indignant outburst of the first two chapters, it is obvious that these teachers also belittled Paul's authority as an apostle: indeed, they probably denied him the title. Instead, they magnified the position of the Jerusalem apostles, particularly of the 'three pillars', Peter and James and John (2:9). That may give us a hint as to their origin and nature, and indirectly therefore as to their teaching. To them, the authority of their gospel depended on the authority of its apostolic proponents, and they seemed to have claimed Jerusalem and the 'Jerusalem apostles' as the source of their 'gospel', as distinct from that of Paul.

This of course will be denied both by Paul and the Jerusalem apostles themselves, for both of whom there was only one gospel, although it had admittedly two different 'target areas' (2:6–9), but that is not the point at the moment. It seems to be mistaken exegesis to assume that 'the gospel to the circumcised' (2:7) means a gospel which also preaches circumcision: it means 'evangelism of Jews' and no more: 'the mission to the circumcised' (2:8), in spite of Betz.

There is one other passage in Galatians that may help us: it is the passage dealing with the confrontation between Paul and Peter at Antioch (2:11 onwards). At first, Peter and the other Jewish Christians there had eaten freely with the Gentile Christians at Antioch, whether the reference is to ordinary meals or to the Lord's Supper, or more probably to both. This would involve ignoring, for the time at least, the Jewish ceremonial food laws, for these were certainly not being observed by the Gentile Christians. However, when 'certain men came from James', Peter, along with the other Jewish Christians, stopped eating with the Gentile Christians, for fear of 'the circumcision party' (or possibly just 'the circumcised'), something which aroused both Paul's anger and his rebuke (2:14). Indeed, it is in this context that Paul uses the verb 'to Judaize' in the slightly different sense of 'to live like Jews' (2:14) with reference to Peter's present behaviour, in opposition to his previous propensity to 'live like a Gentile'.

It is important to note that, irritated as Paul may have been by the pre-eminence accorded by his adversaries to the three 'Jerusalem pillars', he, unlike some modern scholars, does not accuse either James or Peter or John of holding such 'Judaizing' views, still less of propagating them. Indeed, it is Peter's 'hypocrisy' (or 'play acting'), by behaving in a way which is contrary to his real beliefs, which annoys Paul particularly (2:13). How could Peter ever have believed this, after his experience with Cornelius, recorded in Acts 10? After all, this very matter of eating with non-Jews, and therefore presumably of eating ceremonially unclean food, had been the point at issue on that occasion too (Acts 11:3).

We may therefore assume that this 'circumcision party', in addition to insisting on circumcision and the observance of Jewish festivals, also pressed strongly the Mosaic food laws, whatever else they did about the rest of the Torah. After all, Sabbath, circumcision, and food laws were the three most obvious distinguishing features among the Jews of the Dispersion, and in that sense at least were the heart of the Torah.

The only other evidence in Galatians itself as to their teaching concerns again this basic demand for the circumcision of Gentile converts, of which we have already spoken, and which Paul had successfully opposed in the case of Titus (2:3). It seems wrong-headed exegesis to claim that Titus was indeed circumcised, but that he accepted it voluntarily rather than compulsorily: see the Commentary for details here. Titus, in fact, obviously represented everything that these new teachers opposed: he was an uncircumcised Gentile Christian, non-observant of the Jewish ritual law, yet fully accepted at Jerusalem as a brother.

All the evidence of Acts agrees with what we have gathered from Galatians so far. In Acts, Cornelius the centurion had been an uncircumcised Gentile like Titus, and yet the Spirit had come on him (Acts 10:44). He had been baptized (Acts 10:48), and Peter had thereafter eaten with him (Acts 11:3). This fact was bitterly resented by 'the circumcision party' at Jerusalem (Acts 11:2), a group clearly not simply equivalent to 'the Jewish

Christians' in total, and equally clearly distinguished in the context from 'the apostles and the brethren' (Acts 11:1).

Who were the circumcision party, then? Almost certainly, they were the same as the 'believers who belonged to the party of the Pharisees' (Acts 15:5), who had laid down at the very outset of the Council of Jerusalem the demand that Gentile believers must be circumcised and taught to keep the law of Moses (Acts 15:5). If this is so, it is very reasonable to suppose that it was some of the same group who 'came down from Judea' to Antioch, and were equally bluntly teaching there that, without circumcision in accordance with the Torah of Moses, salvation in Christ was impossible (Acts 15:1). It is not surprising that teaching like this, in a mixed yet largely Gentile Christian church (Acts 11:20–21), caused a furore.

But if they were teaching like this in Antioch, it is also reasonable to suppose that it was some of the same group, or at least those with similar views, who were the source of the troubles in Galatia (1:7), for the teaching seems to have been the same. Certainly, in Paul's later days, teachers spreading similar views seem to have travelled very widely in the wake of Paul (Phil. 3:2), and there is no reason why they should not have done so at an earlier stage also.

But if all this is true (and it is simple, consistent and likely), then, with apologies to Ropes and the title of his book, there is no 'singular problem of Galatians' to consider. The source of the teaching attacked by Paul is obvious, and its nature equally so. There is no need to postulate in Galatia (whatever the evidence of other places at a later period) Jewish-gnostic sects with their syncretistic teaching, or to suppose that the source of the Galatian problem was not Jewish Christians but Gentile Christians, possibly even some of the very Galatians themselves, in misdirected zeal for Jewish orthodoxy, as Ropes argues. Still less need we argue, with him, that there was also a 'radical' group of Gentile Christians in Galatia, who wished to reject the Old Testament roots of the gospel, and that Paul therefore had to fight on two fronts at once: in Galatians he fights on one front only.

III. WHEN WAS THE LETTER WRITTEN?

If we start from the evidence of the letter itself, clearly it was written some time after the evangelization of the area by Paul. The duration of this gap is not certain, in spite of Paul's expressed surprise that the Galatians had turned 'so quickly' to another gospel (1:6). This phrase might cover a period of months or a period of years, for Paul, in his indignation, may be speaking figuratively, not literally.

Nevertheless, a shorter rather than a longer period is more likely, as being the simplest interpretation. If, as most scholars assume, *to proteron* in 4:13 should be translated 'on the former occasion', and not simply 'at first' (see RSV), then at least two visits by Paul to the region must be assumed, although BAGD denies that any distinction is being drawn here between an earlier and a later visit. In any case, although in this letter Paul tells us much of his early life and of his relations with the Jerusalem apostles, whether at Jerusalem or at Antioch, he tells us absolutely nothing of the history of his visits to 'Galatia', wherever it was. Presumably this was because the chronology of their own evangelism was already well known to the Galatians themselves, whereas Paul's exact relations with the Jerusalem apostles were hitherto unknown to them, and therefore needed to be explained, to avoid possible misunderstandings, and to strengthen Paul's position.

For external information on Paul's Galatian visits we must therefore turn to the book of Acts which, as we have seen, describes in detail the evangelism of South Galatia only, saying nothing of the north. This southern evangelism was done on the outward 'leg' of the first missionary journey by Barnabas and Paul (Acts 13 and 14), who then retraced their steps through the same area on the way home (Acts 14:21–23). This conceivably could be interpreted as the two Galatian visits, although admittedly, if so, they were undertaken very close to each other. The next possible date for a visit to the area would be after the Council of Jerusalem (Acts 15:41), which seems too late, and would pose other problems.

If these are accepted as the two visits mentioned in the letter, and if the situation addressed by Paul arose very soon after this initial evangelism, the letter to the Galatians could be very early. Indeed, it could just conceivably be the earliest of Paul's letters. Incidentally, an early date, whether well before or during the early stages of the Council, would account for the otherwise puzzling fact that Paul nowhere appeals, in the letter to the Galatians, to the decrees of the Council, which, if quoted, would surely have ended the whole argument at once. However, if this visit on the way home is judged to be too close to the first visit to be counted as a separate occasion, we must see the required second visit as coming at the beginning of the second missionary journey when Paul, with Silas, traversed the area again (Acts 15:40). In that case, the omission of any reference to the decrees of the Council would be even more remarkable, since Acts 16:4 records the missionaries as publishing the decrees of Jerusalem among the churches on this visit. Of course, Paul may have had special reasons for not wanting to refer to this 'conciliar' weapon in writing to Galatia itself at the time.

If on the other hand we insist on a purely North Galatian destination for the letter, then both possible visits to the area recorded in Acts (16:6 and 18:23) would have been even later than this last postulated visit to the south, and well after the Council of Jerusalem. In that case, the letter must have been written considerably later, perhaps from Ephesus during Paul's long Ephesian ministry (Acts 19:10), when the absence of any reference to the Jerusalem decree is a real problem. Of course, even if the destination was South Galatia, this place and late date of composition would be possible, provided that the interval between the initial evangelism and the fall of the Galatians into heresy was not thereby made too long to fit the wording 'so quickly' (1:6), for it is obvious that Paul must have written his letter as soon as he heard the bad news. There is therefore no necessary connection between destination and date: however, a northern destination makes an early date impossible, while a southern destination allows it, without compelling it.

Are there any other external criteria by which to date the letter? To travel further, along this road, we must enter on highly debatable country. For instance, the letter to the Galatians clearly stands in some relation to the letter to the Romans, even if it is not a mere 'rough draft' of it, as some commentators have claimed: there are too many important differences to allow that. Nevertheless, all scholars would agree that the Galatian letter is earlier than Romans: and Romans can be dated to between 55 and 58 AD. How much earlier then is Galatians? Further, there is the obvious relationship of Galatians to the Corinthian letters, especially perhaps to 2 Corinthians, in particular to 2 Corinthians 10 to 13, although it is not necessary to the argument to claim that these chapters constitute a separate letter, as many, including Bruce, have done.

While Romans may have deep theological links with Galatians, the Corinthian letters (and especially these particular chapters of 2 Corinthians) have equally deep emotional links, perhaps because both deal with Paul's personal relationships, whether with his converts or with Jerusalem. From this internal evidence, some scholars have tried to argue an order of Corinthians, Galatians, Romans, or even to 'sandwich' Galatians at a slightly earlier date between various parts of the Corinthian correspondence. This last is probably to put too much weight on the evidence, which after all is largely based on subjective judgments.

Indeed, equally tenable on these grounds would be an order of Galatians, Corinthians, Romans. A good case could be made for the view that, in the Corinthian letters, Paul is carefully qualifying some of the general statements that he has already made in Galatians (contrast, for instance, 3:28 with 1 Cor. 11:1–16), presumably because indiscriminate application of the new principle in local conditions had led to abuse in the Corinthian church. However, this is again somewhat subjective. In each of the letters, Paul is dealing directly with the problems of the particular church involved, and it may simply be that, in one church, Paul was basically addressing theological problems, and, in the other church, practical moral issues. That he will ultimately deal with both sets of issues theologically is characteristic of Paul.

While therefore it seems clear that Galatians is earlier than Romans, it is by no means as clear (while still possible) that Galatians is earlier than 1 and 2 Corinthians, although it certainly hangs closely with them.

One other suggestion based on stylistic and theological grounds is that Galatians is datable (history permitting) as being after the Thessalonian letters, because of their general simplicity and their central interest in eschatology. While the main lines of Paul's theological thought were undoubtedly set by the initial revelation of Christ on the Damascus Road, to which he appeals on several occasions, and his subsequent period of reflection in 'Arabia' (1:17), there is no need to deny the possibility of progression in the deeper understanding and fuller expression of that faith as Paul's life and Christian experience continued. If, for instance, we accept Ephesians and Colossians as Pauline in the full sense, such development seems incontrovertible: indeed, it seems obvious even in a 'prison' letter like Philippians.

If this is allowed, it would certainly be hard to date Thessalonians after Galatians. But the letters to the Thessalonians could obviously not have been written till some time after the evangelization of Thessalonica on the second missionary journey (Acts 17:1–10), so that already we are approaching the period of the Corinthian ministry and therefore the date of the Corinthian correspondence.

However, as Bruce wisely points out, the total span of years involved is not great, since most of Paul's earlier letters seem to have been written within a decade. Even if we include the 'captivity letters', that adds only a few years more, which does not allow much time for major theological development within the period of the letter-writing. If, as Bruce guesses, Paul was converted in his thirties, and wrote the letters in his fifties, he has already had plenty of time to mature his thought, while his theological interests, as shown in the different letters, may well have varied, possibly according to the local needs.

The third and last way to approach the problem of dating is to compare the account of Paul's visits as given in Acts with that given in Galatians itself, although this is notoriously difficult. Naturally, in his letter, Paul is describing past events. If we can identify the last event recorded in Galatians, then at least we shall have a date after which the letter must have been written, although we do not know how long afterwards. Contrariwise, if there is some significant and datable external event which is not mentioned in the letter, it is probable that the letter was written before that date, unless, of course, Paul omitted reference to the event, either accidentally or deliberately for some particular purpose of his own.

Such an event is the Council of Jerusalem of Acts 15, to be dated fairly certainly as about 49 AD. Paul in Galatians certainly does not refer explicitly to the Council, but some editors see oblique references in the opening chapters, either to the council itself, or to the cluster of hurried and semi-official meetings that doubtless preceded and accompanied it (Acts 15:4): for this possibility, see the Commentary. This again would be a pointer to the date.

All that we can say for certain is that (with deference to Bruce) Galatians is not likely, to judge from internal evidence, to be Paul's earliest letter; that it was certainly written before Romans; that it belongs to the general thought-world of the Corinthian letters, but, if anything, is slightly earlier; that it could have been written either in the immediate context of the Council of Jerusalem or just after it.

As will be seen from the Commentary, this interpretation depends on a satisfactory harmonization of the accounts of Paul's Jerusalem visits as recorded respectively in Acts and Galatians. At face value, Acts records three such visits (Paul's initial visit, Acts 9:26; the so-called 'famine visit', Acts 11:30; and the 'council visit', Acts 15:2), and Galatians records only two: here again see the Commentary at 1:18 and 2:1. Yet Galatians 2 certainly describes the same theological climate as that recorded in Acts 15:1, which seems to have arisen only shortly before the Council of Jerusalem took place. This would involve equating the 'second visit' of Galatians 2:1 with the 'third visit' of Acts 15:2. These are not of course insuperable problems, but they do make absolute certainty difficult, in view of the insufficient evidence contained within the pages of the new Testament. For a detailed discussion of this complicated problem, see Marshall, pp. 243–248. It may perhaps be best to assume that Paul in Galatians omitted reference to the so-called 'famine visit' of Acts 11:30 as irrelevant to the question, and not concerned with theological issues at all. Otherwise, we should have to assume that Galatians 2:1 refers to the 'famine visit', and this would pose even more problems than it solved.

IV. WHY DID THE GALATIANS FALL AWAY SO SOON?

This is in many ways an even more interesting question, because it introduces at once the question of the relevance of the letter for Christians today. Various illuminating suggestions have been made by modern editors, not least by Betz, in addition to the obvious answers directly drawn from the text, already familiar from the older editors.

Of course, as Paul frequently says, the cross is always 'a stumbling block' and 'folly' to 'natural' men and women (1 Cor. 1:23). 'Judaizing' in the Galatian sense may not remove the cross altogether, but it does save from persecution because of the cross (6:12), and no doubt the desire to escape persecution was one Galatian motive for accepting circumcision, as Paul bluntly says. After all, most of the early persecution of the Christians in South Galatia was instigated, according to Acts, by those of Jewish faith, not by pagan religions or government officials (Acts 13:50; 14:19). It is very likely that pressure from this quarter continued, or even intensified, after Paul's departure from the scene, although, as Cousar points out, such persecution was rarely directed to Gentile Christian converts, but rather to those converts won from Judaism.

Perhaps another reason for the rapid fall was the subtle attraction of trying to do something to earn their own salvation, impossible task though that might be. Human pride finds it very hard to accept free grace. Perhaps too there was something of intellectual pride in being now able to dismiss the simple Pauline gospel (1 Cor. 1:21) as a crude 'first stage' only: here was something to add to it, to ennoble it, to 'respectabilize' it in the eyes of the world. Perhaps there was also something of the lure of the outward and impressive as opposed to the inward and spiritual. Judaism was a very 'visible' religion in many ways in the ancient world, and even to keep Jewish festivals and food laws would give Gentile Christians a 'stake' in an impressive external system, as impressive outwardly as anything in their former paganism (compare the temptation faced in Hebrews).

All this to Paul was merely 'to glory in your flesh' (6:13), which must have been as attractive an option then as now.

Triumphalism is never dead, even within the Christian church, though Paul tries to restrict all such triumphalism to the cross of Christ (6:14) by a typical and deliberate paradox.

But all of these possible reasons, valid though they may be, have been long recognized as factors, still operative today. What are the newer insights that modern editors have given us? It is only fair to say that, as with all 'modern insights', we may simply be reading back our own contemporary interests and current problems into the letter to the Galatians: that is always a danger. But, if Christian life and experience are eternally the same, and if fallen human nature has not changed over the centuries, it is highly likely that what are basic problems and tendencies today were also problems then, even if the outward expression of these tendencies was not the same. By using these methods, we may be able to see an immediate possible application of Galatians to the church of our own day, apart altogether from its great central doctrines, with their eternal relevance.

For instance, it may be that the Galatian problem sprang from misunderstanding of, or over-emphasis on, one aspect of biblical truth. To judge from the letter, the Galatian churches appear to have been what we would nowadays call somewhat 'charismatic', in the same way, although not perhaps to the same degree as, for example, the Corinthian church was. True, this aspect is not as prominent in Galatians as in the Corinthian letters, since it had not become an issue as it had at Corinth. We can tell the charismatic nature of the Galatian churches not only from the way in which Paul confidently appeals to their initial experience of the reception of the Spirit by faith (3:2), but also from the way in which he appeals to the performance of *dynameis*, 'miracles' (3:5), among the Galatians by the same Spirit as evidence of his continuing presence. This is indeed made doubly clear by the present tense of the two verbs, 'supplies' and 'works' (3:5).

Now, while it is perfectly true theologically that *dynameis*, 'acts of power', do not have to be physical miracles, that is the usual meaning in the New Testament, and it may well have been this that the Galatian church had come to expect. As the birth of the church at Lystra had been associated with one such act of power (Acts 14:10), this mention here is not surprising. This does not say that 'miracles' in this physical form should necessarily and universally mark every Christian church at all times: there are differing views on this matter held by equally godly Christian brothers and sisters. But it does seem from Scripture that this was the initial experience of the Galatian church in early days, as can be seen from the way in which the subject is mentioned so casually, indeed, almost incidentally here.

Have we perhaps therefore, as Betz suggests, an example of 'discouraged charismatics' in Galatia? One cannot live for ever on a continual diet of spiritual excitement and thrill, legitimate part of the Christian life though they may be. Indeed, as Cousar wisely observes, these things do not in themselves necessarily prove that God's Spirit is at work. Steady persistence in the faith in difficult circumstances is the true test of spiritual life. Paul had warned at least the elders of the South Galatian churches in very sober words that they must 'continue in the faith', and that they must enter the kingdom of God 'through many tribulations' (Acts 14:22): had they perhaps not sufficiently heeded his words? The church of Galatia had been born in persecution (Acts 14:5, 19), a fact to which the letter also may refer (3:4). That this was continuing persecution may be shown by 4:29, and such persecution could only have increased their general discouragement.

It has been a common occurrence in church history for a church or group of this 'pneumatic' nature, when discouraged either by the sheer grind of continuance in everyday tasks, especially if accompanied by persecution, or by the lack of systematic Bible teaching, or possibly by the discontinuance of the experience of miracles as a regular part of their ongoing church life, to turn to outward and sometimes heavily structured forms of church life for spiritual reassurance: is that what was happening now in Galatia? It may have seemed to them that there was a security and religious continuity in the thousand years and more of Israel's spiritual history, with its well-known and tested religious precepts and practices.

In subsequent church history, disillusioned 'enthusiastics', as the sixteenth century would have called them, have often either abandoned the Christian faith entirely, or joined a church with a clearly-set structure of creed and ritual, as indeed the Galatians were tempted to do in this case. This is in no sense to compare any branch of the Christian church to Judaism: it is simply to give an example of a similar psychological tendency, in similar circumstances. In either case the disappointed 'enthusiastic' is seeking external reassurance for faith, no longer in the exciting and the miraculous but instead in the organizational.

However, if, on this reasoning, one reason for the problem in Galatia may have been the misunderstanding by the Galatian converts of the doctrine of the Spirit, and of the place of the spectacular in the Christian life, perhaps a second cause was the misunderstanding of the closely associated doctrine of Christian freedom. Bruce, in the title of one of his books, has aptly called Paul 'the Apostle of the Free Spirit', and this he certainly was. The whole contrast in the letter to the Galatians is between freedom and imprisonment, whether it is the old imprisonment under the law before conversion to Christ, or the new imprisonment into which the Galatians were unconsciously slipping back. This, to Paul, is also the contrast between 'the Spirit' and 'the flesh', the spiritual world and the natural world (3:3). But he is equally concerned to assert that the liberty of the Spirit is not licence (5:13): that would equally be of 'the flesh', and therefore an equal bondage.

Perhaps the Galatians had not yet realized the truths of Romans 7, that even after conversion and filling by the Spirit, even after the possible occurrence of *dynameis*, 'miracles', or 'acts of power', every Christian man or woman is still at one and the same time both justified and yet a sinner, to quote a great Reformation doctrine. Did they think, as many have thought since, that they could never sin again after reception of the Spirit? Had they therefore failed to realize that liberty in the Spirit could only too easily become licence? So several modern commentators have suggested.

If so, one can easily imagine both their disillusionment and their frustration when they found that sin still remained as a force with which to reckon, both in their own lives and in the lives of other Christians around them. Liberty, so easily become licence, may have seemed to them to be too dangerous a concept to hold without stricter guidelines. Had Paul misled them after all, or had he over-simplified the position?

If, at this moment, they were faced with eager Jewish-Christian missionaries who offered them a detailed system of moral and ritual rules designed especially to control these manifestations of 'the flesh', this rigid outward discipline must have seemed very attractive to earnest souls who had come to the conclusion that the path of freedom did not work for them, as indeed the Judaizers had probably always maintained, and that their basic natures had not changed. The Corinthian correspondence gives examples of the gross moral lapses perfectly possible in the most 'spiritual' of young churches, especially where there are no strong past traditions of moral conduct, as there were in Judaism, but not in most forms of paganism.

Of course, Paul would demolish this spurious argument for Judaizing by pointing out that mere outward observance of formal rules was just as 'fleshly' as the immoral situations with which it was supposed to deal (Col. 2:16–18), but that would not lessen its appeal to the disillusioned and yet earnest. Practical antinomianism to them was not a vague possible danger, but an observed and experienced result, although it is unlikely that, as some editors hold, there was actually an organized 'antinomian party' in Galatia, with whom Paul also had to contend. Nevertheless, Paul would deal with this issue by his concept of 'the law of Christ' (6:2), the new law of love (5:14), which would make any form of selfish licence impossible, as well as by the doctrine of the indwelling Christ, whose living presence alone makes conformity to this new 'law' possible. Ultimately, the answer lies in Paul's concept of Christian experience as being a sharing in Christ's cross and resurrection (2:20). Not unconnected is the fact that, in Galatians, despite the mention of *dynameis*, 'miracles', as occurring (3:5), Paul does not dwell in this letter on the gifts of the Spirit, as he does in Corinthians. Rather, he stresses the fruit of the Spirit (5:22–24) as the truest proof of the Spirit's presence, and as that which makes antinomianism impossible.

That raises the further question, Had Paul never dealt with these topics before? If he had, how could the Galatians have forgotten them so completely and so quickly? The latter is precisely Paul's own despairing question (1:6); but first let us ask, If he had not dealt with them, what was the reason for it?

Had Paul perhaps not had time to develop these 'protective' doctrines in his hurried initial visit or visits to the South Galatians, as some have suggested? Or had he as yet had insufficient experience of 'raw Gentile' evangelism (as distinct from evangelism of Jews) to realize the necessity of steady and developed teaching on these points? Did he first raise these issues in the letter itself? This would not of course be theoretically impossible, and would in no way conflict with the doctrine of revelation, but it does not seem likely. There does indeed seem to be a steady development and increasing many-sidedness in Paul's theological thought over the years, whereby he never denies anything that he taught in early years, but often seems to amplify it. Those who follow this train of thought would claim with some justification that both Corinthians and Romans amplify, and, to that extent, qualify the simple all-embracing statements made within Galatians. If this is so, could not Galatians itself be amplifying the still simpler teaching given initially and verbally to the converts? Even within Galatians, the statements made by Paul to correct the error are somewhat blunt and unqualified (see Commentary for examples), compared with those of the later letters.

But all this bluntness and the rough-hewn nature of the statements does not necessarily mean that Paul had not made similar statements already in his initial preaching to the Galatians, still less that he was ignorant of the need for making them. After all, before his career as a peripatetic missionary, Paul had worked for a long time in the largely Gentile atmosphere of Antioch (Acts 11:26, with 11:20), where such moral problems must have existed. The reason for the sweeping statements may be simply that this letter was forged white-hot in the fires of controversy. Strong, bold pronouncements needed to be made anew to the Galatians, not qualified and carefully balanced theological statements, covering all possible later misunderstandings and eventualities. Further, Paul does not seem to be conscious of any new aspects in his teaching: rather, he appeals confidently to it as something already well known (1:8 and 5:21).

The pastoral situation faced in the Corinthian correspondence, or the reflective theological presentation of the letter to the Romans, were more suitable for these measured statements than the spiritual life and death struggle in Galatia. Besides (as hinted above), the whole stress in the letter to the Galatians is that the converts seem to have forgotten all the most elementary teaching given them by Paul. Their whole attitude is as much beyond Paul's comprehension as it is puzzling to us today. They must have been 'bewitched', he says simply (3:1): no merely logical explanation of such total forgetfulness would suffice.

But unfortunately this is a situation only too familiar to any teacher of the Bible or indeed of anything else that runs counter to humanity's natural wishes and inclinations. Paul's great task in this letter is therefore to continually remind the Galatians of what he has already told them (1:9), and what they should know well already, rather than to introduce new and deeper doctrines, as in 1 Corinthians 3:1–2. That being so, it is gratuitous to assume that Paul in this letter is hastily applying theological 'sticking-plasters', the need for which he had not foreseen previously. We cannot make easy excuses like this to explain away the total misunderstanding by the Galatians of the nature of the gospel, for, if we do, we shall even more readily make them for others or even for ourselves. The theological value of the letter to the Galatians lies in the fact that the Galatians are so similar to Christians of every age.

V. WHAT IS THEOLOGICALLY CENTRAL TO THE LETTER?

In the sixteenth century, a question like this would have been answered by Protestants directly and unanimously as 'the doctrine of justification by faith'. Indeed, some of the greatest giants of the Reformation (like Luther and Calvin) virtually based this whole doctrine on Galatians and Romans. In more modern and critical times, the centrality of this doctrine to the letter has often been questioned. Justification by faith, it is sometimes said, is only one of many themes contained within Galatians, and not necessarily central to it.

Part of this reluctance is no doubt due to the ecumenical and eirenic spirit of the age, along with a reluctance to reopen old historical battles. Nevertheless, precisely because church reunion negotiations are widely taking place today, both the doctrine and Galatians itself are coming afresh under intense study, especially by Roman Catholics, Lutherans and Anglicans. Recent Lutheran-Catholic negotiations in the United States for instance have produced a very scholarly study on the doctrine, which is fully theological and does not minimize the wide differences that exist even today between the various viewpoints held on the matter.

More typical however is a product of the Anglican-Roman Catholic negotiations. Equally intended to deal with the doctrine of justification by faith as a possible point of difference between the churches today as it certainly was in Reformation days, it appeared under the title 'Salvation and the Church', maintaining that justification by faith was only one minor sector of Christian doctrine and should not be handled in isolation either from the general theme of salvation or from the overarching theme of the church. If justification by faith is denied a place as a central doctrine in theology, it is not surprising that its central place in the letter to the Galatians is questioned.

Now, to say that in Galatians Paul is dealing with the doctrine of justification by faith is probably a misnomer. Paul actually deals with the Christian experience of justification by faith and reception of the promised Spirit, and undergirds and vindicates this theologically by Scripture. Also to say that he deals with the doctrine narrowly or in isolation would be incorrect. It is true to say that there are numerous other topics also treated in the letter – salvation through Christ, union with Christ, unity in Christ, liberty in Christ, the promised gift of the Spirit, the fruits of the Spirit, the consequent practical demands of Christian living in everyday circumstances, and so on. Yet all of these stem from the new, totally transforming relationship with God in Christ which is enjoyed through faith, and Paul's word for this is 'justification', which for him is no legal fiction, but a transforming spiritual experience.

There can be no doubt that the central topic of Galatians is the question as to how and why we are accepted by God initially, and how and why we continue to be acceptable to God thereafter: both of these have been challenged by the Judaizers.

43

Modern commentators often show their own theological position by whether they translate the Greek word *dikaioutai* (2:16) as 'justified' (RSV), or 'reckoned righteous' (RSV mg.), or 'put right' (GNB), or even 'made right': but, important though these theological distinctions are, they pale into insignificance for Paul compared with the question as to how this new status is to be achieved and maintained.

Here Paul is clear and unequivocal. Our new standing is achieved only by faith in Christ (2:16), which is also faith in the cross as God's chosen means of reconciliation (6:14–15). This faith in the finished work of Christ results in the promised gift of the Spirit (3:2), who is ours because we have become sons and daughters of God (4:6), and this brings in turn the new freedom of the Spirit (5:1). But, because faith in Christ also means union with Christ (2:20), this new liberty can never become licence to do as we please: the faith that justifies is a 'faith working through love' (5:6). This union with Christ by faith unites all humankind; differences of sex and race and status have become irrelevant in Christ (3:28), as has even the religious distinction between 'circumcision' and 'uncircumcision', Jew and Gentile (5:6). No reader of the letter can doubt that this is Paul's message to the Galatians and, in this sense, justification by faith does indeed lie at the very heart of the letter, although the doctrine itself may not be stated in Galatians as clearly and unequivocally as in Romans 5:1, at a later period. But after all, Romans is basically a theological treatise, while Galatians is an emotional theological appeal.

If it is argued that this centrality of justification by faith is only so because the letter to the Galatians was written in controversy, the answer is that it was written in a controversy about the very nature of the gospel. So, if justification by faith is central to this letter, it is only because justification is central to the gospel itself. Always there will be the danger of leaning on our own efforts to win salvation, always there will be the temptation to lean on outward observances to secure it. Whenever this is so, Galatians will still speak to the church, and Paul's impassioned arguments will still be as compelling as ever.

VI. THE VALIDITY OF PAUL'S ARGUMENT FROM EXPERIENCE

Another thing very clear on a plain reading of the letter to the Galatians is the use that Paul makes of Christian experience, as an argument. Whether it is an appeal to the experience of the Galatians before their conversion (4:8), or after their conversion (4:15), or to their experience of the Spirit both initially and continually at work in their midst (3:2–5), or to Paul's own experience at and after his own conversion (1:13–17), or to his experience in connection with the Jerusalem apostles (1:18 – 2:14), it is basically always the same argument. How valid is this appeal?

It could be dismissed as a mere passing reference, and the consideration of plain remembered facts, if it were not so frequent and so fundamental to Paul's argument. But is such argument from experience legitimate at all, in matters theological? Could not such experiences be illusory and deceptive, not in the sense that they never occurred, but in the sense that they are capable of other explanations? The modern reaction to 'cheapjack' theologies of 'feeling' and 'experience', aided by psychological explanations of that religious experience, is to distrust and totally denigrate the use of Christian experience as a theological argument. However, this extreme position clearly goes far beyond Scripture, including Paul. To say, with some, 'You may have the doctrine, but I have the experience', is rightly rejected as unconvincing, but, rightly understood, this contrast is false.

For instance, if 'miracles' (3:5) are to be adduced in themselves as a proof of the reality of Christian experience, the theologian of today might point to many other possible explanations of the events, psychological as well as physical. The student of comparative religion might point to the occurrence of such phenomena among those of other faiths besides Christianity, and even among those of no religious faith, and so on. This is a wise caution, but it is important to realize that Paul does not use bare experience in itself as an argument, still less as a proof. He uses as evidence that kind of experience which is enjoyed through believing response made by us to acts and words of God recorded in Scripture, which are themselves external to, and independent of, that experience. Such experience can therefore be both tested and verified by the Scriptures. Christian experience is to Paul a confirmation or seal of God's truth, not an independent entity: Christ must still be accepted initially by faith, if he is to be accepted at all (2:16).

Yet Paul's previous experience of bondage under Jewish law, and the Galatian experience of similar bondage under pagan superstitions, were real and remembered experiences, to which he could appeal. The joy and freedom which had been brought, not magically or irrationally, but by the knowledge of acceptance and forgiveness by God, was just as real a fact in either case. The continual presence of the Spirit in the hearts of the Galatians was demonstrated to them every time that they prayed (4:6). The fruits of the Spirit in their lives were plain for all to see (5:22–23). Nor were these fruits something laboriously produced by them, like 'good deeds' under the law, or indeed like the 'bad deeds' of unregenerate humanity; they were the spontaneous product of the new spiritual force at work within them. In that sense, to Paul, the fruits of the Spirit are a surer sign of God's work in us than even the gifts of the Spirit, highly though he values them (1 Cor. 12 – 14).

This is therefore no shallow humanistic argument drawn from casual experience. Results of this kind, rightly seen and analysed, are the surest tokens of the spiritual forces that produce them. Christianity, in the last analysis, is not magical, but it is truly supernatural, since the transforming power of the Spirit lies at its heart. A new work of creation has been done in the Galatians (6:15) by God. Nothing less than this could account for the changes produced in the human life which has been brought into contact with God through the gospel, and this transforming power of the Spirit is basically Paul's argument for the truth of his gospel.

VII. IMPORTANT ISSUES IN THE LETTER

When read in a contemporary context, Paul's letter to the Galatians raises a number of other important issues in many minds.

A. THE ATTITUDE OF PAUL TO COMPROMISE

In our modern ecumenical age, the necessity for Christian compromise is much in the air. We often wonder, for instance, if our Christian ancestors could not have avoided the bitterness, and even the bloodshed, of the religious wars of the past, by more readiness to exercise compromise, especially in matters which we can see clearly today not to be essential.

Approaching from this angle, it is natural to ask whether Paul's approach to the Galatians (not to mention his approach to the Jerusalem apostles) was perhaps unnecessarily polemical. If the Galatians were being persecuted not so much for being Christians as for being uncircumcised Gentile Christians, and if the acceptance of a simple rite of circumcision would assure them of freedom from this persecution, was it not sheer stubbornness on Paul's part to refuse? What if circumcision did lead to an obligation to observe certain Jewish festivals and certain ceremonial food laws? After all, there was nothing wrong or inconsistent with Christianity in these laws in themselves: many, if not all, Jewish Christians still observed them, as they had in their pre-Christian days.

This was notably true of the great mother church in Jerusalem, where many of the members had previously been Pharisees (Acts 15:5) or priestly Sadducees (Acts 6:7) before conversion, and who, for different reasons, would be equally shocked to the core at any failure to observe God's law, for such it clearly was, if it had been given by God to Moses, and enjoined on God's people. Would it not have been an act of self-sacrificing love on the part of Gentile Christians in Galatia to make a small surrender of religious 'liberty' in order to avoid putting a stumbling block in the path of these Hebrew fellow Christians? Indeed, was this not precisely the course which Paul himself advocated in 1 Corinthians 8:13, with reference to Jewish food laws? Was it not the course which he actually took, when he circumcised Timothy (Acts 16:3), before taking him as a travel companion? Why not allow it in Galatia, then? And why refuse to circumcise Titus now (2:3)? So some will argue.

The problem for the Jewish Christians can also be seen from another angle. The Christian church was still living in a very uneasy relationship with the Temple and with orthodox Judaism, not to mention with the extremist political groups within Israel. Obviously, the parent church of Jerusalem would do everything in its power not to jeopardize this delicate relationship, endangered as it already was by false rumours of Paul's attitude to law and circumcision (Acts 21:20–24). Was it not more important to maintain this Christian relationship with the parent body of Judaism than to enjoy some so-called liberty? They may well have hoped that perhaps Israel would yet heed the gospel and turn to her Messiah: the awful days of AD 70, with the consequential irreconcilable break between Christianity and the new 'monochrome' Judaism, were yet to come.

We can see how tempting, and even appealing, this line of argument might have been to the Galatians. We may be sure that this was one of the lines followed by the Judaizers of Galatia, and no doubt sincerely believed by them; but Paul would have none of it, as is clear both from the contents of this letter and his relations with the Jerusalem apostles (1:16 – 2:24). To him therefore there must have been a far deeper theological principle involved, outweighing all these considerations: compromise here, despite his flexibility elsewhere, was impossible.

With hindsight, we can see that Paul was right: had he yielded on this point, 'then Christ died to no purpose' (2:21), for Christianity would have become merely one more Messianic sect within Judaism. But the strange thing is that Paul seems to have been alone, or nearly alone, in this stand against the circumcision of Gentile Christians, which must have increased the suspicions of his Jerusalem opponents that his position on this matter was merely only one of stubbornness and intransigence. True, when the question was first raised at Antioch, which was a largely Gentile church, there was apparently widespread opposition to it, led not only by Paul but also by Barnabas, as is shown by the fact that both of them were sent to Jerusalem to plead their case (Acts 15:1–2). Paul certainly did not stand alone at that stage.

Indeed, when the matter was discussed at the Council in Jerusalem, Peter actually supported Paul and Barnabas in a typically forthright manner, quoting as precedent his own experience with the uncircumcised Cornelius (Acts 15:7–11). But on another undated occasion recorded in Galatians, Peter had been at Antioch, where he obviously had not been observing the Jewish food laws, for he, like the other Jewish Christians, had been enjoying table fellowship with the Gentile Christians there (2:12). However, when some of these 'weaker brethren' with Jewish scruples came ('certain men from James', 2:12), he 'separated himself' at once from his Gentile brothers and sisters in Christ, as did all the other Jewish Christians of Antioch, even Barnabas himself (2:13). Paul says bluntly that they did this 'fearing the circumcision party' (2:12): but it could also have been seen by Peter and the rest as a temporary compromise, designed to avoid offending the scruples of the Jerusalem Christians. No doubt Peter saw this gesture as something quite different from the circumcising of Gentile Christians: but Paul would have none of this temporary compromise either. Was he perhaps being a little extreme, or was he right?

The well-known case of Titus could be compared, as another instance of Paul's refusal to compromise, for instance. When the case for uncircumcised Gentile Christians was being argued at Jerusalem, Acts 15 mentions only Barnabas and Paul by name as delegates from Antioch, although 'some of the others' (15:2) are recorded as going with them. Would it not have made sense for this difficult and sensitive question to be argued at Jerusalem by circumcised Jewish Christians from Antioch, men like Paul and Barnabas, who could plead for their Gentile brothers and sisters without exacerbating the issue?

But instead of following this course, Paul came up to see the apostles in Jerusalem on this occasion, whenever it was, deliberately bringing with him the uncircumcised Titus who was 'a Greek' (2:3), that is 'a Gentile' and, at that, not even a Greek like Timothy, who, because he had a Jewish mother, would be counted by Hebrew law as a Jew (Acts 16:3), and was therefore circumcised by Paul. More, Paul actually flaunts the uncircumcision of Titus in the letter. The simplest reading of the text in 2:3 is that there had been some considerable pressure from the circumcision party to have Titus circumcised, but that Paul had steadfastly refused. To assume, with some commentators, that Titus had voluntarily accepted circumcision would be to adopt a very unnatural interpretation of the words 'was not compelled to be circumcised', and would destroy Paul's position.

In contrast to this seeming intransigence on some occasions, it was the apparent readiness of Paul to compromise on other occasions which the Jerusalem party must have found hard to understand. He had already circumcised Timothy (Acts 16:3), but now he refused to circumcise Titus (2:3). At times he kept the Jewish ritual law (1 Cor. 9:20), at times he did not. He was prepared to appear before the Jerusalem Christians as a law observer (Acts 21:20–24), while obviously this was not always true overseas. Indeed, inconsistency was a charge often made against him, as we can see from the Corinthian correspondence (2 Cor. 1:17). Why then was he so stubborn in the case of the Galatian controversy? It can only be that, in their case, he regarded any such compromise as fatal to the gospel (5:3–4), for Paul would only compromise when 'the truth of the gospel' was not directly involved (2:5).

However, that Paul was perfectly ready to accept compromise in areas which he did not regard as essential can be seen clearly from Acts, if not from Galatians. In Galatians, the agreement at Jerusalem was merely that Paul and Barnabas would evangelize the Gentiles, while Peter, James and John evangelized the Jews (2:9). The gospel was thereby recognized as a unity: it was only the spheres of operation which were different, for it cannot be seriously argued that two different gospels were involved. The question of the need for circumcision would not enter into the case of evangelism of Jews. It looks as if the whole subject was delicately avoided, or even tacitly dropped, in the case of Gentile evangelism, although the 'Jerusalem pillars' must have known well what was Paul's mind, and therefore what his attitude would be. But if this is so, then neither side can have viewed the issue as essential, and the position of Paul had therefore been vindicated. This in itself shows that any opposition to the reception of uncircumcised Gentiles as full believers and full brothers in Christ came not from the leaders of the Jerusalem church, but from a section (possibly a considerable section) of the rank and file.

There was therefore no compromise involved in any of the decisions recorded in Galatians, for even the agreement to 'remember the poor' (2:10) was something already dear to Paul's heart, as he says, especially if, as probable, 'the poor' refers to 'the poor among the saints at Jerusalem' (Rom. 15:26), for whom he was to make his famous collection later. Likewise, there was certainly no compromise visible in the events at Antioch recorded in 2:11–14: outright confrontation is described there, with Paul utterly refusing to yield ground. We cannot therefore find evidence for Christian compromise on the part of Paul in this letter.

But in contrast to these two occasions described in Galatians, the decision of the Council of Jerusalem as recorded in Acts certainly was a Christian compromise on non-essentials, and one apparently accepted (one trusts, whole-heartedly) by Paul and Barnabas as well as by the Jerusalem church at the time. Without going into the exact meaning of the details (for which see the commentaries on Acts), circumcision was certainly not demanded of Gentile Christians, although certain ritual and moral requirements were specified (Acts 15:20, 28–29, with Acts 21:25). These are not said to be essential to salvation, as circumcision had apparently been claimed by the Judaizers to be (Acts 15:1), so perhaps this was the reason for their ready acceptance by Paul on this occasion. But they are nevertheless described as 'necessary' (Acts 15:28), so that they were obviously still considered by the Jerusalem Christians as of some considerable importance.

Whether these requirements were regarded as belonging to the covenant of Noah or to the covenant of Moses makes little difference: they seem in either case to be considered by Jerusalem as universally obligatory for Gentile Christians, not a mere matter of optional acceptance on occasions to avoid offending tender scruples. This compromise therefore goes much further than Paul's advice to the Gentile Christians in 1 Corinthians 8, even if still not touching 'essentials'. Perhaps this is why Paul tacitly dropped the whole arrangement later, but his is a question pertaining more to a commentary on Acts than one on Galatians.

Paul rightly and strenuously opposed any circumcision of Gentile believers; it was not that he regarded circumcision as wrong, but that it was totally irrelevant now, in the face of the new life in Christ (6:15), as irrelevant indeed as was the state of uncircumcision. The whole question was totally outmoded; to re-introduce it was to take a step backwards, to the old time of 'preparation' for the gospel (4:1–11). To accept circumcision meant to Paul to be bound to keep the whole law (5:3). This inevitably involved moving back into the sphere of thought where salvation was dependent on, and earned by, keeping that law (5:4). It is true that to earn salvation in this way was an impossibility, but that was what made the very attempt so wrong and indeed so ridiculous.

For a Jewish Christian, already circumcised, the position was completely different. Paul held that such a person was free to observe the law, as most if not all of the Jerusalem Christians apparently did (Acts 21:20), or to ignore the law, which Peter often did, in later days at least (2:12), or to keep it at times, and ignore it at times, as Paul himself obviously did (1 Cor. 9:20–21). This to him was not only a matter of Christian expediency, directed by the nature of his company at the time: it was also a matter of theology, since these things were now irrelevant.

If the Council of Jerusalem was Paul's greatest compromise, what happened afterwards? Did Paul quietly drop the whole matter? Did he regard the compromise involved in the Jerusalem decree (at least in the ceremonial and ritual area) as being a mere temporary expedient, to avoid schism in the church, and to facilitate social and religious fellowship between Jewish Christians and Gentile Christians? It is striking that Paul never appeals to the Jerusalem decree in any extant letter (unless the opening chapters of the letter to the Galatians contains oblique references), even in situations where to quote it, and so to invoke the authority of the Jerusalem church, would have settled the argument at once. Acts 16:4 mentions the promulgation of the decree in the South Galatian churches, but that is all: why does Paul never mention it himself?

Of course if the letter to Galatia was written either before the Council of Jerusalem, or in its early stages, there would be no problem, for the Jerusalem decree would have not yet been issued. If Galatians was written after the date of Acts 15, there certainly is a problem. But the Corinthian letters, not to mention the Roman letter, or a prison letter like that to the Philippians, were written long after the Council of Jerusalem, and Paul still makes no reference to the decree. Indeed, in the Corinthian correspondence at least, he seems to give advice which does not go nearly as far as the Jerusalem decision, if it does not actually run counter to it.

There can be only two possible answers. The first possibility is that Paul accepted the practical compromise of the Council of Jerusalem for the time being, but did not think it a final solution, and therefore dropped it quietly as soon as possible, particularly in the largely Gentile churches further away from Jerusalem, and therefore less subject to visits from Jewish church members, whether they were well disposed or trouble-makers (2:4). The second possibility is that he did not wish to settle any argument simply on the authority of Jerusalem and its apostles, however estimable they might be (2:6): that would run counter to his whole theology.

The first of these assumptions may possibly be correct; the second certainly is, as we can see from the opening chapters of Galatians (1:11 – 2:10). Paul wanted to settle this and other similar questions not by an appeal to an external earthly authority but by the law of love (Ro. 14:1–12), as interpreted by Scripture, not by a return to old legalism. That to him was the path of maturity. Nevertheless, Paul's basic position remains clear: he was perfectly ready for compromise on non-essentials, but completely intransigent when the nature of the gospel was at stake.

B. JUDAIZERS, NOT JEWS

One of the darkest stains on the history of the Christian church has been anti-Semitism, all the more inconceivable when practised by those who claimed to be followers of the Christ who was born a Jew and who wept over Jerusalem (Lk. 19:41). No reader of the letter to the Romans (Rom. 9:3) could ever accuse Paul the Jew of anti-Semitism: and yet sometimes commentators on Galatians or Romans have been accused of being tainted by it.

Now, it is true that some of the greatest of the classical

commentators on Galatians may have been guilty of this bias at times (Martin Luther is one example): but, if so, they did not learn the attitude either from Galatians or from Paul himself. For such a grievous aberration, we must all express our sorrow, and utter abhorrence. That should be the more easy for any commentator on Galatians, since Paul in this letter asserts that the division between Jew and Gentile has lost both meaning and relevance 'in Christ Jesus' (3:28).

But, like other such 'natural' distinctions overarched in Christ, although the difference has been transcended, it has not been abolished. The existence of 'Gentile Christians' and 'Jewish Christians', as two mutually distinct and distinguishable groups within the early church, proves this, as does the very possibility of the conflict that led to the Council of Jerusalem (Acts 15:1–2), and therefore to the letter to the Galatians. Had early Christianity been homogenous and monochrome, the question of Judaizing could not have arisen.

We have seen that it is probable that the Jerusalem Council did not settle the issue finally as far as Paul was concerned: it is certain from the later pages of the New Testament that it did not end the question as far as the Judaizers were concerned (Phil. 1:17). It is reasonable to suppose, in the absence of other evidence, that these 'men . . . from James' (2:12), the hard core of Pharisee 'irreconcilables' (no doubt with many orthodox sympathisers overseas), had accepted the council decree grudgingly as a temporary setback, but were still anxious to push the matter to its conclusion. This group, probably the same as those from Judea originally active at Antioch (Acts 15:1), and certainly those vociferous at the Jerusalem Council (Acts 15:5), continued to dog Paul to the end of his days (Phil. 3:2). Probably Paul's words 'let no man trouble me' (6:17) are a reference to his ongoing harassment by the same group.

Small wonder, therefore, if Paul expressed himself very strongly on occasions concerning these 'Judaizers' (Phil. 3:2). Even when he does, there is not a trace of any wider anti-Semitism in his thoughts or words: he is concerned only with his theological opponents at the time. After all, these opponents were not even Jewish by religion, but Christian; that was what made their behaviour all the more inexplicable to Paul. As

Cousar says, Paul's polemic is not with the Jews, but with Jewish Christians. The irony is that it does not seem as if Paul himself held to the provisions of the Council of Jerusalem either, but for quite different reasons. Certainly there is no evidence for his use or publication of the decree in later years. Nevertheless, in spite of this, he seems to have enjoyed good relations to the last with the bulk of the Jerusalem Christians: schism in the church had been avoided, for the Judaizers had been isolated from the support of the main body of Jewish Christianity.

But, having said that, it is necessary in an ecumenical age devoted to religious dialogue to say bluntly that Paul did not regard the religion of Judaism as a continuing parallel alternative to Christianity, nor did he regard those who were Jewish by religion as already being in a state of grace and salvation. Otherwise, not only would his whole stance in Galatians on circumcision and law-keeping be inexplicable: his own conversion to Christianity and subsequent missionary work would be meaningless. It is not that Judaism was a false faith: but, to Paul, it was only a past step along the road that finally led to Christ (3:24). To go back to Judaism now would be unthinkable (3:3), while to remain in Judaism after Christ's coming would be to refuse to accept Israel's Messiah (Acts 18:5–6). Still more unthinkable would be a return to the old ways of paganism (4:9): so Galatians becomes a charter for the uniqueness of Christianity and the need for evangelism of all humanity, Jew and Gentile alike. Again, we may compare the letter to the Hebrews.

To Paul, preaching Christ to Jews, like preaching to Gentiles, was not therefore merely one possible option, but a divine necessity, and indeed always a priority in his own evangelistic work (Acts 13:46). Only in the light of this knowledge can we understand the fervour with which in the letter to the Galatians he opposes what to him was a total rejection of the Christian gospel in favour of a virtual return to the old way.

C. SIGNS AND WONDERS

Galatians gives us surprisingly little evidence as to this phenomenon in the life of the local church. With the exception of 3:5, there is no reference to the performance of any miracles in the local church, and it is theoretically possible (though most unlikely) that even this verse refers only to the initial evangelism of Lycaonia, where Paul's miraculous healing of a lame man started what we would nowadays call a 'people movement' towards Christianity, even if it did not last for long (Acts 14:8–13). Nevertheless, the present tense of the two verbs *epichorēgōn*, 'supplies' (the Spirit), and *energōn*, 'works' (miracles), in 3:5 suggests a continuous ongoing process. We may therefore assume that the gifts of the Spirit were just as widespread among the Galatians as among the Corinthians, especially as Paul refers to the 'miracles' here so casually in passing, without any particular emphasis: it looks as if he is almost taking them for granted.

Why then is there no detailed discussion in this letter of the gifts of the Spirit, of their function and their control, even of their abuse, as there is in 1 Corinthians 12? One reason may be that, at the height of a theological controversy, Paul has no time to turn to a secondary issue, important though it might be. A second possible reason has already been suggested in this Introduction, in the section dealing with Paul's argument from Christian experience. If the Galatian Christians, for any reason, were 'disillusioned charismatics', then this was the last doctrine in the world to discuss at the time. Instead, Paul concentrates on discussing with the Galatians the fruits of the Spirit (5:22–23), those other signs of the Spirit's presence which, although unspectacular, guarantee holiness of life in a way that spiritual gifts do not necessarily do. It is possible, even in the New Testament, to be a false prophet (Mt. 7:15) and to perform 'great signs and wonders' to deceive (Mt. 24:24): it is not possible to produce the fruit of the Spirit without the transforming work of the Spirit within the heart (Mt. 7:15–18). In that sense, Galatians is a useful balance to Corinthians. Paul in Galatians affirms the existence and reality of *dynameis*, 'miracles', and appeals to them amongst other signs of the Spirit's presence (3:5). But he does not concentrate on them, or see them out of this context: he carefully balances them (indeed, in this letter, some would say, he almost overbalances them) with the fruit of the Spirit. As mentioned above, there may well be a particular local reason for this, either in the controversy as to the very nature of the gospel, which was rocking the church to its foundations, or in the spiritual predicament of the Galatians at the time.

But it also corresponds to a deep spiritual principle of the New Testament that such manifestations, real and valuable though they are (Rom. 15:19; 2 Cor. 12:12), should not be given undue prominence, but should be seen as part of the whole Christian 'packet'. Paul had realized very early that Satan too could work 'pretended signs' (2 Thes. 2:9), and Christ himself had warned that many who had prophesied, cast out demons, and done mighty works in his name, would yet be rejected at the last day (Mt. 7:23). In themselves, therefore, signs are not decisive.

D. MEN AND WOMEN IN CHRIST

Galatians is not a letter which provides us with abundant evidence on this issue of men and women in Christ, which is so interesting and relevant to modern Christians. This again is not surprising: Galatians is not primarily a pastoral letter like the Corinthian letters, dealing with the questions and problems of a struggling local church, but a theological refutation of a heresy that, if accepted, would have destroyed the whole church, men and women alike. One cannot and should not therefore expect a balanced theological presentation of every aspect of Christian truth here.

Yet, in spite of this, it is remarkable that one of the most far-reaching statements on this subject in the whole of the New Testament is made in 3:28: 'there is neither male nor female; for you are all one in Christ Jesus.' Now admittedly the spanning of this particular gulf is not the sole point of Paul's remark. Indeed, it could even be argued that it is not his primary or initial thought. In view of the general run of the letter (and especially of chapter 2), it is likely that, for his argument at the time, the opening clause 'There is neither Jew nor Greek' was his basic point, but that thereafter he extended the principle to the over-arching by Christ of other equally deep divisions observable in the 'natural' world of his day.

That of course does not in any way lessen either the truth or the importance of the later clauses, including that dealing with male and female, but it is wise to realize that this is not the point at issue at the time: that is why there is no detailed discussion in this context of the practical implications of this sweeping statement. There is, for instance, no discussion of the married state, with its rights and duties, in Galatians, as in Ephesians 5:21–33: there is equally no discussion of sex in relation to church order, as there is, say, in 1 Corinthians 11:2–16 and 14:33–36, however we interpret the evidence there. It is therefore not fair to use Galatians in argument in this area, except in so far as it propounds a great basic principle, the application of which may well vary at different times and in different situations. Perhaps we might lay alongside 3:28, as an equally generally relevant principle, the dictum 'through love be servants of one another' (5:13), which suggests the voluntary mutual subordination of 'clothe yourselves, all of you, with humility toward one another' of 1 Peter 5:5.

However, having said this, several points should be noticed. First, Paul is clearly referring in this context to 'as many of you as were baptised into Christ' (3:27): it is therefore, to him, because we have 'put on Christ' that we 'are all one in Christ Jesus' (3:28). Paul is not talking of some radical re-understanding of gender achieved by 'natural' thought, but of a spiritual transformation produced by our new oneness in Christ. He is not denying an existing 'natural' distinction (like that between Jew and Gentile), but in a sense affirming it, and at the same time, affirming that it is now transcended in Christ. Further, he is not saying that men and women are now the same, but that they are 'one in Christ'. Here the Greek *heis* could be translated as 'one person', not even as 'a unity', which would have required the neuter form *hen*. Man and woman together form a unity in the body of Christ, just as man and woman together in Genesis 1:27 are created 'in the image of God'. Although Paul's wording here is concise, this seems to be his meaning: man and woman are complementary in Christ.

It is also important to realize that for Paul the difference between men and women has not been obliterated, even in Christ, any more than the difference between Jew and Greek has been: it is their attitude to each other that has been completely altered, so that their relationship has also been radically altered. This can be seen very clearly for instance in Ephesians 6:5–9, where Paul has elaborated the implications of the new relationships for masters and slaves, but for the reasons mentioned above, there is no similar working out of any detailed relationships between the sexes in this letter. However, it should be noted, as mentioned elsewhere in the Introduction, that, although transcended in Christ, the difference between Jewish Christian and Gentile Christian still persisted within the church, not only in the case of the Judaizers where it seems to have taken a sinful turn, but also in the case of the 'orthodox' Jewish Christians of Jerusalem headed by James, where it was innocent. But this difference was now apparently characterized by a mutual acceptance of each other in love (5:13–14), fully acknowledging the difference that existed and yet conscious of their fundamental underlying unity in Christ. Perhaps this is a good parallel.

Further than this, Paul does not take us in Galatians. It would be grossly unfair to invest his great statement 'there is neither male nor female' in 3:28 with a literal significance which would have been far from his mind, although the later Gnostics carried it to this conclusion. Paul is making in this context a theological statement which is true at the deepest level, not a physiological or psychological pronouncement. He must not be misunderstood, here or elsewhere, in a crudely literalistic way. This is shown by his detailed discussion in other contexts both of the situation now obtaining within marriage (Eph. 5) and in church order (1 Cor. 11), in both of which he accepts sexual differentiation.

It would be beyond the province of a commentator on Galatians to enlarge on these discussions in other letters, and to give an opinion as to whether Paul's applications of the new principles are to be regarded as universal rules or merely as temporary injunctions in the light of the local situation of the day. They may nevertheless be mentioned as examples of Paul's consciousness of the continuation of a difference between the sexes, and the consequent need to work out the implications for Christians, whether men or women, of being at one and the same time in the 'natural' and 'supernatural' orders. There are for instance some commentators who hold that, in such other or later letters, Paul fell below the high level of the principle enunciated by him in Galatians: but those who have a high view of Scripture and of the doctrine of inspiration will be loth to adopt this view. A more convincing view is to hold that, as in several other areas (*e.g.* that of spiritual gifts), Paul was led in later days to explain and qualify the theologically true generalizations of Galatians in the light of local cultural conditions, because of the abuses which had subsequently arisen in the local churches. This, after all, is what Galatians itself is doing in connection with the doctrine of Christian liberty, if our reconstruction of the circumstances of writing the letter is correct. But, in any case, Paul's attitude is in sharp contrast to that of contemporary Judaism: the 'Judaizers' could offer little or nothing to women.

ANALYSIS

I. THE ARGUMENT FROM EXPERIENCE (1:1 – 2:21)

A. GREETING (1:1–5)

B. THE SUBJECT OF THE LETTER INTRODUCED (1:6–9)

C. PAUL'S CONVERSION (1:10–24)

    1. Paul's protest (1:10–12)

    2. Paul's life before his conversion (1:13–14)

    3. Paul's conversion and subsequent events (1:15–24)

D. LATER RELATIONS WITH JERUSALEM CHURCH LEADERS (2:1–10)

E. THE CLASH WITH PETER (2:11–16)

F. DEATH AND THE NEW LIFE (2:17–21)

II. THE ARGUMENT FROM THEOLOGY (3:1 – 5:1)

A. INTRODUCTION (3:1–6)

B. ABRAHAM'S FAITH (3:7–9)

C. WHO IS UNDER THE CURSE? (3:10–14)

D. DOES LAW ANNUL PROMISE? (3:15–18)

E. WHAT IS THE PURPOSE OF THE LAW? (3:19–29)

F. THE DIFFERENCE BETWEEN SON AND INFANT (4:1–11)

G. A PERSONAL APPEAL FOR BETTER RELATIONS (4:12–20)

H. AN ARGUMENT FROM RABBINICS (4:21 – 5:1)

III. THE ARGUMENT FROM RESULTS (5:2 – 6:18)

A. THE GOAL OF THE GOSPEL (5:2–6)

B. A PERSONAL ASIDE (5:7–12)

C. THE TRUE USE OF FREEDOM (5:13–18)

D. THE 'NATURAL RESULTS' OF NATURAL HUMANITY (5:19–21)

E. THE HARVEST OF THE SPIRIT (5:22–26)

COMMENTARY

I. THE ARGUMENT FROM EXPERIENCE (1:1 – 2:21)

A. GREETING (1:1–5)

'Paul, an apostle, not an apostolate from humans, nor through any human, but through Jesus Christ and God the Father, who raised him from among the dead, and all the Christians with me here, to the churches of Galatia: grace to you, and peace, from God our Father and the Lord Jesus Christ, who gave himself for our sins, to take us out of this present wicked age, in accordance with the will of our Father-God, to whom be the glory for ages of ages. Amen.'

1. *Paul* is the sender of this letter: the one simple word is quite enough to introduce him to the recipients, to whom he was obviously well known. Any letter of the time will begin with the name of the sender, closely followed by that of the recipient. Normally, the bulk of the letter will then be written by a scribe,[1] and it will only be in the closing lines that the author will pick up the stylus himself, and add a sentence or two in autograph. Forgery was a danger even in the days of Paul himself: certainly, in the sub-apostolic days, 'pseudepigraphy' became a menace.[2]

---

[1]Often, this would be a professional scribe, but this expensive luxury was not likely in the case of a Christian letter. See Rom. 16:22, *I Tertius, the writer of this letter*, where the 'scribe' was obviously a fellow Christian.

[2]As shown already by 2 Thes. 2:2, where Paul must have had reason to believe that such forged letters were already circulating under his name. But see M. R. James, *The Apocryphal New Testament* (Oxford: Clarendon Press, 1924) for the remark that, while apocryphal gospels are common, apocryphal letters are rare – perhaps because of these precautions.

Even without such evidence, it is certain that the Galatians were in no doubt as to the writer of this letter: from beginning to end, the letter breathes Paul. Not only has it been described as an earlier 'rough draft' of Romans,[1] it also contains so many other Pauline idiosyncrasies that, along with Philippians and the Corinthian correspondence, it has always been regarded as belonging to the indisputably Pauline 'core'. Even those who nowadays attempt to solve the problem of authenticity by the use of computers usually start with this letter as base, although this only shows their belief in its genuineness, not the genuineness of the letter itself.

Paul (in its full form of *Paulus* or *Paullus*) is a common enough Roman surname (never a praenomen or distinguishing name), found frequently in classical literature, inscriptions and papyri, as BAGD shows. Even in the New Testament, the Sergius Paulus of Acts 13:7 bears it. Originally an aristocratic Roman name, it was later borne by many newly enfranchised citizens, whether because their ancestors had originally been slaves of some member of this house, or as a compliment to some provincial governor of that name. Perhaps we may compare the way in which third-world Christians, when wanting to take a 'foreign' name in addition to their own, will frequently adopt either that of a much-loved missionary, or of some prominent foreign statesman. Beyond the fact that Paul was born a Roman citizen, we know nothing of the origins of citizenship in his family.[2] He certainly had no drop of Roman blood in his veins; but none made the proud name of *Paullus* more illustrious.

It is just possible that Paul was not even the name used by his enfranchised family, but chosen by him because of its assonance with his Jewish name, Saul. Many instances of this sort of assimilation occur in the New Testament: for instance, the Hebrew 'Simeon' (Acts 15:14) appears in Greek form as *Simon* (Mt. 16:17). We do not know whether Paul continued to be known as

---

[1]This may be unfair, for some aspects are developed quite differently in Romans. Nevertheless, the basic theological content is the same in both letters, while the highly charged emotional atmosphere is closer to Corinthians (especially to 2 Cor. 10 to 13).

[2]Perhaps it was, as often, the reward for illustrious service by his ancestors as local civic officials in Tarsus. Perhaps, however, they had attained it by less noble means, like the tribune of Acts 22:28.

Saul in Jewish-Christian circles; it is very likely. Certainly when Simon Peter is mentioned in Jewish Christian contexts he is more commonly called 'Simeon' or 'Cephas', the latter being the Semitic name corresponding to 'Peter'.[1] Nevertheless, it is only before the first missionary journey that Luke uses the name 'Saul' to describe the apostle of the Gentiles. After Acts 13:9, he is always 'Paul', and this is the name that he himself uses in all his letters. It is as though his acceptance of the Gentile mission to which his conversion led him demanded the renunciation of his Jewish past (although see 1 Cor. 9:20, 'to the Jews I became as a Jew'). His Jewish name, with its reminder of Saul, the first king of Israel, the pride of Benjamin, stands for that heritage. When writing to what are presumed to be Gentile, not Jewish, converts in Galatia, the Gentile name 'Paul' has peculiar appropriateness. He is reminding them that for Christ's sake he had already identified himself with them (4:12), or 'become as you are'.

But Paul is also *an apostle, apostolos*. In spite of all the theological battles over this word in recent years, it is probably best to leave it, in this transliterated Greek form, untranslated, although etymologically it corresponds to the Latin term 'missionary', which might well be used for it. A term like 'emissary extraordinary' may recapture some of the atmosphere, but is too clumsy for use. To us, the word 'apostle' means first and foremost the twelve men chosen by Christ to be near him, and whom he might send on his tasks (Mk. 6:7). But the Scriptures merely say that Christ named the twelve 'apostles' (Lk. 6:13); that is, he used an existing word to make clear their status and functions. Within Judaism, the corresponding word was well defined; a *shāliach* meant a special messenger, with a special status, enjoying an authority and commission that came from a body or person other than the person himself.[2] So in the days of the New Testament the word 'apostles' had a meaning far wider

---

[1] It seems to be over-exegesis to try to trace fine distinctions of meaning in the use of these different names: probably the local circumstances and locally used language dictate their use at any given time.

[2] See Bruce for the various senses and usages of the Hebrew corresponding words. The *shāliach* seems to have been essentially a legal representative, whether of an individual or a group. Hence the Talmud can say repeatedly 'A man's *shāliach* is as it were himself', since he could act on behalf of his sender in sales, betrothals, *etc.*

than 'the twelve', or 'the eleven' after the defection of Judas. It is used of the twelve, but it can also be used of James the brother of the Lord, who is not found in any list of the twelve, and also of a wider, indefinite group, called 'the apostles of the churches'[1] (2 Cor. 8:23, RSV mg.; *cf.* Ro. 16:7).

Yet Paul uses the word here deliberately to make a point, not merely to inform them that this letter is from 'Paul the missionary' as distinct from any other Paul. It is from Paul the apostle as distinct from a body at Jerusalem, the members of which equally call themselves apostles. Yet to him, 'apostle' is not so much a title of office as a description of function and he makes that plain by what follows.

His apostolate, he tells them, is *not from men nor through man* (NIV, 'by man'). It has neither human source nor human agency (NEB, 'not by human appointment or human commission'). There is probably no significance in the change from *men* to *man*. Paul may be recalling, however, that a Jewish *apostolos* or *shāliach*, to use the Semitic form, although usually representing an individual, would sometimes be sent from a group (perhaps the Sanhedrin), and would in that case have received a commission from the high priest or some similar high official. When Paul went on his journey to Damascus, his Jewish commission or 'apostolate' had been of this nature (Acts 9:1). No longer is it so; now, his Christian apostolate is *through Jesus Christ and God the Father*. It is therefore from this source that he has received his commission. It is impossible to say how far the title '*Christos*' (originally a passive form from *chriō*, 'I anoint') had already advanced in the direction of becoming a proper name, as it is in modern English; usually in the New Testament, when it has no definite article, it is so treated. When it has the definite article, it is probably better to translate as 'the Messiah' or 'the Anointed', although it is uncertain how much of this sense the Gentile Christians would have understood. But the important thing is that for Paul the source of his authority is Christ; and this Christ is a Christ deliberately set side by side with God. Among ancient witnesses, only Marcion the heretic here omits the clause *and*

---

[1]For a detailed discussion, see the appendix in Burton. It seems over-punctilious here to refuse James the full title of apostle, merely because he was not one of the original twelve.

God the Father; and this was certainly from doctrinal considerations on his part.

In Paul's writings, it is rare to find any bare or unqualified reference to God. God is usually further characterized at once as the one who has revealed himself in such-and-such a way. Normally for Paul, this revelation is in connection with his work in and through Christ; and this passage is no exception to the rule. He is the God *who raised him from the dead*: this is the normal New Testament form of expression, rather than saying, as we do, that Christ rose from the dead. Always in the New Testament, the resurrection of Christ is central to the Christian faith. Since Paul sees the Christian life in terms of sharing in the death and resurrection of Christ, the resurrection has an even greater relevance for him.[1]

Why does Paul describe himself as this sort of apostle? Certainly not in direct opposition to the apostles at Jerusalem, for they did not owe their commission to humans any more than he did. They too could have claimed that they were appointed by Christ, in accordance with the will of God the Father. Rather, Paul's aim is to show that his apostolate stands or falls with theirs, for it rests on exactly the same basis. It is extremely unlikely that any of the Jerusalem apostles 'stood on their dignity' as against Paul, but it is highly likely that some of their more enthusiastic followers did so, on their behalf. We know, for instance, that these extremists seem to have accused Paul of being no true apostle, or, at best, a self-appointed one (1 Cor. 9:2; 2 Cor. 11:5). No-one who reads the story of his conversion could take seriously this charge of self-appointment; perhaps this is why Paul more than once refers to the story of his conversion in his defence (Acts 22 and 26). Indeed, the whole of the first part of Galatians will be an appeal to past experience, first and in particular to Paul's own spiritual pilgrimage, and secondly to the history of his relations with the Galatian churches.

To put it in modern terms, the validity of Paul's apostolate is being questioned. He replies by showing that, put in this way,

---

[1]Because Paul's conversion was for him, as for others, a meeting with the risen Christ on the road to Damascus (Acts 9:5, 27), the resurrection of Christ has a deep personal significance to him.

the question is invalid since, in asking it, the questioners implicate themselves also. If the Jerusalem apostolate and Paul's apostolate to the Gentiles, and, indeed, Peter's apostolate to the Jews, have all one and the same source, how can such a question even arise? It was, it is true, the sort of question that greatly exercised first-century Judaism. Both John the Baptist and Christ had been asked by what official authority they acted. Both had made the same answer, whether explicitly or implicitly; it was by the authority of God (Jn. 1:25 and Mk. 11:27–33). Their ministry found its proof and vindication in the working of God through them, and this is Paul's thought too. The proof of the 'validity' of his ministry is to be found in the working of the Holy Spirit that accompanies it, in the results of a ministry rather than in its antecedents.[1] If any at Jerusalem should challenge this, they would at once be aligning themselves with Jewish theology rather than Christian. Paul's apostolate and his gospel belong together: that is the reason for the introduction of the topic here.

2. Paul wants to show that he does not write alone. *All the brethren who are with me* (NEB, 'I and the group of friends now with me'), also join in the salutation. Much study has been devoted to 'Paul's travelling circle' in recent years, of which Judge's book[2] is one example. While it is true that there are a group of Christians whose names appear constantly in the New Testament in connection with that of Paul on his travels, we should beware of seeing him as some sort of wandering Hellenistic philosopher, surrounded by a circle of pupils. The more casual translation of the NEB given above may well be correct,

---

[1] This introduces the vexed question of 'signs and wonders'. While Paul appeals to the very existence of his converts as proof and seal of his ministry (2 Cor. 3:3), he also appeals to accompanying 'signs and wonders' as proof of the Spirit's working through him (Rom. 15:19). One school of opinion has always held that these signs ceased to be given, and indeed, were not needed, after apostolic days: another school holds that they should and do continue today. Neither doubts that they took place in Paul's day. Whatever our view, we should note that Paul lays no exclusive emphasis on these spectacular proofs: they are but one sign among several (2 Cor. 12:12, where the unspectacular proof of 'patience' is added).

[2] E. A. Judge, *The Social Pattern of the Christian Groups in the First Century* (London: Tyndale Press, 1960). Interesting though his views are, they need some qualification: there are important differences between Paul and a travelling Hellenistic philosopher, and we should not confuse them.

rather than any translation which would emphasize the distinction between an assumed 'inner circle' of Paul's friends and the main body of the church, usually called 'the saints'. But 'friends' is inadequate as a translation for *adelphoi*, 'brothers'. The word has a long history in Judaism, as may be seen from the Old Testament. In the new Christian family, it took on a richer and deeper meaning. Brothers, sisters, saints, chosen, Nazarenes, Galileans: the names used for Christians were many, but the sense of 'belongingness' was common to all of them. True, Paul often does associate some younger member of his circle with himself in the writing of a letter. But it is unlikely in most cases that the association extends further than the greeting, the more so as in verse 6 Paul will drop at once into the first person singular. Probably he merely wishes to show the Galatians that he does not stand alone in opposition to the Judaizing heresy that has crept into the churches of Galatia; he speaks for the whole Christian church, from which he writes, wherever it is: that is the point of saying 'all the brothers' (NIV).

The letter is addressed *to the churches of Galatia*. This was a perfectly adequate address in its day, but has puzzled scholars greatly since. For a summary of different views as to its meaning see the Introduction, pp. 18ff.[1] Whatever the exact geographic location, the phrase clearly refers to a number of local *ekklēsiai* or 'churches', which form part of the one great *ekklēsia* or church. This is consonant with Pauline usage throughout. If the letter is a circular, the question arises as to whether only one copy was sent, or several. If only one copy was sent, presumably the various local churches were expected to hand it on from one to another when read, possibly first making a transcript themselves. In view of 6:11, where stress is laid on Paul's handwriting, it seems improbable that there was more than one original autograph copy. Paul elsewhere exhorts local churches to pass on and share with one another similar apostolic letters of general interest and relevance.[2] If the recipients were 'South

---

[1] Betz points out that the churches concerned must have been close geographically and must also have been linked organizationally in some way not clear to us: they were not simply disconnected local congregations.

[2] See Col. 4:16 for instructions to share with Laodicea a letter sent to Colosse, and vice versa. Perhaps this took place more widely than we think.

Galatians', we know of at least four such local churches, and there may well have been more.

3. The greeting from Paul is *Grace to you and peace.* The juxtaposition of these two nouns is thoroughly Jewish and was now to become thoroughly Christian. It is therefore a mistake to see here a junction of the Hellenic and Semitic worlds.[1] It seems as if Paul at first had only intended to say 'Grace be to you', and then added 'and peace', almost as an afterthought. Since, for Paul, *charis* ('grace') is almost synonymous with 'Jesus Christ', for he knows nothing of impersonal grace, and since we enjoy peace with God through Christ, the distinction is not great. 'Peace' is the Greek *eirēnē*, the promised gift of Christ to his troubled disciples (Jn. 14:27); it corresponds to Hebrew *shālōm*, that spiritual well-being that comes from a right relationship with God. Wherever Arabic has brought the greeting 'salaam' into other languages across the world, there is a verbal echo of this great truth.

This *grace* and *peace* come *from God the Father and our Lord Jesus Christ.* It is probable that by the common construction known as chiasmus (which could be translated as an 'x-shaped' construction), the source of grace is seen as Christ, and the source of peace as God the Father. Again, however, the main theological point is the close association of Christ with God. Indeed, the use of the word *Kyrios*, 'Lord', as a title of Christ would in itself be sufficient to assure this. Much study has been devoted to this Greek word, the one chosen by the early translators into Greek of the Hebrew Bible to stand for the divine name YHWH, which might not be pronounced by the pious Jew, and for which the Hebrew *adōnai*, 'my Lord', had already been substituted. *Kyrios* varied in meaning from the polite 'sir', used in formal address to a stranger, to the full sense of 'Lord', in confession of the deity of Christ. When the early Christians used the phrase, 'Jesus is Lord', as a baptismal confession, they cannot have meant less than this.[2]

---

[1] The pagan Greek did not say *charis*, 'grace', as a greeting, but *chaire*, 'be joyful', although the words sounded somewhat alike, and so the one may have led to the other: see Betz. 'Peace' as a greeting is fully Semitic, and so is 'grace', in its Hebrew form.

[2] BAGD has a full discussion of these various meanings, under *kyrios*: Betz has a further bibliography; the literature is vast. However, the full sense is clearly meant, when applied to Christ, and that is all that is important here.

4. As Paul has particularized God the Father as the one who raised Jesus Christ from the dead, so here he particularizes Christ as the one who *gave himself for our sins.* NEB has 'sacrificed himself', but this seems to give *dontos* too narrow a meaning, correct though the interpretation may be. Is Paul thinking of the unique and crucial self-giving of Christ on the cross as *hyper*, 'on behalf of', our sins? If so, then the thought must be that of the Mosaic sin-offering. Or does he think of the continuous and exemplary self-giving of Christ throughout his whole life? In that case, the suffering servant of Isaiah 53 must be in his mind. But there is no contradiction between the two, and both ideas may be included here. This is not so much here a theological definition, as it is a confession of infinite indebtedness to Christ.[1]

This self-giving of Christ is always seen in the New Testament as producing a positive result. Here, the purpose is stated as *to deliver us* (NIV, 'rescue us') *from the present evil age.* The division between 'the present age' and 'the age to come' was familiar to every Jew, and therefore to the Christian. What we are accustomed to translate as 'everlasting life' means literally 'life of the age (to come)'. As in John's Gospel (Jn. 12:31), the thought that this present age is under the power of the evil one is frequent. Thus, what Christ's death has done is to transfer the Christian from one age to the other, from the sphere of Satan's power to that of God. While still living physically in this present *evil age*, therefore, we enjoy already the life of the age to come. This is for Paul the victory of the cross. But it is just possible that the Judaizing heresy that was troubling the Galatians also made great play of the Greek word *aiōn*, 'age', as the later Gnostics certainly did.[2] In that case, Paul would be deliberately using a

[1]Whether or not this formed part of some early pre-Pauline Christian formula or creed, as sometimes claimed, is not certain: see Bruce for the arguments. Betz points out that the statement can appear in three forms: either God is depicted as the agent, or Christ (as here) is the agent, or the plain passive of the verb may be used ('Christ was given up'). There is no discernable theological difference between these three different forms of expression. Of course, if Martin Hengel (*Crucifixion* [ET, Philadelphia: Fortress Press, 1977]) and G. Ogg (*The Chronology of the Life of Paul* [London: Epworth Press, 1968]) are right in dating Paul's conversion within a year or two of the crucifixion, 'pre-Pauline' would cease to have any significant meaning.

[2]In spite of W. Schmithals (*Gnosticism in Corinth: an investigation of the letters to the Corinthians*, ET by John Seeley [Nashville: Abingdon Press, 1971]) there is no real evidence

word familiar to his opponents, and showing how even this is caught up into the wonder of the Christian gospel. There are two ways of defeating an opponent which are used by Paul. One way is to show that the ideas propounded are incompatible with revealed Christianity; the other way is to show how they are not only embraced but also transcended within the gospel.

But lest he should, even unintentionally, give the impression that atonement was the unaided activity of God the Son, Paul hastens to add that all this was 'in accordance with the will of the God who is also our Father' (for there is only one article for both *Theou, God,* and *Patros, Father*). Here is no possibility of an unreal antithesis between a harsh Father and a loving Son. The action of the Son was the very proof of the Father's love, as John 3:16 makes clear. Christ came to fulfil the Father's will, and thus to reveal him. The concept of *to thelēma, the will of God,* is one of the most profound concepts in the whole New Testament. This rescues our Christian calling from being merely subjective response, and roots it deep in the plan of God.

5. To any Jew, it was natural to slip into reverential *berākhāh,* or 'blessing', after any mention of the divine name. For instance, 'The Holy One – blessed be he' is one of the commonest of such blessings used by later Jewish commentators. So here, after the mention of the name of God, it is natural to add *to whom be the glory for ever and ever* (literally, 'for ages of ages', where the same word *aiōn* is used). Just as in old days the name of Yahweh, with its association of salvation from Egyptian bondage, stirred a Jew to praise, so now the name of Jesus Christ stirs Paul to similar response.[1] If the Jew of old was a 'Yahwist', to use modern theological jargon, then Paul and those to whom he wrote were 'Christians', whose whole understanding of God was dominated by the revelation in Christ.

It is just possible that this clause should be translated not so

---

that the heresy in Galatia was a form of Jewish Gnosticism, however true that may be in the case of the heresy of Colossians. Here, orthodox Jewish beliefs seem involved, although of an apocalyptic school. It is doubtful whether Gnosticism, in the full sense, had yet developed.

[1] It is of course true, as Betz points out, that no other Pauline 'prescripts' end with a doxology, as Galatians does. He suggests that the doxology takes the place of the usual praise of the recipients of the letter, which would have been out of place in this instance.

much as an ascription of praise, but as a glad affirmation of faith: 'his is the glory.' In that case, it might be compared with the ending of the Lord's Prayer which, whether part of the original text or not, certainly represents a very early liturgical 'response', like that made by Paul here. In either case, *doxa, glory*, is not the empty praise that humans can give: *doxa* corresponds to the Hebrew *kābōd*, the unutterable effulgence of the divine glory, the outward sign called the *shekīnah* that to a Jew denoted the very presence of God (Ex. 40:34).

The *Amen* at the end (like *Hosanna, Hallelujah, Maranatha* and *Abba*) is one of the 'fossilized survivals' of the original Hebrew and Aramaic languages of worship, transmitted through the Greek-speaking church of New Testament days to the later Latin-speaking church, and ultimately to most languages of earth. BAGD discusses this word, usually translated in the LXX as *genoito* (we may compare Paul's common *mē genoito* for the negative wish) with the sense 'let it come to pass'. It may be, however, that the Hebrew word contained theological overtones, referring not only to the steadfast faith of the one who prays, but also the changeless faithfulness of the one to whom the prayer is made.[1]

B. THE SUBJECT OF THE LETTER INTRODUCED (1:6–9)

'I am astounded that you are so quickly turning away from the one who called you by Christ's grace – to a different gospel. Not that there really are two sorts of gospel; it is only that there are certain parties who are throwing you into confusion, actually aiming at the distortion of the gospel of the Messiah. But even if it were I myself, or a very messenger direct from heaven, who should bring a gospel to you other than the one that I actually preached to you, you must turn in horror from him, as being one under God's curse. As I have already told you, so now I repeat: if anyone is preaching a gospel different from that which you received, let him be under God's curse.'

[1] So, in Galatians, *pistis* can either mean 'faith' or 'faithfulness': the meaning must be determined by the context: this probably reflects the same Hebraic background.

6. After the opening greeting,[1] Paul normally in his letters moves onwards to some prayer for the local church. He very often first finds some point on which he can commend them. Then he gradually introduces the real purpose of the letter, which is not always so pleasant to the recipients. All this was not only the normal construction of a first-century letter, but still is the typical pattern in many non-Western lands today. But on this occasion there is no easy and gradual transition to the subject: Paul is too deeply moved for that. 'I marvel', he begins (AV): it is incomprehensible to Paul's own nature that anyone should be capable of such conduct as the Galatians; *thaumazō, I am astonished*, is a strong word, and Paul means it. What conduct on the part of the Galatians is it that so moves him? Not gross moral lapse, but that *you are so quickly deserting him who called you in the grace of Christ and turning to a different gospel*. For *metatith-esthe, deserting*, other suggestions are 'changing your mind' or 'turning away' (BAGD). The verb is in the present tense. This is a process which is still taking place as Paul writes: he may still not be too late to arrest it. Also, the verb is probably middle voice, not passive. It is therefore something that the Galatians are themselves doing; they cannot say that they are compelled to do it by others, even if the false teachers are present and persuasive.

All this increases their culpability, so every clause in this verse is like another whiplash. They are doing this *so quickly*: it is not because with lapse of time, the gospel has lost its freshness. Some scholars on the basis of the words *houtōs tacheōs* have attempted to fix the date of the letter more exactly (see the Introduction, pp. 31ff.). But Paul may not mean 'so soon after I have evangelized you' (though this would be the simplest inter-pretation).[2] He may mean 'you have capitulated to these false teachers so soon after their arrival in Galatia'. There had been no long struggle in which the Galatians had been gradually worn

[1]Again, this is a standard part of the pattern of the secular letters of the day. After this, Paul should come to the expression of some good wish for the recipients, and then to the main body of the letter, if he followed secular analogies. But there is no reason to tie Paul woodenly to a set pattern, as some commentators do.

[2]It is of course possible that the word is used to mean 'so soon comparatively'. That might, for Paul, cover a period of years, if it is purely rhetorical (Betz).

down. They had apparently surrendered at once and had actually become enthusiastic over this new 'gospel'. That this corresponded to some cultural characteristic of the Galatians (so Jerome) is possible but unlikely. In many other areas of the world where response to the gospel has been swift, so has the lapse into heresy, especially in animistic areas where life is still tribally organized. *Him who called you* is, of course, God, not Paul. The apostle or missionary was only the herald, the ambassador, who brought the proclamation of the gracious offer (2 Cor. 5:20). The Galatians have not simply abandoned a theological position; they have abandoned a personal, loving God, who has manifested that love by calling them *in the grace of Christ*. Elsewhere, Paul can speak of Christians being chosen 'in him', *i.e.* 'in Christ' (Eph. 1:4). Since Christ is the very grace of God personified, there is no contradiction between the shorter and longer forms. It is typical of Pauline theology that *kalesantos*, 'called', is an aorist participle, which conveys the idea that God's call has been decisive, a historic fact in time. Perhaps there is a grain of comfort here for the Galatians, if they are ready to receive it. We might translate, 'who called you once and for all'.

Some ancient witnesses to the text read only 'him who called you by grace' (so NEB); this makes no real difference to the sense. Others read 'from Christ who called you by grace'; but this, while equally true, is not a typically Pauline phrase.

Paul sees the teaching of these Judaizers as *a different* (v. 7, 'another'[1]) *gospel*. We may leave the consideration of their actual teaching until later in the letter, where Paul seems to be dealing with it in some detail. Here some may ask, Is Paul perhaps being narrow-minded?[2] After all, these Judaizers certainly did preach salvation through Christ, although perhaps not through Christ alone. They never denied, as far as we know, that it was necessary also to believe in Jesus as Messiah and Saviour. How, then,

---

[1]Betz sees no semantic difference in Hellenistic Greek between *heteron*, 'another', and *allo*, 'different', citing Barton in support.

[2]There is a tendency, in some modern commentators, to be more broad minded than Paul, in dealing with the Judaizers: see Bruce for some examples. But to take this line is to fail to see Paul's basic theological point: the 'gospel' of the Judaizers is not a 'gospel' because it lacks 'grace' as its sole component, adding 'works of the flesh'.

can Paul say that this is *a different gospel*? It is true that the Judaizers seem to have in addition insisted on the observance of certain Jewish rites and ceremonies unknown to the Gentile churches founded by Paul. But did this really mean any more in those days than the 'denominational differences' in Christendom mean today? One church may use written forms of prayer, while another prefers extempore prayer; but we do not normally think of denying to our fellows the name of Christian because of this. Furthermore, it is highly likely that the Judaizers observed no Jewish customs other than those observed by the bulk of the Jewish Christian church at Jerusalem; and Paul certainly never accused James or John or Peter of preaching 'a different gospel'. Indeed, his whole point in this letter is that Jerusalem and Antioch preach exactly the same 'good news'. Why then is he so vehement in his opposition to the Judaizers? So would run the argument of some.

7. Perhaps the best way to see why Paul attacks their teaching so vigorously is to read carefully the next few clauses. He has said in verse 6 that this Jewish-Christian preaching is 'a different gospel' (*heteros*, properly in Greek 'the second of two alternatives', although in Hellenistic Greek such finer distinctions are blurred[1]). He now goes on to say *not that there is another [allo] gospel*: it is only that there are some who *trouble you*, who are 'throwing you into a state of mental confusion' (*tarassontes*) and actually *want to pervert the gospel of Christ*. Here Paul is questioning not their sincerity but their theology: sincerity in itself is not enough, and indeed, if misdirected, may do more damage, as here.

There are several possible interpretations of this sentence. It is probable that for a moment, in the heat of the argument, Paul has allowed to this false teaching the name of *euangelion*, 'gospel', and that he now wants to retract this name. A different gospel? How can there be any such thing, if there is only one gospel truly so called? This can then be only a distorted gospel, not another gospel. But, in so saying, is Paul allowing that the Judaizers preach essentially the same gospel, distorted though it

---

[1]BAGD, and also Bruce, give several examples of this blurring of distinctions.

be? Or is he totally condemning their message? The latter seems the more natural interpretation, to judge from what follows. None were more sure than these Jewish Christians that they preached 'the gospel of the Messiah' in all its fullness: they saw themselves not as perverting the gospel but as re-asserting it. But in truth, says Paul, none mangled the gospel more. There may be a deeper stress in the *thelontes, want to*: Paul may mean that this is a wilful distortion of Christian truth, and thus the more culpable, although indeed in the Bible all spiritual blindness is seen as wilful. Alternatively, he may mean that, while this is their desire, they cannot succeed. In spite of all their distorted presentation, the gospel still remains, eternally valid, eternally the same.

Tarassontes, trouble you (NEB, 'who unsettle your minds'; NIV, 'throwing you into confusion') is an interesting word. The various forms of this root always describe the opposite of that typical gift of Christ, *eirēnē*, peace of heart (Jn. 14:27). A 'Galatian gospel' can bring only unsettlement, doubt, lack of inner harmony, because it strikes at the nerve-centre of the great New Testament doctrine of assurance of salvation, which alone brings peace.

Who are these trouble-makers? *Tines, some*, is vague in the Greek, perhaps deliberately vague, with the use of the plural.[1] In 5:10 Paul uses the singular, as though it were one particular person, perhaps the ringleader, who is to blame. We cannot tell who he or they were; we do not know whether even Paul himself was sure of their identity. But it is likely that the source of the trouble was the extreme 'right wing' group of the Jewish-Christian church, probably emanating from Jerusalem and claiming James' authority, though no doubt James was perfectly correct in disclaiming any connection with them (Acts 15:24).

8. Paul's answer to this challenge is direct. The Galatians must learn to pay no attention to the outward qualifications of the messenger. No doubt they had been overawed by these august figures from the 'mother church' in Jerusalem, who apparently

---

[1]Betz suggests that this vagueness was to avoid giving to the trouble-makers any unnecessary publicity, but this seems a rather modern concept, too sophisticated for the context.

claimed apostolic authority for their message. So far from receiving them, says Paul, they must not even receive Paul himself if he should return preaching a gospel like this. When we realize the closeness of the link that bound Paul, the lonely bachelor, to the early converts who were his spiritual children (2 Cor. 6:13), and remember the esteem in which they held him, we can appreciate the force of this injunction. It is not just that Paul, in a burst of spirituality, is begging his spiritual children to correct his doctrine if he is ever wrong. The principle goes far beyond this. He is teaching them that the status or person of the messenger does not validate his message; rather, the nature of the message validates the messenger. Later, he will stress this again. To Paul, the test of 'apostolic ministry' is to be found in its fruits.

But this test of preachers does not only apply to Paul. Even if *an angel from heaven* were to preach any gospel to them other than that which they had already received, Paul's prayer is that such a messenger should be *anathema*, which conveys the same idea as the Hebrew *ḥerem*, that of being 'under the curse', 'under the wrath of God'.[1] From a person or object under God's curse, the Galatians should turn away in horror: so they ought to turn in horror from preachers such as these. But this is the very opposite to what they have done. They have in fact listened with 'itching ears' to this false gospel (2 Tim. 4:3), as Paul warned Timothy.

Why introduce *an angel from heaven*? It may be that Paul is thinking of the general meaning of *angelos*, which is 'messenger': from any such messenger, whether human or apparently divine, they must turn away. It may be, however, that it is a reference to the Judaistic nature of the heresy. It was common Jewish belief that the Mosaic law had been given through angelic mediators,[2] and these new teachers may have stressed

---

[1] For the whole concept of the curse, see the excursus in Betz, and the section which follows.

[2] This is of course not actually stated in the Old Testament, unless we so interpret verses like Ps. 68:17, 'with . . . thousands upon thousands, the Lord came from Sinai', where the reference is to the angelic host. But it certainly seems to have been commonly held by Jews of New Testament times, and, if so, they must have used some biblical text to justify the view, even if the exegesis was far-fetched. The tendency in later Judaism was to make God himself more remote, by introducing mediators in his dealing with Israel.

this point when urging the simple Gentile Christians to keep the Mosaic law. Later Judaism, especially when tinged by Gnosticism, made greater play still of angels. Again, Paul may be using this particular word to show them the possibility of Satan himself appearing 'as an angel of light' to deceive them (2 Cor. 11:14). It was to one who suggested a 'false gospel', a gospel without a cross, that the Lord said, 'Get behind me, Satan!' (Mk. 8:33). If, on the other hand, this letter was written to those living in the southern part of the Roman province of Galatia, then *angelos* might possibly be a reference to the circumstances of Paul's evangelism of them and their attribution of divinity to him on that that occasion (see Acts 14:11).[1] The word *euangelizō*, *preach*, involves the *euangelion*, 'gospel', of which BAGD says: 'originally a reward for good news, then simply good news . . . also in religious use . . . in our literature only in the specific sense God's good news to men, the gospel.'

9. Perhaps Paul fears that the Galatians do not yet understand the seriousness of the matter, so he reiterates it. *As we have said before, so now I say again*. There is probably no significance in the switch from plural to singular in the sentence, a switch common to Paul. In the New Testament, the plural 'we' is often used for the singular 'I'.[2] In modern English, the 'we' has an authoritarian sense; but in some languages, the use of 'we' is more modest than the use of the blunt 'I'. If the 'South Galatian' theory as to the letter's destination is adopted, then it may be that Paul's mind is going back to the time when Galatia was evangelized by himself and Barnabas (Acts 14:7), and he is pleading with the Galatians to remember their common gospel on that occasion.[3] In that case, the *before*, conveyed by the preposition *pro-* before the verb, *legō*, 'say', would refer to the

[1]Some editors challenge this. True, Paul was initially seen by the Lycaonians as Hermes, who was the traditional messenger of the Greek gods, but not an 'angel' in the Hebrew sense. Since Paul's later stoning gave the lie to this view, it is probably better to see the phrase as pure hyperbole.

[2]BAGD under the word *egō* draws attention to the literature dealing with this question. Whatever the explanation, the fact seems undoubted.

[3]Editors have often remarked on the singular lack of reference to Barnabas throughout the whole letter, except in connection with the Antioch episode. Perhaps the cause is embarrassment, because of the dubious part played by Barnabas in that incident.

circumstances of the initial evangelization. We would have to assume that Paul had warned the Galatians from the start about the possibilities of subsequent distortion of the gospel. We cannot say that this was impossible, in view of his similar warning delivered at Miletus to the Ephesian elders (see Acts 20:29–30). Nevertheless, it seems more likely that Paul is here referring to his own statement already made in the sentence before. He is in that case simply saying, 'Let me repeat what I have just said.' That Paul would cheerfully repeat advice or instruction, we know from his own words in Philippians 3:1.

The phrase *ho parelabete, which you received*, is interesting. In one sense, Paul's own experience represents a decisive break with religious tradition, as seen in its Jewish form.[1] He will describe himself, before conversion, as a great traditionalist (1:14), obviously in contrast to his later behaviour. Further, in the Gospels, Jewish religious leaders are accused of neglecting God's plain command in order to keep their own cherished traditions (Mt. 15:1–6). But Paul does not condemn all 'tradition'; what he condemns is religious tradition which is in conflict with the word and command of God. When tradition is 'independent' in this sense, not under the control and testing of the word of God, then it comes under utter condemnation. Elsewhere, Paul commends his churches for observing 'the traditions' which they have received from him (2 Thes. 2:15), whether by word or letter. But the word *paradoseis* in that particular context seems to refer to 'handing down of doctrine', not of practices in the church. It is thus not untrue to say that the only 'apostolic tradition' known in the pages of the New Testament, and commended there, is in the realm of doctrine. Those who hold that, hold the true 'apostolic tradition'.

In the passage immediately before us, the aorist tense of *parelabete*, 'you received', while it should not be overstressed, probably conveys something of the thought of the 'once-for-all' nature of the faith delivered to the Galatians. Paul preached it;

---

[1] Paul's whole attitude to tradition is an interesting study. In one sense of the word, his conversion was a direct act of God, quite independent of any Christian or Jewish tradition (1:12). In another sense, he hands on to the Corinthians what he has 'received' from Christ (1 Cor. 11:23). For the technical Hebrew words probably lying behind the Greek here, see Betz. See also F.F. Bruce, *Tradition Old and New* (Exeter: Paternoster, 1970).

they received it. That was a decisive experience, not a tentative
or temporary position, to be outgrown later, as perhaps suggested by the Judaizers.

There are two other points that we should note here: the first
is that the Judaizers in their preaching in Galatia would have
undoubtedly laid great stress on 'tradition', as Paul the Rabbi
knew well. He must meet this emphasis by showing that, in
some circumstances, this 'tradition' can become a stumbling
block, as it had been in his case and still was with the vast
majority of his fellow countrymen. But Paul is never content
with a merely negative attack. His second point will be that his
gospel is the true biblical 'tradition', for it goes back to God's
promise to Abraham, centuries before the giving of the law,
through Moses.

C. PAUL'S CONVERSION (1:10-24)

The gospel is a truth; but for Paul and the Galatians alike, it is far
more than an abstract truth. It is a truth proven in experience,
and Paul's argument here will be to recall to the Galatians their
own rich spiritual experience in early days compared with their
present spiritual poverty. After that, he will turn to theological
argument, using the very Old Testament Scriptures that the
Judaizers were doubtless quoting to such effect. Finally, in the
closing chapters of the letter, he will use his culminating argument – the transforming moral and spiritual power of the true
gospel. These are practical arguments that none can gainsay; but
before he uses any of them, he will appeal to the undoubted
facts of his own experience, to which they can bear witness.

1. Paul's protest (1:10-12)

This could be paraphrased as follows: 'Now when I talk like this
am I trying to win human approval – or God's? Or am I trying to
please mortal men?[1] If I were still trying to give satisfaction to a

[1]Both 'persuading' and 'pleasing' tend to have a bad sense in Paul, when the words are
used with humans as object (Betz).

human master, I would not be Christ's servant. I pronounce solemnly to you, fellow Christians, that the gospel which was preached by me is no human gospel. The proof is that I neither received it by human tradition, nor was I taught it by rote: it came through an unveiling of Jesus Christ.'

10. There is probably considerable stress on *arti, now*. It seems likely that the Judaizers accused Paul of being 'all things to all men', in a sense very different from that in which he used the phrase (1 Cor. 9:22). They seem to have insinuated that when he was among Jews, he preached the need of circumcision and law-keeping in order to 'curry favour' with them (NEB). He was simply, they said, trying to 'canvass for their support' (NEB), doubtless, they felt, conscious of his own insecure position as being no true 'apostle'. In the same way when he was speaking to Gentiles, he preached freedom from the restrictions of the law in order to increase his following among them. To the Judaizers, Paul was an ecclesiastical politician, not a theologian. He was simply canvassing for high office in the church. Naturally, such an untrue charge must have cut Paul to the quick. He hated inconsistency above all else, as we can see from his summary dealing with Peter at Antioch (2:11). But he has learned not to waste time over his own hurt feelings; he appeals to well-known historical facts instead.

Of course, no person in their right mind could accuse Paul, in the writing of this letter, of going out of his way to curry favour with anybody. Indeed, if he had desired to antagonize the Judaizers and Galatians alike, he could hardly have done it better: so much is clear. But Paul is probably referring to something much wider than this letter. His whole life is open to their examination. Since his conversion he has deliberately renounced all aim of pleasing humans in favour of that of pleasing God alone. He has long ago learned that mere 'eye-service' of fellow humans is utterly inadequate, and this was indeed one of the first truths that he taught his converts (see Eph. 6:6; Col. 3:22). Of course, he was not alone in this attitude. The Jerusalem apostles had already enunciated the principle boldly in Acts 5:29, and several sayings of the Lord lie at its root (*e.g.* Mt. 6:24). So concerned is Paul with pleasing God alone that he not only refrains from seeking to please himself; he does not even judge himself (1 Cor. 4:1–5).

There is a world of meaning in the short word *eti*, *still*. Paul now sees clearly that the whole course of his life in Judaism was at heart designed not to win the praise of God, but human praise. The 'religious' person is often praised by the world outside; the Christian is very rarely praised. But, even here, Paul does not say these things to praise himself. He is simply admitting, to paraphrase his meaning, 'There was a time when this charge that they make against me would have been justified. But that was when I taught as they taught; it is not true now.' He brushes over the charge itself by simply showing the utter inconsistency of service of humans (in the sense of trying to curry favour with them) with that unique and complete devotion to God which is the only fit response to the manifestation of God's love in Christ. A slave can have only one master; that was axiomatic in the Graeco-Roman world of the first century (*cf.* Mt. 6:24).

11–12. But surely even Paul must serve some human masters in the gospel? No doubt the Judaizers claimed that Paul had learned the gospel initially from the apostles and elders in Jerusalem; surely therefore he was dependent upon them for approval and support? How then could he challenge any teachers from Jerusalem, the mother church? It is the same sort of argument that has often been used in the past, singularly without profit, in theological controversy as to the relationship of Bible and church. Admittedly Paul has had a personal transforming experience of Christ: but from where did that experience come? So Paul will outline the steps that led to his conversion and the experiences that immediately followed, to prove the independence of the work of the Spirit.

I would have you know translates *gnōrizō*, a word which often means 'reveal' (so BAGD). Hence NEB, 'I must make it clear to you'. What follows is a declaration of more than usual solemnity. Paul has a variety of ways with which he introduces such 'statements at law'; this is one of them. Once again, it is noteworthy that the apostle does not try to defend some theological position; he simply appeals to the sort of gospel which they, as well as he, know to have been preached in Galatia with well-remembered results. But what does he mean by saying that it *is not man's gospel*, in Greek *ouk estin kata anthrōpon* (NIV, 'not something that man made up')? Paul himself explains this paradox by saying that he had not received the gospel as a 'tradition', in the way in which Jewish beliefs and practices had been handed down. This is a direct blow to the Judaizers, but more follows. Neither was Paul's gospel something learned by rote and repetition, as doubtless Paul had learned rabbinics in the school of Gamaliel at Jerusalem. This is a warning to us today not to overstress the importance of oral *katēchēsis*, 'baptismal instruction', in the early church, as is fashionable today. No doubt such Christian teaching and learning by rote existed in the early church, as it exists in third-world churches today, but Paul is concerned here to show that no-one can be educated into the kingdom of God. This was another blow to the claims of the Judaizers. Paul had not, he says, learned his gospel in the presumed Christian catechetical schools of Jerusalem. Where then had he learned it? It had come directly through a *revelation* (*apokalypsis*, 'unveiling') *of Jesus Christ*, he says.

Is the phrase *of Jesus Christ*, *Iēsou Christou*, subjective or objective genitive? Is this a revelation made by Christ to Paul, or a revelation of the true meaning of the Christ made by God to Paul? Perhaps it is better to leave the meaning as ambiguous in the English as it is in the Greek. Of the alternatives, the second seems slightly better, but it need not rule out the first. On the road to Damascus, Paul had received a transforming revelation. The source of all revelation is God; and the content of this revelation was Christ (Acts 9:5). From that moment, the veil that had obscured the Messiahship of Jesus was drawn away from his eyes and Paul saw clearly the true spiritual meaning of historical facts with which he had long been acquainted. It seems impossible that Paul could have lived in Jerusalem from boyhood (the probable meaning of *anatethrammenos*, 'brought up', in Acts 22:3) without knowing at least the outline facts of the life of Jesus. It is equally impossible that Paul should have persecuted the church without knowing the interpretation which the church gave to these facts about Jesus: that was the reason for the persecution. Indeed, some scholars have held, on the basis of 2 Corinthians 5:16, that Paul had met or seen Jesus in the days of his Jerusalem ministry. If, as is probable, Paul was a younger contemporary of Jesus, that is by no means impossible, and even likely.

However that may be, Paul does not seem to be claiming here any supernatural direct acquaintance with the historical facts of the gospel story. That would savour more of magic than of revelation, and anyway we have seen that it is unlikely that any special revelation of such a nature would be necessary in this area. But no-one could see Jesus to be the Christ, God's Messiah, without the illumination of the Holy Spirit. This had been as true of Peter in Matthew 16:17 as it was of Paul; and Paul soon saw that this principle was to be generalized (1 Cor. 12:3). This 'revelation' in Jesus of the suffering Messiah, God's Son, and the 'Lord', is itself the gospel, and this revelation no mere humans can impart by teaching, however much we may desire to do it.

2. Paul's life before his conversion (1:13–14)

How can Paul prove to the Galatians the essentially supernatural nature of the gospel which he preached to them, and still preaches? He does it by direct appeal to his own known experience of that gospel: nobody can deny this as a fact.

'For you have heard about the sort of life that I lived when I was of the Jewish faith in days gone by – how I persecuted and raided the church of God beyond all measure and proportion.[1] I was making great strides in Judaism, outdistancing many of my own age-group among my people, since I was a regular extremist as far as ancestral traditions were concerned.'[2]

13. Paul is concerned to show that, before his experience on the road to Damascus, he certainly did not believe this gospel.

---

[1] BAGD, under the word *hyperbolē*, supports this sense.

[2] With deference to Betz, Paul almost certainly had not studied oratory, nor read Quintilian, the stock classical work on the subject. Any resemblance between his defence and the stock 'defensive' approach of oratory is therefore either accidental or instinctive, if not something read into the text by us. Apart from all else, Paul was too agitated to follow set rules of composition at this time.

Moreover, he was in no way disposed to believe it. So far from accepting it, he was infuriated as a Jew by what he regarded as a blasphemy, just as a pious Moslem would be today. Later, he was to sum this period of his life by describing himself as 'in pious zeal, a persecutor of the church' (Phil. 3:6, NEB). How had the Galatians *heard* of all this? There are several possibilities. First, since in Acts Paul refers on two occasions to his own conversion in some detail (Acts 22 and 26), he may well have also done so when preaching to the Galatians initially. He was always ready to reinforce theology by experience, as he does in this letter. Secondly, the Galatians might have heard the news themselves, as the rumour spread from church to church. The conversion of such a notable opponent must have made a great impression everywhere (1:24). Thirdly, the Judaizers themselves may have mentioned it scornfully: 'The man is only a convert,' they may have said; 'have you never heard that he actually used to persecute the church in early days?' The fourth possibility is that this was the first that the Galatians had heard about the matter. Paul would then be simply introducing his own experience for the first time, with this apology for mentioning it at all.

My *former life* translates *anastrophē*, a word very frequently used in the New Testament, always of 'conduct, way of life, moral behaviour', whether good or bad. Paul's use here of the word *Ioudaismos*, 'Judaism', is full of pathos. It is not until the days of the apostolic fathers that the word will be used in direct contrast to *Christianismos*, 'Christianity', but it is quite clear that already Paul regards Judaism as a different religion.[1] For him it belongs to the past; for him, as already in John's Gospel, the term 'the Jews' has become a term to describe those in Israel who have not responded to the gospel (see Jn. 10:31, *etc.*). The rejection of their promised Messiah had turned Judaism from the main stream of God's plan and purpose to a stagnant backwater. It is a tragedy that the misplaced and mistaken zeal of the mediaeval church turned this plain statement of fact into a theological principle, and initiated that Christian anti-Semitism

---

[1] Betz is incorrect in saying that, at that time, Paul was only 'changing parties' within Judaism, from Pharisaism to Christianity: the break was too total and violent for that, and both sides were clearly conscious of it.

which has been the shame of the church of God in some centuries: see the Introduction, pp. 53ff.

The word *ediōkon, I persecuted,* is the very word used in Acts 9:4, 'Saul, Saul, why do you persecute me?' It has often been noted, especially in recent years, that this context comes very close to identifying the church with the body of Christ, though no such formal identification is made here. But this has roots in dominical sayings like Matthew 10:40, 'He who receives you receives me', and does not necessarily represent any further doctrinal development. It does seem unlikely, however, that Paul could use this same verb *diōkō* without being at the same time vividly reminded of his own experience at Damascus. He could have brought out the point mentioned above (that persecution of the church is persecution of Christ) by calling the church 'the church of Christ', as he usually does. But here he obtains the same effect by calling it *the church of God, ekklēsia tou Theou,* 'God's company', just like Israel in the Old Testament. Opposition to the church is not only opposition to Jesus as Messiah: one who did not accept Jesus' claim might perhaps make light of this. It is also opposition to God, the God who, in Old Testament days, had chosen Israel as his 'company', and who now has chosen the Christian church, whether Jew or Gentile. This is again a direct challenge to the Judaizers. All the past, as well as the future, belongs to the Christian church, not to them. This was a point that the early fathers delighted to make in controversy.

14. But Paul had other more solid qualities in those days to commend him as a Pharisee, besides his zeal in persecuting the church (of which it is unlikely that Gamaliel at least approved, see Acts 5:38). *Prokoptō, advanced,* translated in the paraphrase on p. 85 as 'making great strides', is a neutral word in Greek. The apostle does not say whether this road which he was taking was leading to a good or bad destination, but merely that he was well advanced on his journey. If religion be seen as a race, a kind of competition, then Paul was well ahead in the lead; NEB well translates as 'outstripping many of my Jewish contemporaries'. These latter are probably his rabbinic fellow students at Jerusalem. All the 'men of his year' could bear him witness, if only they were willing to do so (*cf.* Acts 26:5). But it was only an outward progress in Judaism, a formal religion. Something of Paul's accompanying inner torment of conscience in those days can be seen from Romans 7.

Such progress in a young rabbi would be shown mainly by knowledge and practice of the 'traditions' of Israel, the increasing body of material that had, over the centuries, grown up around the Torah like a protective fence. This was collected and summed up, first in the primary collection of the Mishnah, then in the secondary and later collection called the Gemara, the two together forming the Talmud. Of it, in later days, the rabbis would say: 'The Scriptures are water; the Mishnah, wine: but the Gemara, spiced wine.' How early this attitude had begun to develop, we cannot say; but passages like Mark 7:6-13 suggest that it was not unknown even in New Testament days. It is probably these traditional explanations of the law which Paul describes as *traditions of my fathers*, *i.e.* 'of my ancestors' (NEB). Some have preferred to translate as 'my own family traditions', and scent a reference to Paul's known family connections with the Pharisaic party (see Acts 23:6). Whichever explanation be adopted, Paul says that he was a *zēlōtēs*, a zealot for these traditions. He may be using the word in a general sense, or he may be thinking of the fanatical zeal displayed by the later party in politics, usually called 'the Zealots', who were finally responsible for the catastrophe that overwhelmed Jerusalem. Christ had probably already numbered one such among his twelve; compare Mark 3:18 with Luke 6:15. Now Christ is to number a second such among his apostles, one whose fanatical zeal had been just as great, although it had been in the realm of religion, not politics.[1]

3. Paul's conversion and subsequent events (1:15-24)

'But when it was the gracious will of God, who had set me apart when I was an unborn babe, and called me through his grace, to reveal his Son in my case, so that I might preach the good news

[1] It is of course most unlikely that Paul had any actual connection with this extremist party in his pre-conversion days, even if it existed at such an early date. It is his 'zeal' that is emphasized (Betz: but contrast, less probably, Lightfoot).

about him among foreigners, at once I did not consult with any human being, nor did I make the journey up to Jerusalem to those who had been apostles longer than I. Instead, I retired to Arabia, and then came back to Damascus. Then, after three years, I did go up to Jerusalem, to make the acquaintance of Cephas, and I stayed with him for about a fortnight. Not one other of the apostles did I see, except James, the Lord's brother. On my oath before God, what I am writing is true.

'After that, I went into the general area of Syria with Cilicia. But I was unknown by sight to the Christian churches of Judea: all that they had heard was that their former persecutor was now preaching the good news which he had formerly tried to destroy, and they continually praised God for what he had done in my case.'

15. What had changed this young man from a blind if fervent follower of religious tradition to a devoted servant of Jesus Christ?[1] It was the gracious will of God. To Paul, the origin of all human salvation lies in the mind and loving purpose of God. That is always his sheet-anchor, but equally he never denies the reality of the response to which we are summoned. Before Herod Agrippa he refers to this occasion, and immediately adds 'I was not disobedient to the heavenly vision' (Acts 26:19). But all this is within the *eudokia* of God, his loving purpose of salvation. The clearest use of the noun itself is to be found in Luke 2:14; and, while it is the verb that is used here in verse 16, the theological force is just as strong.

Like Jeremiah, Paul is one 'set apart'[2] and called from his mother's womb, by the prevenient grace of God. This may refer to Paul's call to the prophetic office, in view of the parallel with the wording of Jeremiah (Je. 1:5), but it may equally well refer to his general Christian calling. Romans 9:11 shows how strong a theological position Paul was prepared to adopt. Here, as in Romans, the reference is to a child as yet unborn.

[1] For various 'Freudian' interpretations of Paul's conversion, ancient and modern, see Betz, who rightly rejects them as inadequate.

[2] Many scholars have seen here a reference to the Hebrew verb *pārash*, 'to set apart', the root which probably underlies Paul's old title as a 'Pharisee'. This however, while possible, is not necessary.

16. *To me*, or, following the Greek, 'in me' (NIV). In either case, God's gracious purpose of salvation is shown to be accomplished by a revelation of his Son: that is his pattern of working, and it is as true of Paul as of any other Christian. If we translate 'in my case', we will preserve the ambiguity of the Greek *en emoi*. The NEB, somewhat periphrastically but perhaps wisely, translates both meanings side by side, 'to me and through me'. Again, there is no theological contradiction. What begins by being a revelation of Christ to Paul becomes a revelation of Christ in Paul, as the Spirit produces his fruits in unaccustomed soil. As Paul preaches to the Gentiles the unsearchable riches of Christ, so Christ is revealed through him. In view of the fact that a consciousness of his task followed so closely upon Paul's conversion, probably 'through me' is the best translation, if we must restrict ourselves to one. For Paul is clear that the purpose of this revelation, this unveiling of Christ, was *in order that I might preach him among the Gentiles.*[1] The phrase *en tois ethnesin* is probably better translated in modern English as 'among the foreigners'; it literally means 'among the peoples', with the meaning of non-Jewish peoples. Acts 9:6 and 15 show how early in Paul's Christian life was his sense of God's calling to the Gentile mission. The Galatians and his other Gentile converts were not only his spiritual children (Gal. 4:19): they were the fruits of his apostolate to the nations (Rom. 1:13, *cf.* Je. 1:5), his 'letters of introduction' to those who asked him by what authority he preached. They were the Spirit's seal on his apostolate; they were his special missionary sphere. No wonder he reacted so violently against Judaizing interference here (2 Cor. 3:2).

17. There are some slight difficulties in fitting the events which Paul here says followed his conversion into the highly compressed account of Acts. But his main point is that he retired immediately to think out by himself and for himself the implications of the new discovery: he did not seek teaching from others. By *Arabia*, he presumably means here the district in the

---

[1]Although, in Hellenistic Greek, the senses of purpose and consequence are often confused, and the appropriate prepositions are therefore frequently used interchangeably, this clause is clearly one of aim and purpose. See Bruce for this breaking down of grammatical categories in later colloquial Greek.

immediate vicinity of Damascus, although Nabatean 'Arabia' covered a far larger and ill-defined desert area as well. This whole general area was under the rule of Aretas, and might thus be fairly so described. Damascus itself was not controlled by Aretas at the time, but his resident 'ethnarch' there represented his interests and obviously had influence (2 Cor. 11:32). But the exact location of Paul's stay is unimportant. It is however important that, whatever part Ananias had played in Paul's actual experience (Acts 9:17), Paul did not have help from him or from any other of the Damascus Christians at this later stage. This is a further proof that the gospel is essentially supernatural. By the Spirit the first illumination came to Paul, and by the Spirit the light would grow. Paul would already be familiar, of course, with all the Old Testament Scriptures dealing with the Messiah. He would probably also be familiar with the Christian use of such Scriptures, from his old days of controversy with the church. All that now remained was to rethink his whole position in the light of the new revelation. For this, not advice from others but quiet thought was needed.

If Paul felt no need of consultation with the Christians of Damascus, he felt still less need of consultation with those of Jerusalem. To the argument of the Judaizers that the apostles were at Jerusalem, Paul would make the retort that he, equally with them, was an apostle. He did not deny the priority in time of their apostolic calling; but, apart from the fact that they *were apostles before me*, he would admit no difference. If, as is probable, Paul in these words is here referring to the 'inner ring' consisting of the twelve, and not to the wider apostolic group, then an interesting point arises. Upon what did Paul base his claim to be an apostle in this peculiar, almost exclusive sense? Undoubtedly, upon the will of God and the call of Christ.[1] And, without having met the risen Christ, how could this be? We can only say that Paul seems to have regarded his meeting with the

---

[1]For the qualifications for membership of the twelve, see Acts 1: 21–22, where the question arises over the appointment of Matthias. We may dismiss the view adopted by Betz that the roots of Paul's concept of apostolate lie in Syrian Gnosticism. The *shāliach*, or 'official envoy', concept is too deeply rooted in orthodox Judaism for that (Bruce), although Lampe considers it to have arisen later than the time of the New Testament (see G. W. H. Lampe, *A Patristic Greek Lexicon* [Oxford, Clarendon Press, 1961–68]). By the fourth century, it was common, and it may well have existed for some time before that.

risen Christ on the road outside Damascus as being just as 'real' and objective an experience as any confrontation of Christ by Peter or Thomas in post-resurrection days (*cf.* 1 Cor. 15:8). He was thus just as able to bear witness to the reality of Christ's resurrection as they were.

The importance of this for us today is considerable. For it means that, at least in a secondary sense, any true Christian today can bear similar testimony to the risen Christ. It is necessary to say 'in a secondary sense', not because our experience is any less real than theirs, but because Scripture is clear that the original twelve apostles had a peculiar function in bearing this witness to the life, teaching, death and resurrection of Jesus Christ (*cf.* Acts 10:41). That is why any authentic Christian experience must conform to the apostolic faith and practice. Indeed, the New Testament itself is the abiding record of the eye-witness testimony of this vital first generation. There was, however, in the eyes of the Jerusalem church, although not of Paul, a further qualification apparently considered necessary for the position, and a qualification to which Paul could lay no claim, as not being one of the twelve. It was to have been in the company of Christ from the days of John's baptizing until Christ's resurrection (Acts 1:22). Those who interpret 2 Corinthians 5:16 as an indication that Paul had met or seen Jesus during the days of his earthly ministry,[1] might conclude that Paul would probably have answered in the words of that verse. Mere knowledge of the physical events of the life or person of Christ had for him paled into insignificance compared with the flash of spiritual insight by which alone one could rightly interpret those events.

18. Nevertheless, Paul would be the last person in the world to deny the importance of such knowledge: it was perhaps to gain it that he finally sought the company of Peter, one great 'fount of tradition' at Jerusalem.

It is often Paul's way, after a sweeping denial of the kind he has just made, to introduce some qualification which is

---

[1]But for a different interpretation of the meaning of the phrase, see Tasker, *2 Corinthians*, TNTC (Leicester: Inter-Varsity Press, 1963); compare also NEB translation.

demanded by his rigorous sense of honesty, even if it might seem to be damaging to his case. So in 1 Corinthians 1:14, after he has roundly denied that he has baptized any Christians at Corinth except Crispus and Gaius, by 1:16 he has added the Stephanas family, and possibly others. Here then he freely admits that after three years he did go up to Jerusalem to *visit Cephas*, or perhaps 'to make the acquaintance of Cephas', staying with him for about a fortnight (*fifteen days*, by Semitic reckoning).

Once again, we are faced with unsolved and indeed, with our present evidence, insoluble questions of chronology. The *three years*, for instance, may be counted either from the date of Paul's conversion, or from his return from Arabia to Damascus. On a first reading, the account in Acts sounds as if all these events took place in a very short time. But we can tell from the speed at which the narrative moves in Acts that it is a highly compressed account. If we had the full history of Paul's movements in early years, we might well find that they present a far more complex pattern than that found in either Galatians or Acts. We do not know, for instance, whether this was the visit of Acts 9:27 paid by Paul to Jerusalem following his conversion (for verse 23 of Acts 9 warns us that since Paul's conversion 'many days' had passed, which might well cover three years), or whether it was the so-called 'famine relief' visit of Acts 11:30.

If we take the biblical text at its face value, this should be the first visit, the more so as the second visit was apparently paid from Antioch, not Damascus. But again, Acts does not actually say that Paul spent all this very early period at Damascus. It states only that the period ended and began with Damascus. Nor does it even say that, when expelled from Damascus because of the hostility of both the local Jews and Aretas (possibly arising from Paul's evangelism not only in the city itself but also in nearby 'Arabia'), Paul went immediately to Jerusalem. Jerusalem is merely the next point at which the story is taken up. Nevertheless, on Paul's own testimony, the main point is clear. For the first few formative years after conversion, he had not even revisited Jerusalem; and, by that time, Paul's gospel was fully developed. Indeed, we have seen that it was because of preaching this gospel that he had been forced to flee

Damascus and seek refuge in Jerusalem (Acts 9:22–26). So he could hardly be said to owe his gospel to the Jerusalem church.

Nevertheless, fair is fair; Paul admits that he *went up*[1] to Jerusalem. No doubt the Judaizers would seize on this admission: let them seize upon it. He has a further admission to make which will be still more damaging to his case. He did it *to visit Cephas*, or 'to get acquainted with Peter' (NIV). The verb *historēsai*, while originally meaning something like 'to enquire of', means in Hellenistic Greek 'to visit for the purpose of coming to know someone' (BAGD). Paul meets the anticipated Judaizing attack by explaining why he visited Peter, and indeed, why he stayed with him for 'a couple of weeks' (for *hēmeras dekapente* is possibly only a vague term of time). Still, it was certainly not because he thought of Peter as 'prince of apostles' that he sought him; why then did he want 'to get to know' Peter? It is tempting to see the reason in the possession by Peter of the sole qualification for apostleship which Paul was lacking in the eyes of the Jerusalem church. Paul apparently had no firsthand knowledge of the life and ministry of Jesus save that which any outsider might have, even a religious dilettante like Herod Agrippa (see Acts 26:26). Peter must have been a priceless fount of knowledge in this area. Indeed, tradition makes him the source behind Mark's Gospel. Anyone who spent a fortnight lodging with Peter must have heard much about the earthly Christ, and the first letter of Peter gives some idea of the kind of reminiscence to which Paul would have been able to listen.

19. Be that as it may, having admitted that he met Peter, Paul will go no farther. He makes the astonishing point that *I saw none of the other apostles*,[2] even though he admits that he was in Jerusalem and apparently was living in Peter's lodging there. It is not certain whether we should translate the next phrase *except James the Lord's brother*, or as 'only James, the Lord's brother'

---

[1] 'Go up' is the usual word to denote going to a capital, in this case, a religious capital, as Paul readily accepts and acknowledges. But this does not extend to an admission that the 'Jerusalem apostles' were a religious hierarchy.

[2] Trudinger, quoted in Betz, translates this as 'other than the apostles I saw no-one except James, the Lord's brother'. But this does not seem a natural translation. James the son of Zebedee would of course have been already martyred by Herod by this time (Acts 12:2).

(NIV); it all depends on whether Paul reckoned this James as an 'apostle' like his namesake, James the son of Zebedee. One of the twelve he was certainly not. He had not, like the others, followed Jesus from John's baptism and was apparently brought to belief only after the resurrection, possibly by one of the appearances of the risen Lord. He therefore lacked one of the necessary qualifications for recognized membership of the twelve just as much as Paul did, and would therefore have been useless for Paul's presumed purpose of gaining information about Christ's ministry. In any case, apart from these two (at least two seem demanded by the plural 'apostles' in Acts 9:27), he met none of the original apostolic circle.[1] This, if accepted, would make the claim of the Judaizers slender.

20. *Before God, I do not lie:* Paul would not have said this, if he had not realized that his statement would be challenged. But not only is Paul's statement conceivable, it also fits perfectly with the little that we know of conditions in the Jerusalem church of the day. For one thing, Acts 9:26 mentions specifically that all the disciples at Jerusalem (and this, no doubt, included the apostles) were terrified of Paul when he arrived. Those who remembered his persecuting activities of only a few years before might be pardoned if they suspected another trick now. Christians in many parts of the world today learn to be wary of 'false brethren' (2:4), who turn out to be nothing but secret police informers. To our cost, we can now fully understand the disciples' reaction more easily than our predecessors could. Had it not been for the introduction by Barnabas (presumably to Peter and James), it is very unlikely that Paul would have met even these two. We see then that it may not have been by Paul's own choice that his initial contacts in Jerusalem were so restricted, though no doubt at this later stage he realizes that God's hand was in it all. Perhaps the other apostles were not yet convinced of the reality of Paul's conversion. Alternatively, they

---

[1] We may reject views that a wider circle than the twelve is meant here, although of course the term could be used more widely elsewhere (see Rom. 16:7). Indeed, in Romans, out of thirty-four uses of this term, only three refer to the twelve (according to correspondence from Morris), and, in the whole of the New Testament, out of some eighty uses, seventy are outside the Gospels, and usually have this wider reference.

may not have been in Jerusalem at the time. We know extra-ordinarily little of the movements of these other, more shadowy, members of the twelve, apart from various late traditions. True, Acts 8:1 tells us that the apostles did not join in the general flight after Stephen's death: but Acts 12:1-3 suggests that only James, the brother of John, and Peter were in Jerusalem at the time of Herod's persecution of the church. Certainly, the aftermath of that persecution was that even Peter fled 'to another place', almost certainly somewhere outside Herod's jurisdiction (Acts 12:17), possibly even, as suggested elsewhere, Antioch.

Whatever we may guess to have been the probable reasons for the circumstances, Paul has given us the blunt facts. He must realize how unlikely they sound, for he adds (paraphrasing for the sake of clarity), 'On my oath, what I am writing is true.' After such a solemn assertion, we do well to pay special heed, for Paul is not giving a casual account of his movements. Everything here depends on whether he has had prolonged personal contact with the leaders of the Jerusalem church before his own gospel was formed. He denies this by what was a virtual form of oath to a Jew, more binding still to a Christian who followed the Lord's injunction (see Mt. 5:34).

21. So far, so good. Paul has proved his point that, in early days at least, he had no sustained contact with the acknowledged leaders of the church at Jerusalem. But had he perhaps had contact with them elsewhere? Or at the least, had he had such contacts with the scattered local churches of Judea? This question would become the more important if, as suggested, the twelve were at this time scattered more widely. *Then*, says Paul, *I went into the region of Syria and Cilicia*: to the churches of Judea, he was *still not known by sight*.

If, as seems demanded, the visit to Jerusalem which he has just described was that recorded in Acts 9:26-30, then Paul has omitted the brief stay at Caesarea, and is now referring to his return to Tarsus. He is certainly at Tarsus in Acts 11:25 when Barnabas seeks him out and brings him to Antioch to share in the ministry there. But it does not necessarily follow that Paul had remained in the city all the time in between. As it is certain that he had preached at Damascus (and probable that he had also preached in 'Arabia') in the period immediately following his conversion, so it is very likely that he had preached both in Tarsus itself and the surrounding area during this later period. Otherwise, it is hard to see at what point in Paul's recorded journeys he could have evangelized Cilicia, as seems demanded by Romans 15:18–23, and elsewhere. It is uncertain whether *ta klimata, the regions,* is to be understood in a broad sense as 'the general area', or whether it means 'the province of Syria and Cilicia' in which Tarsus was situated.[1] This will have bearing on the meaning of the word 'Galatians' as recipients of the letter, but is not directly relevant here. For even if it meant the Roman province, it is not necessary to assume that Paul preached in every corner of it. Antioch itself, for instance, was in Syria, properly so called. At various times, the province extended far enough to the south to include Jewish-Christian churches. All that is necessary is that Paul should actually have preached in this period, while he was still uninfluenced by any Jerusalem interpretations of the gospel, whether 'right-wing' as of the Judaizers, or 'central' as of James, or 'left-wing' as of Peter, who may well have observed the food laws in early days (Acts 10:14), but later bluntly called the whole law of Moses an intolerable burden (Acts 15:10).

22. For *not known by sight (agnooumenos tō prosōpō)* NIV has 'personally unknown', which is probably a better translation. Many members of the Jerusalem church must have had good reason to know what Paul looked like, after the persecution of Acts 8:1–3, but would not have known him personally. But, since this persecution appears to have been confined to Jerusalem itself, it may well have been that the country churches of Judea were still completely ignorant of Paul's personal appearance,[2] in which case RSV would be correct. If the traditional (but late) description be accepted, he was short, bald-headed, with

---

[1] Betz, probably rightly, takes the word as 'regions', not 'province'.

[2] In spite of views to the contrary expressed by some commentators, 'Jerusalem' was usually considered within Judaism as quite distinct from 'Judea', though geographically and politically part of it. This usage had its roots in the Old Testament with the separate origins of Jerusalem (2 Sa. 5:6): for a similar use in the New Testament, see Acts 1:8.

bushy eyebrows and piercing eyes, and with slightly bandy legs. Such a man would surely be remembered well, if once seen.

The *churches of Christ in Judea* is literally 'the congregations of Judea which are in Christ'. The plural *ekklēsiai* is used to denote local churches, local expressions of the one great *ekklēsia*, the church of God. Our use of 'churches' to express 'denominations' has of course no warrant in Scripture. While it is true to say that what we call 'denominations' did not as yet exist, yet certainly great differences of usage (and perhaps church government) existed between the Jewish-Christian churches (as of Jerusalem) and the newer Gentile churches (as for example of Corinth). In 1:13 Paul has spoken of the 'congregation of God'; here he uses his more common expression 'the congregation(s) of Christ'. It was perhaps necessary for him to add some such word to make clear their distinction from the purely Jewish synagogues, for no reader of the Old Testament denied that these latter had an equal right to the more general title 'congregations of God' (*cf.* 1:13). The use of the word *Judea* here has bearing on the meaning of the phrase 'the churches of Galatia' in 1:2. If the one means a Roman administrative district, then the other ought to do so likewise.

23–24. There is, however, another point which is sometimes forgotten. Not only was Paul unknown by sight to the Judean churches, but also his gospel had certainly not been learned from them. Yet they recognized his gospel at once as that which they preached, and as that which he had previously attacked when he persecuted them. This means that what Peter and James are recorded as doing in 2:6–7, the country churches of Judea had already done long ago. They had accorded Paul full status and recognition. This is inescapable logic if we take Paul's position that the message validates the messenger. That this was the view of the Judean churches is shown by their praise to God for what he had done in Paul: as he says, *they glorified God because of me.*

D. LATER RELATIONS WITH JERUSALEM CHURCH LEADERS (2:1–10)

'Then, fourteen years later, I went up again to Jerusalem with Barnabas, taking Titus along with me too. I went up because of a revelation. And I laid before them for consideration[1] the gospel which I am preaching among the nations (though I did this in private before the powers that be, for fear that by any chance my race might have been vain, or still be in vain).

'But not even Titus, who was with me, for all that he was a non-Jew, was forced to be circumcised. But, because of the "planted" false Christians, who had wormed their way in, to spy on the freedom which we actually enjoy in Christ, with the purpose of bringing us into slavery – not for one moment did we yield ground to them, and become subservient: for our purpose was that the gospel truth might remain for you.

'But from those who seemed to be somebodies – it makes no difference to me what kind of people they were: God cares nothing about "face" – well, these seeming authorities had nothing to add. So far from doing that, because they could see that I had been entrusted with the Gentile mission as Peter had been with the Jewish mission (for the one who had worked through Peter to reach the Jews had also worked through me to reach the Gentiles), and because they recognized the particular spiritual gift that had been given to me, James and Cephas and John, the recognized "pillars", shook hands with Barnabas and me, as a sign that we were one, agreeing that we were to go to the non-Jews, and they to the Jews. Only they were anxious that we should continually bear "the poor" in mind, and this was the very thing that I had been eager to do.'

1. Once again, an exact chronology is impossible to establish on the scanty evidence which we have. It is possible, though not certain, that Paul here means *fourteen years* after his first visit; but he could mean fourteen years after his conversion. Either way, this represents a considerable lapse of time. Paul has already engaged in the Gentile mission for some years and there is no question about the gospel that he preaches being fully developed by now. But does *palin, again,* necessarily mean only a second visit? Or could it refer to a third, or any subsequent visit? Undoubtedly this is possible linguistically. But the whole

---

[1] So BAGD takes it; this seems to be the best interpretation of *anatithēmi*, 'set up', or 'place before'.

point of the argument would seem to be lost if Paul has omitted the account of a second visit and gone directly to tell of a third visit. If the visit of 1:18 is that of Acts 9:26, then this latter visit must be either the visit of Acts 11:30 (the so-called 'famine relief' visit) or that of Acts 15:2 (the so-called 'Council of Jerusalem' visit).[1] If the chronological order of Acts be accepted, then the famine visit was before Paul's first missionary journey, while the Council visit followed it. But in either case, Paul had been engaged in Gentile ministry for some time (notably in Antioch, see Acts 11:26), so that he certainly had a 'Gentile gospel' which might be discussed.

The mention of *Barnabas* here is not decisive, as, according to Acts, he accompanied Paul on both visits. Some have seen the mention of his name here and elsewhere in the letter as a proof that the recipients lived in the southern part of the Roman province. This is because Barnabas undoubtedly accompanied Paul during the evangelization of this area (see Acts 13 and 14), while the hypothetical evangelization of the northern plateau must have taken place, if historical, long after the breach between Barnabas and Paul.

More radical biblical critics find the answer in saying that Acts 11:30 and 15:2 represent variant accounts of the same incident, and that we have here an example of a 'doublet', in fact. But this is an impossible view for those who have a high opinion of the historicity of Acts, a historicity borne out in recent years in many minor aspects.[2] That being so, we cannot say that Galatians 2:1 refers to this one and the same Jerusalem visit. But if this conflation is impossible, what has happened to the account of the second visit? No-one could suspect Paul of deliberately falsifying his statement, the more so as he is virtually 'on oath' by his own choice. On a matter like this, it is inconceivable that his memory could be at fault. He was not travelling so constantly to and from Jerusalem that he could accidentally miss out

[1]Betz (excursus on the Conference at Jerusalem) is very emphatic that we must not call this meeting 'the apostolic council'. His reasons however seem more ecclesiastical than theological or historical.

[2]For details see Bruce, *The Book of Acts*, New London Commentary (Marshall, Morgan and Scott, 1962), and more recently Marshall, *Acts: an Introduction and Commentary*, TNTC (Leicester: Inter-Varsity Press, 1980).

the account of one visit. The only possibility, if this verse does refer to the Council visit and not the famine visit, is that Paul regarded the latter as completely irrelevant to his argument, since it had nothing to do with theological matters, and thus deliberately omitted it without any intention of deceiving. However, this would certainly weaken his argument, and the Judaizers would surely have seized on it, if so.

2. But why did Paul go to Jerusalem at all? The Judaizers would be quick to pounce on this. Better late than never, they would have said, if he was at last recognizing the authority of Jerusalem. Perhaps he was even obeying a summons from Jerusalem to explain his strange non-Jewish behaviour in the north. Paul's answer is quick and to the point. He *went up by revelation*. He does not say how this revelation came. It may have come directly to Paul, or through the 'group guidance' of the local church (as in Acts 13:2), whether mediated through local prophets or not, or through some travelling prophet like Agabus (as in Acts 11:28). The New Testament never says that 'direct' guidance is more spiritual than 'indirect' guidance; and Paul makes no such claim here. At first sight the circumstances of the famine visit (Acts 11:27–30) would seem to fit this wording better than the events that preceded the Council of Jerusalem in Acts 15:1–2. The 'revelation' would in that case be the prophecy, made by Agabus, of the coming famine in Judea. But it would be unwise to be over-dogmatic. We do not know what were the exact reasons for the decision to appoint the Antioch delegation in Acts 15, and it may well be that the voice of some local prophet brought guidance here too. Whatever the circumstances that lay behind the delegation, Paul sees its true reason as the mind and will of God. But, having arrived at Jerusalem, he says, *I laid before them* (*anethemēn*; *i.e.* 'declared', 'referred', 'communicated for their consideration') *the gospel which I preach among the Gentiles*. By this time the Jerusalem apostles could not influence Paul's gospel: it was too late for that. They could only accept it as the same as their gospel or reject it; there was no other alternative. In fact, they were to accept and acknowledge it whole-heartedly. Paul does not say whether this conference was the main purpose of his going up to Jerusalem. If that was

so, then the visit must have corresponded to the Council of Jerusalem, with its attendant opportunities of talk with church leaders. On the other hand, if we opt for this being the famine visit, he may simply have seized the opportunity afforded by the famous visit to satisfy his own mind on this matter; the somewhat casual language of Paul could perhaps be used to support this interpretation.

The use of *anethemēn* here (NIV, 'set before them') is perhaps a deliberate echo of *prosanethemēn*, 'confer', in 1:16 (see also 2:6 for the same verb). Paul now goes out of his way to do the very thing that he had so sedulously avoided long before. That is typical of Paul. The circumstances have now entirely altered, and he is not afraid to act in a diametrically opposite way. This is precisely what lays him open to the charge of inconsistency in the eyes of lesser men, and perhaps this danger was why he needed the assurance of a revelation before going to Jerusalem, however that revelation came.

Even granted that Paul did go up to Jerusalem, and did discuss his gospel there, he makes plain that this was not before the general body of the church, *but privately before those who were of repute*.[1] This was not some 'general synod', before which he was being taken to task; these were personal talks between the acknowledged leader of the Gentile churches and two who were generally acknowledged as leaders of Jewish Christendom. The phrases *kat' idian, privately*, and *tois dokousin, those who were of repute*, are both significant here. We will discuss later exactly what he means by the latter, but the sense of 'influential people' is common to all explanations. To those who see in this visit a reference to the Council of Jerusalem, these words present some difficulty. Everything was public at the Council, in a highly controversial atmosphere. However, it is always possible to say that these were private meetings with the leaders, which either preceded or accompanied the main public discussion of the matter. So long as we do not think anachronistically in terms of modern 'sub-committees', this is quite conceivable.

It is typical of Paul that he does not see the danger as being

---

[1] As pointed out by Betz, this phrase 'those who were of repute' is in itself neutral, and can be used positively or negatively. Only the context can decide how it is to be taken in any given case.

merely lest Jerusalem should fail to approve his gospel, thus resulting in a rift in the church. It is characteristic of him that he is not concerned with obtaining the approbation of mere humans: the approval of God is all that he covets (2 Tim. 2:15). Paul frequently uses *trechō*, *run*, in this moral sense (as indeed the Stoics had used it before him in their moral philosophy, as BAGD shows). 1 Corinthians 9:24–26 is one instance; Philippians 2:16 comes even closer, also with *eis kenon*, *in vain*, while in Galatians 5:7 he will apply the same metaphor to the Galatians themselves. It is also typical that he uses the occasion to point out to the Galatians that his gospel has not changed. As he runs now, so he ran then. It is the Galatians who have moved ground, not Paul. This will be important if, as is probable, the Judaizers are accusing him of being a shifty fellow (2 Cor. 1:17), always adapting his gospel to his hearers or the situation of the moment.

3. The next three verses constitute a notoriously difficult passage, not made any easier by Paul's obvious emotional excitement which, as often, leads him into involved grammar and unfinished sentences. These, in turn, lead to some textual confusion; and so the circle of difficulties widens. It is clear that some group, presumably the Judaizers, had pressed for the circumcision of Titus the Gentile whether before or during the Jerusalem visit. It is also clear that Paul opposed this. We cannot be absolutely certain, however, whether Titus was actually circumcised or not,[1] although the natural meaning of the text would be that he was not. With the whole spectrum of Pauline thought before us, we can well understand why Paul was willing to circumcise Timothy (already regarded as a Jew, since he had a Jewish mother) 'because of the Jews' (Acts 16:3), *i.e.* to facilitate work in a Jewish milieu, but was violently opposed to any proposed circumcision of Titus. Certainly the reason for this apparent discrepancy would not have been equally plain to James and the great 'central block' of the Jerusalem church, who were still orthodox Jewish Christians, although not Judaizers.

---

[1] In all fairness, the most logical thing to assume is that Titus was not circumcised. Otherwise, Paul's whole argument would seem to fall to the ground, or, at the very least, to be greatly weakened.

The only serious textual difference here is that some 'Western' manuscripts (including D: see Metzger) omit *hois oude*, 'to them . . . not', at the beginning of verse 5. This has the effect of making it theoretically possible that Titus was actually circumcised. NEB mg. therefore translates 'I yielded to their demand for the moment'. Verse 3 would then have to be translated 'Titus was circumcised, but not because he was compelled to be circumcised, it was only because . . .', *etc*. Paul would then be saying that, in what he later regarded as a mistaken moment of compromise, he had agreed to the circumcision of Titus as a gesture. As he looks back now, his anger boils over at what he regards as the treachery and insincerity of those who led him to take such a step (2:4).

Had Paul actually gone as far as this, his emotional excitement would be very understandable. Also, as far as Titus was concerned, the retreat from principle could not exactly be described as 'temporary'. Titus was now for life a circumcised Gentile and the Judaizers could point to him in triumph as a living argument for Paul's two-facedness. But there is another possibility. If Paul had originally agreed to the circumcision of Titus, and later refused permission, all conditions necessary for the assumed scenario would be met. Both Paul and the Judaizers might well be indignant with each other for what they would regard as 'bad faith', and the Jews could accuse Paul of inconsistency again. This explanation is possible whether or not we keep the negative in verse 5. For whether we translate 'I yielded for the moment' or 'I did not yield for a moment', the ultimate result for Titus was the same: it would have been only a momentary aberration, and Titus was not circumcised. The fact that manuscript evidence is divided at all on the question as to whether the negative should be read here or not probably reflects the fact that the early church was as puzzled by the matter as we are today. However, the evidence is overwhelmingly in favour of its retention, which NIV supports ('we did not give in to them', v. 5) and this is certainly preferable.

4. NEB probably correctly amplifies *because of false brethren* by adding, 'That course was urged only as a concession to . . .' (although the NEB marginal suggestion 'The question was later raised because of . . .' is also possible). Who were these *pseudadelphoi*, 'false brothers'? As Paul has already addressed even the erring Galatians as *adelphoi*, 'brothers', in 1:11, it is tempting to see in this a denial that these Judaizers are acting the part of true 'brothers' at all. They are utterly lacking in love. So BAGD interprets the word, comparing its similar use of those who are undoubtedly Judaizers in 2 Corinthians 11:26. But the NEB may be right in going further with its blunt translation 'sham-Christians'. In this case, Paul would be denying the very reality of the Christian faith of the Judaizers. This is a serious charge; but Paul knew them far better than we can ever do, although it is true that in theological controversy he sometimes uses extreme language (Phil. 3:2). But why are these 'bogus Christians' described as *pareisaktoi, secretly brought in*? The word almost means 'smuggled in', and, if we press its passive force, it suggests that these Judaizers were 'planted' on the church by some person or persons outside. We would dearly like to know who at Jerusalem stood behind the Judaizers. It was certainly not James, the Lord's brother, who vehemently denied it (Acts 15:24); it was equally certainly not Peter, in spite of the views of one school of critical scholarship, now outmoded. It was possibly not any one great apostolic figure, but simply the group of Jerusalem Christians who had formerly belonged to the Pharisaic party (Acts 15:5) or perhaps the large bloc of ex-priests (Acts 6:7), those 'zealous for the law' (Acts 21:20). In any case, *pareisēlthon, slipped in*, almost 'sneaked in', while equally uncomplimentary, is active in sense, not passive. The Judaizers were not unwilling participators: they were active agents, committed to their beliefs.

It is not clear into what meeting or group these agents had wormed their way, nor indeed in what place it was. Presumably the reference is to the Jerusalem church, and not to the church from which Paul had come to Jerusalem (which was Antioch on each of the two possible occasions). The book of Acts does not mention Titus at all, so that we can look for no help from there in fixing the place. But such a Gentile convert might well have been early associated with Paul in the largely Gentile ministry of Antioch. Titus appears constantly in 2 Corinthians as Paul's trusty agent, especially in connection with the collection for the poor saints at Jerusalem (again, a collection from Gentile churches), and by the date of the letter to Titus he is responsible for an almost purely Gentile church, that of Crete. Indeed, at this time Titus must have been associated with Paul at Antioch (as he had been at Corinth) or Paul could not have taken him up with him to Jerusalem as a delegate. But that does not necessarily prove that the tussle over the circumcision of Titus took place at Antioch. The plain reading of this passage suggests that the strife broke out as soon as the Antioch group had arrived at Jerusalem, although it is certainly hard to see how Judaizers could be spoken of as being 'planted' on the Jerusalem church if that was their home base. It would be more natural if they had been 'planted' on Antioch. But if Paul regarded them as 'sham-Christians', he might have concluded that they had wormed themselves into the Jerusalem church, rather in the way in which the apostles had originally suspected Paul himself of worming his way into the church there after a 'conversion', the genuineness of which they apparently doubted (Acts 9:26). If we could apply the reference to Antioch, it would certainly fit much better. For we do know that some Jerusalem brethren had entered that church and caused strife immediately by their Judaizing doctrine: indeed, it was such behaviour that had necessitated the holding of the Council (Acts 15:1). Probably the answer is that Paul is thinking of the activities of these Judaizers at Antioch, even if at the time describing his Jerusalem opponents, especially since they were probably the same people.

Whoever they were (and ultimately they were the same group, wherever they were active), Paul is vehement that their whole purpose was only *to spy out*, to peep and pry into Gentile Christian liberty and bring converts back again into a new slavery, this time to the law of Moses. He will deal with this question at greater length in the next main section of the letter ('The argument from theology', 3:1 – 5:1), so that the details need not detain us now. Of course, no Judaizer would ever admit that his deliberate purpose was to 'enslave'. Such people were no doubt genuinely shocked by the carefree attitude of Gentile Christians to the law of Moses, their own most treasured possession. It is highly likely that they thought themselves to be enriching the spiritual lives of Gentile converts immeasurably. But from his own experience Paul knew that this action was but a return to slavery. True, the Galatians had not been slaves to this particular Jewish system before: as pagans, they had had their own system of religion and morals. But a change of masters is not an escape from slavery: that is Paul's whole point.

5. *For you*: Paul is not fighting this battle on behalf of himself; it is for the sake of his Gentile converts with the aim of ensuring that the gospel truth shall remain for their enjoyment. Judaizing is not to him merely another aspect of truth; it is a lie, diametrically opposed to *the truth of the gospel*.

6. Verses 6 to 10 again constitute a very involved passage, both in thought and language, although the difficulties in the language are almost certainly due to Paul's emotional intensity at the time. That being so, some kind of paraphrase is the best hope of understanding it, rather than the literal translation of the RSV. Though at times the NEB is considerably fuller here than the Greek, it reproduces the probable thought sequence well: of the older translations, Moffatt is best, although again interpretative rather than directly translative. The NIV is a good compromise between the positions, with a fairly literal translation as against the 'dynamic equivalent' of the NEB.

Three times within a short space Paul will use the participle *hoi dokountes* (in various grammatical cases), 'those who were of repute', meaning something like 'the influential men' (BAGD). But in each case the expression is slightly fuller and stronger, as though Paul's rising indignation is finding the studied courtesy of 2:2 impossible to maintain. There, they are simply described as *hoi dokountes*, 'the somebodies'. By verse 6, they have become *hoi dokountes einai ti, those who were reputed to be something*, or 'those who seemed to have some official position', although Paul at once bursts out in indignant expostulation that God cares nothing about any such 'rating'.[1] By verse 9, they are *hoi*

[1] Betz is puzzled by so convoluted a sentence in such a well-composed letter: but the answer is easy. Paul is dictating at speed, and his emotions and thoughts have run away with him. The scribe, not Paul, may be at fault here: he may have accidentally omitted a clause or two.

dokountes styloi einai, who were reputed to be pillars, or perhaps 'those who are rated as pillars of the church'. The veil of anonymity is now completely dropped: they are Peter, James and John. It is as though Paul deliberately refrains from giving them the honoured name of 'apostle' here, although he had done so in 1:17, where he had also included himself. To use it here would have played into the hands of the Judaizers: perhaps, however, he is simply using instead a local Jerusalem title of 'pillar', a typically Jewish metaphor.

What they were, hopoioi pote ēsan: how much this conceals is uncertain. It may simply mean 'whatever you may like to call them', referring to the title of apostle or even 'pillar' (v. 9). It may, however, mean 'whatever they once were', referring to the peculiar position of privilege during the earthly ministry of Christ to which they owed their present eminence.[1] To Paul, this earthly knowledge of the Christ meant little compared with the transforming miracle of spiritual knowledge of the Messiah. To the Jewish Christian, on the other hand, such knowledge seems to have meant everything. Not only were the twelve original apostles venerated as the earthly companions of Christ; the earthly brothers of Jesus were apparently accorded a similar veneration. This was so much so that James, brother of the Lord, seems to have automatically taken the place of the martyred James, brother of John (Acts 12:2), in a sort of Christian 'Caliphate' at Jerusalem. To Paul, all of this would doubtless have been recognizing 'personal distinctions' (NEB) which, by definition, is not the way that God works: to him, *God shows no partiality.* It was precisely because of this attitude at Jerusalem that it was possible for a movement like that of the Judaizers to arise.

There is another key root in Greek, which, with prepositional variations, is used three times in this passage: it is *tithēmi*, 'to place' or 'to lay down'. It too gives a clue to the links in Paul's thought. In 1:16 Paul had said *ou prosanethemēn*, 'I did not consult any man' (NIV); 2:2 had *anethemēn*, 'I laid before them (my

---

[1]This is much more probable than the view of Heussi, quoted in Betz, that these apostles had already passed away at the date of writing, and hence that the past tense *ēsan*, 'were', or 'used to be', is used to describe them.

gospel)'. Here in 2:6 we have the defiant *emoi ouden prosaneth-ento, added nothing to me.* NEB mg. has paraphrased this as 'gave me no further instructions'; NEB, 'did not prolong the consulta-tion', is also possible. Paul has been asserting his independence throughout, not because he primarily wants to claim an independent position for himself, but because he wants to prove the supernatural origin of both his gospel and his apostolate. To Paul, both propositions stand or fall together.

7–9. The attitude to Paul of the orthodox Jewish-Christian church leaders, as distinct from that of the Judaizers, is an interesting study for which there is, unfortunately, somewhat scanty evidence in Scripture outside Galatians. The way in which Paul was spirited by the church from place to place in early days (Damascus, Jerusalem, Caesarea, Tarsus), usually as a result of the violent opposition which his bold preaching stirred up, may suggest that the leaders of the church were somewhat apprehensive of the consequences of the enthusiasm of this young convert, but not that they had any doubts as to the orthodoxy of his gospel (Acts 9:20–30). We know nothing of earlier relations between Paul and John, but Peter is treated very summarily by Paul in 2:11. This is confirmed by 2 Peter 3:15–16, which shows what may be regarded as a very cautious attitude on the part of Peter towards 'our beloved brother Paul'. This was doubtless characteristic of Peter in later days at least: no doubt it was a case of 'once bitten, twice shy'. Acts 15 shows a puzzled but loyal James accepting the palpable differences of approach and method between Paul and Jerusalem in a kind of 'interim agreement'; but his real embarrassment with Paul is only manifest in Acts 21:17–26. All this is perfectly consistent with the picture in Galatians.

Nevertheless, on this particular occasion, whether it was before the Council of Jerusalem, or during the Council of Jeru-salem, or at the close of the Council (for all three views are held), there was full and glad recognition by the orthodox leaders that there was only one gospel, shared alike by Jeru-salem and Antioch.[1] This sense of common 'belongingness' was

---

[1] It is unfair exegesis to see 'the gospel of the uncircumcision' as being substantially

sealed by giving *the right hand of fellowship*. Clasped right hands were the sign of friendship and trust (so BAGD), and this action on the part of the church leaders in Jerusalem must have been a blow to the Judaizers. A heavier blow was still to follow. If Paul's gospel was accepted, then his apostleship must be accepted too. So it was that the handclasp was also the seal on an agreement; Paul and Barnabas were 'accepted . . . as partners', as the NEB has it. By this action, Paul's apostolate to the Gentiles was recognized as fully as Peter's to the Jews (v. 7), the latter being apparently an apostolate in which the other members of the college of twelve shared as well. They took this course not as a result of a complicated process of reasoning, but from direct observation of spiritual facts. Just as Peter's apostolic ministry to the Jews had been sealed by the work of the Spirit in the hearts of his hearers (as in Acts 9:32–42, for instance), so the seal of Paul's apostolic ministry was the harvest of the Gentiles given him by God. Paul had realized this all along, as we see from Acts 15:3 and 12. When he is approaching Jerusalem for the great tussle at the Council of Jerusalem, he knows that his strongest argument is to report the conversion of the Gentiles: no-one can gainsay that, as Peter points out in Acts 15:8. To close one's eyes to such spiritual evidence would have come dangerously near to the sin against the Holy Spirit and neither James nor Peter were in danger of that, although perhaps the Judaizers were.

That this is the true meaning of the passage is shown by the use of the verb *energeō, worked* (v. 8), and the noun *charis, grace* (v. 9), or perhaps 'spiritual gift', both associated with the work of the Spirit in and through Paul, as well as in and through Peter. Another irony of the passage, not lost entirely on Peter (Acts 15:7), is that, in a sense, Peter's original mantle had now fallen on Paul. It was Peter in the first place who had seen the seal of the Spirit upon his Gentile work, and this had convinced him of the authentic nature of the Gentile mission (Acts 10:47; 15:8–9). Later at Antioch, all Peter's own arguments will be turned against him by Paul (2:14); but at Jerusalem there was no

---

different in content from 'the gospel of the circumcision', with some editors. The context here plainly denies such a view. We should do better to simply translate the two terms 'evangelism of the Gentiles' and 'evangelism of the Jews' respectively.

need. Peter himself used them stubbornly in the support of Paul.

Again, the attitude of the strictly orthodox Jewish Christians of Jerusalem would make an interesting study, if only the materials were a little richer. At best, they must have regarded Peter as a doubtful ally, especially after the Cornelius episode. This seems to mark a breach between him and the 'circumcision party' (Acts 11:2–3). After his outspoken words at the Council (15:7–11) they must have been even further estranged from him.

10. The Jerusalem 'triumvirate', we have already been told, 'added nothing to me' (v. 6). This verse adds however: *only they would have us remember the poor; which very thing I was eager to do.* Perhaps 'God's poor' would be a better, if loose, translation of *the poor*, for the reference is not only to the general duty of almsgiving, binding on all good Jews in any case, but to the special obligation towards the 'poor saints' of the Jerusalem church (so NEB amplifies it as 'their poor'). There is no hint of this particular item in Acts 15 (although there is no reason why such an injunction should be included in the 'findings' of the Council), and the indignation expressed by Paul in the second half of the verse would admittedly be much more understandable if this occasion were the 'famine relief' visit of Acts 11:27–30. It should have been, to say the least, unnecessary to invoke such an 'Inter-Church Aid Team' to remember the duty of mutual help: that was the whole purpose of their presence in Jerusalem. *Hoi ptōchoi*, 'the poor', is one of the early names for Christians which does not seem to be used outside Jewish-Christian circles in Palestine. Other names in the same class are 'Galileans' (Acts 2:7) or 'Nazarenes' (Acts 24:5). Early names like 'saints' (Acts 9:32) or 'brothers' (Acts 9:30) or 'disciples' (Acts 9:26) continued to be used in the Gentile churches, even after the new name of 'Christian' came into use (Acts 11:26). It seems a simple deduction that those names were still used in the church which were felt to be still applicable. Naturally, 'Galileans' was no longer appropriate, and equally naturally 'the poor' was not equally applicable. The word had a long history in Israel's past literature, referring to the pious remnant of God's people. They were usually 'poor' not only economically but also in the sense of being in special need of God's help (so BAGD on the meaning of the Greek words; the synonymous words in Hebrew are given in Abbott-Smith). No doubt the use of 'poor' and 'poor in spirit' by Christ in the beatitudes (Lk. 6:20 and Mt. 5:3) had helped to make the word current in Christian circles, as it was already in strictly Jewish circles. If the Christian church was God's new 'remnant', then the Christians were also now 'God's poor'. Paul himself makes use of the concept in passages like 2 Corinthians 6:10 and 8:9, but usually he introduces it only in the context of Christian giving, when it has the literal sense.

The plain fact of the matter is that the Gentile churches might number many poor members in their midst (implied in 1 Cor. 1:26), but there were also some rich members. No Gentile church could be described as 'poor' in the sense of the grinding poverty of the Jerusalem church itself. True, the abuses of the Lord's Supper, mentioned in 1 Corinthians 11:21, could take place only in churches where there was considerable inequality in the distribution of wealth, and this posits some wealth at least. But the greatest proof of the comparative wealth of the Gentile churches is that Paul did in fact manage to raise such a 'collection' for the Christians of Jerusalem. Indeed, it was one of the major concerns in all of his later letters which are of a 'pastoral' nature.

There were doubtless various causes contributing to this chronic poverty of the churches in Judea. Cynics will point to the experiment in communal living recorded in Acts 4:32–35 as a possible cause. But we should notice two things even here: first, those who were able to contribute large sums of money to this common 'pool' seem to have been 'overseas Jews' (like Barnabas of Cyprus, Acts 4:36), not local people; secondly, the poverty of the church had far deeper roots, if the bulk of the members were already so poor. Palestine was at the time over-tilled and over-populated. Chronic rebellions and disturbances had worsened a position already made grave by the generally barren nature of the soil after more than a millennium of deforestation, although the fertility of the great estates of Galilee was still a byword, according to Josephus. Village India or Africa of today, and doubtless many other parts of the world, presents a picture not dissimilar. Added to this, the land was perpetually crowded with pilgrims returning to their home land for festivals. Jerusalem was a bloated religious capital, crammed with hungry, unproductive mouths, which seems to have had little true economic basis for its existence.[1] Finally, the whole evidence of the Gospel is that it was largely the poor and downtrodden, not the rich, who responded to Christ: the letters show the same.

The Greek word *espoudasa*, *I was eager to do*, is ambiguous only in the interpretation of its aorist tense. It may refer either to Paul's subsequent eagerness (NEB, 'I made it my business to do'), or more probably to his past attitude (NEB mg. 'I had made it my business to do'). In either case, it did not represent a difficulty, still less the possibility of a barrier to relationships: on the contrary, it offered the possibility of sharing fellowship.

E. THE CLASH WITH PETER (2:11–16)

Paul has now made it abundantly clear that his presence at Jerusalem in no sense showed any subservience to the apostles there. They had made no contribution to his present position. But now he will go further in order to demonstrate the essential independence from them both of his gospel and of his position.

'When Cephas[2] came to Antioch, I stood up to him, face to face, because he stood condemned. For before some parties came from James, he used to share meals with non-Jewish Christians; but as soon as they had come, he shrank back and made a clear break between himself and them – just because he was afraid of the "Circumcisers". And the rest of the Jewish Christians joined him in acting this false role so that even Barnabas was actually carried away and did it along with them.

'So when I saw that they were not being straightforward about gospel truth, I said to Cephas in front of everybody, "If you, who start from a Jewish position, live like a non-Jew, and

---

[1] See Wacholder in *IDBS*, entry 'Sabbatical Year', for the possibility of the occurrence of a 'sabbatical year' within this period. This would of course greatly increase the problem of poverty.

[2] It is over-exegesis to see, with some editors, theological reasons for the use of the name 'Cephas' here. It was simply the usual name by which Simon Peter was apparently called in Jewish circles. Some witnesses actually do however read 'Peter' in the text here: see Nestlé, noted by Betz.

not a Jew, how can you try to force non-Jews to live like Jews?"
We, who are Jews by birth, and thus not "sinful non-Jews",
because we know that no-one is justified by doing what the law
commands, but only through trust in Christ Jesus – we ourselves have put our trust in Christ Jesus, with the aim of being
justified as a result of our trust in Christ, and not as a result of
our doing what the law commands (because "no-one can be
justified by doing what the law commands).'

11. Unfortunately, we have no idea when or why Peter visited
Antioch.[1] If we translate *ēlthen*, *came*, as 'had come' (which is
just as likely), then Peter may have already been there for some
considerable time when the recorded incident took place. In any
case, for the charge of 'play-acting' to be effective, Peter must
have been there for a period long enough for the local Christians
to observe that this Jerusalem Christian at least had no scruples
about eating with Gentiles, any more than any of the local
Jewish Christians had (v. 13). All that is known is that Barnabas
was also 'on the staff' of the church at Antioch at this time, and
this would suggest an early period before his rift with Paul had
taken place. But since we know almost nothing of the movements of Barnabas it is unwise to be dogmatic here. It is possible
to use the 'psychological argument', *i.e.* to say that it is inconceivable that Peter should have acted in this way after a recent
conference with Paul recorded in Galatians, whether we consider it to have been the 'famine relief' visit, or the Council visit,
or some other visit totally unrecorded in Acts, in which case
'had come' would be the appropriate translation. Another group
of scholars will answer at once that, while it is, of course,
possible that Paul narrates this episode out of its chronological
order and that the events took place before the conference, we
have no proof; anyway, nothing that Peter does is 'inconceivable'. If we protest that this makes Peter a weathercock, they
will reply that this is precisely what Peter is, and that this is why
Paul is so angry. Such circular arguments will take us nowhere.

[1]Betz well suggests that when Peter left Jerusalem for 'another place' (Acts 12:17), that
other place may have been Antioch. It was outside of Herod's control, and probably the
largest Christian centre after Jerusalem. If so, this may have been the occasion to which Paul
refers, but we do not know for how long Peter stayed in Antioch.

Paul makes his point, that he *opposed* or 'stood up to' (*antestēn*) Peter *to his face*: but he wants to show that he had good reason for this. Peter *stood condemned* (*kategnōsmenos*; less strongly in NIV, 'was in the wrong'). He was acting not only against his conscience and against the clear revelation that he had received in Acts 10, but also against his past tradition and custom in Antioch. Paul may have wanted at the same time to show that no Jerusalem church authority was infallible just because he was an 'apostle' or even a 'pillar'.

12. But it is not an honest mistake that stirs his wrath so much as the deceitfulness of it all. Peter's common practice at Antioch had been to share meals with the non-Jewish Christians; all knew that and all had rejoiced in it. After all, Peter had been the first chosen by God to preach to Gentiles, as he would remind, or had already reminded, the Council of Jerusalem in Acts 15:7. No doubt, the church at Antioch had some common feeding arrangement for its members, not unlike the 'community kitchen' of Jerusalem. If this system did not extend to all members, it would certainly have covered those engaged in 'full-time ministry', for they would have had neither a home to cook in nor means wherewith to buy food, apart from the gifts of the Christians to whom they ministered.[1]

Thus *synēsthien, he ate with*, or better, 'used to eat with', must have referred primarily to the common meal, which seems to have characterized the early Christian groups as much as it did the Qumran community. But it cannot have failed to include the Lord's Supper.[2] For if Peter ate with Christians on ordinary occasions, he surely joined with them in that solemn meal at which they remembered the death of their common Lord. By the same rule, if Peter ceases to eat the common meals with them

[1]Although Paul often worked for his own living, he seems to have regarded this as a special case, not to be generalized as far as 'teaching elders' of the church were concerned (see 1 Tim. 5:18). 1 Cor. 9:4–5 shows that Paul realized very well that neither Peter, nor the Jerusalem apostles, nor the Lord's brothers, had any of his own scruples about accepting local church support.

[2]However, to restrict the scope of the words *ate with* to the Lord's Supper (with some) seems impossible. Peter had been condemned by the Jerusalem extremists for eating ordinary meals with Gentiles at Caesarea (Acts 11:3), and Christ had been condemned on exactly the same grounds (Mt. 9:11), for 'tax collectors and sinners' were reckoned with Gentiles, even if Jewish.

now, he also ceases to join them at the Lord's Table. How narrow the line of demarcation was between the 'church feast', or *agapē*, and the Lord's Supper we can see from the very possibility of Corinthian abuses arising at all. In the modern 'abstract' liturgical setting of the Lord's Supper, such things are unthinkable. Peter is therefore refusing to sit at the Lord's Table with fellow Christians. Worse still, he does this not from considerations of conscience, but simply *fearing the circumcision party*.

Who were these *certain men* who *came from James*? Again, it sounds as if Paul is preserving a studied anonymity; he could perhaps have given names if he had so desired, though it is doubtful if they would have meant anything to us now. This is the more likely if, with NEB mg., we prefer the other possible reading and translate, 'a certain person' in the singular. The words 'from James' are not as strong in Greek as in English, but they do express controlled indignation. Paul is not implying that James of necessity sent them (indeed, James denies this in Acts 15:24); but they were certainly men from James' circle, James' group, within the Jerusalem church. The implied criticism is that James should not have tolerated such views. James in Acts 15:24 does accept responsibility for them being of his circle (using the same preposition *apo*, 'from') but denies that he or the Jerusalem church gave them any commission to spread their views among the Gentiles. They were clearly his own 'right wing', the Pharisaic group, and a sore embarrassment even to him. We give much thought to the problems of Paul, but few to those of James. This is scarcely equitable, especially in view of the vast range of opinion among Jewish Christendom. Paul describes this group, here and elsewhere, as *hoi ek peritomēs*, often translated, as here, *the circumcision party*. In our paraphrase above, it has been translated 'the circumcisers', as descriptive of their distinctive practice. The word might, however, mean no more than 'the circumcised', 'those from the Jewish Christian Church', using *peritomē*, 'circumcision', as a collective term for Jewish Christendom. Why Peter should be so afraid of this group of extremists in Antioch, when he was prepared to oppose the same people in Jerusalem, is a problem that we cannot explain.[1] Of course, if this Antioch incident happened before the Council, perhaps Peter had learned his lesson on this occasion: he would not make the same mistake again.

13. Had this piece of 'play-acting',[2] this playing false to his own convictions, been confined to Peter alone, it might not have been so serious. But all the rest of the local Jewish Christians were carried away by the tide, including even faithful Barnabas. Paul had to act quickly, or there would have been 'two communions' in Antioch, two Christian groups existing side by side, one Gentile and one Jewish, unable to share the Lord's Supper together.[3] This was unthinkable to Paul, although today we accept it as a matter of course. He sees Peter's action as arising from fear of the circumcision party: of Barnabas' motives he says nothing. To Barnabas, no doubt, this was simply a matter of love. He did not want to grieve the brethren from Jerusalem; abstention from table fellowship with his Gentile fellow believers was all that would be necessary. Once the Jerusalem emissaries had departed, the old terms of fellowship could be resumed. Was not this a small sacrifice to make for peace? But to Paul, this was 'peace at any price', and he was not prepared to buy peace on those terms. The strange thing is that, at the Council of Jerusalem, Barnabas stood four square with Paul on the matter.

But in this case at Antioch there can be no doubt but that Paul was right in his stand, and he knows it. The one anomaly is that, had not Barnabas been what he was, there might well have been no Paul to withstand him in this way; for, under God, Paul owed to Barnabas both his introduction to the Christian circle at Jerusalem and, later, his introduction to the Christian ministry at Antioch (Acts 9:27; 11:25–26).

[1]Unless, that is, we support the theory that Zealot opposition to Jewish supposed 'collaborationists' with Gentiles was growing, leading to a desire on the part of Jewish Christians to cut any suspicious-looking links with Gentile Christians, and so avoid persecution. There are references in Zealot letters to 'Galileans' as being persecuted by extremists: whether 'Galileans' means 'Christians' or not, we cannot say, but it is highly likely.

[2]See *TDNT* under this word. The charge made by Paul against Peter may be even more extreme: in Jewish usage, Greek *hypokritēs* usually translated Hebrew *hānēph*, 'apostate'.

[3]Was this perhaps what the 'Cephas party' in Corinth also stood for? (See 1 Cor. 1:12.) Although this has been suggested, it is not likely.

14. The word *orthopodousin*, *were not straightforward*, has occasioned some discussion. True, it may mean 'act straightforwardly', as translated above: but the NEB mg. translation, 'making progress', is just possible. We should then take the whole phrase as meaning 'not advancing in the direction of the truth of the gospel'.[1] The main sense is clear, however: NIV well has 'not acting in line with'.

Paul lays stress on the fact that, while his earlier talks with Peter and James at Jerusalem had been *kat' idian*, 'privately' (2:2), this rebuke was *emprosthen pantōn*, *before them all*. Peter's feelings are not recorded, but they can be imagined; his piece of deception had been all in vain. Everybody in the local church at Antioch knew very well that Peter was in the habit of living *ethnikōs*, *like a Gentile*. Probably the main reference is to the complicated system of Jewish food laws which made social intercourse between Jew and Gentile almost impossible. This was indeed Peter's strong point; he had received a special revelation on this matter and its validity had been accepted by part at least of the Jerusalem church (see Acts 11, though the final reaction of the Pharisaic party on that occasion is not recorded): Peter gained nothing by the 'hypocrisy'. Even the very Judaizers must have known his past lapse in this area; and if they did not, there would doubtless have been local church members glad to tell them in hushed tones. But in what way was he trying to compel *the Gentiles to live like Jews*? Presumably, by inducing them too to observe the Jewish food laws as the price of full fellowship. No doubt Peter would have rightly protested that nothing was further from his thoughts. But this was precisely the aim of the Judaizers; indeed, this was their whole purpose in coming to Antioch. Peter's ambiguous behaviour was playing right into their hands, and Paul wanted to shock him into seeing this clearly.

There may be another reason for the violence of Paul's reaction. Peter would not realize it, but this withdrawal from fellowship with Gentile Christians was tantamount to saying that they

---

[1]BAGD has references to several valuable papers and articles on the subject. Note especially the citing of Kilpatrick's rendering 'they were not on the right road toward the truth of the gospel'. There are possible parallels in the Qumran literature, for which see Betz.

were not as good as Jewish Christians, and that in some way they lacked something of the fullness of the gospel. Otherwise, why separate from them? The Judaizers would have admitted this view at once. If Peter were pressed, he would no doubt have denied it. But the action of both Peter and the Judaizers asserted it, for we can be sure that the Judaizers would not join with Gentile Christians at Antioch, still less Jerusalem, at meals of any kind, and it was their action that counted. When we refuse to eat at the Lord's Table with those whom we acknowledge to be fellow Christians, the reason must be because we consider ourselves to have something that they have not, whether it be a mode of baptism, or a theory of apostolic succession, or some other particular theological doctrine. This in effect denies the other the full status of Christian, and, to Paul, that status depends solely on relationship to Christ by faith. Of course, the Judaizers went far beyond Peter, who was concerned only with table fellowship between Jewish Christians and Gentile Christians. They wanted to have the Gentiles actually circumcised, and keep not only food laws, but the whole law of Moses. Paul will deal with this larger issue in the next section of his letter.

From verse 15 to the end of the chapter, there follows a passage of close theological argument, in many ways anticipating chapters 3 and 4. As we try to interpret it, we face the kind of problem which meets us so often in John's Gospel. Where do Paul's words to Peter on this historic occasion come to an end, and where does his later theological reflection on the issue, for the benefit of the Galatians, begin?[1] Probably the answer is that he passes from one to the other easily, without being conscious of the change himself. The opening verses certainly make better sense if we imagine them as part of an expostulation addressed nominally to Peter, but actually to all the Jewish Christians present, whether members of the local church or strangers from Jerusalem. The argument is strictly Jewish; for the moment the Gentile Christians, whether of Antioch or Galatia, have become awed onlookers at a battle of giants.

[1]In either case, we have here no 'tape recording' of the incident, but only a free recollection of the gist of what was said or thought: see Betz.

15. *We ourselves, who are Jews by birth, physei,* or perhaps 'by nature'. Paul starts with the known position of the Jewish Christian, making for the purposes of argument no distinction between the Judaizer and the orthodox Jewish Christian believer, including himself. He had already made it painfully clear that he sees no distinction between the Judaizer and Peter. But now he makes no distinction because to him there is no distinction. Jewish believers had all alike believed in Christ with a view to being saved. That in itself is a confession that the old system of Judaism was not enough. If keeping the law had been an effective way to win acceptance with God, then there would have been no need for Christ to have come. He accepts the fact that they are *not Gentile sinners* or, sometimes more abusively, 'Gentile dogs'.[1] The word *hamartōloi* probably applies more to Gentile shamelessness than to anything else; Paul is of course using, perhaps bitterly, the common terms used within Judaism. By this he means that those coming from a Jewish background were presumably free from the grosser vices of the pagans around them, those vices which were directly restrained by the law of Moses, at least in their outward manifestations.

16. Nevertheless, by believing in Jesus as Messiah, the Jewish Christians had shown that they believed that *a man is not justified by works of the law*. Christ had made it clear that he had no message of salvation for 'the righteous', but only for those who were conscious of their status as 'sinners' (Mt. 9:13). All Jewish Christians, therefore, had initially agreed that it was utterly impossible to commend themselves to God by law-keeping. They had shown this by abandoning law-observance as a possible means of salvation, and turning instead to that salvation offered freely by the Messiah in response to faith. At the end of verse 16 this position is reinforced, suitably enough, by a reference to Psalm 143:2. Now, all Paul has to do is to show that the present insistence of the Judaizers on the keeping of the law is utterly at variance with their own basic belief. It is not only Peter

[1] See Phil. 3:2, where Paul uses this Jewish term of abuse, not for Gentiles, but for Judaizers. It is only fair to say that it probably arose, not as mere abuse, but because of what appeared to Judaism to be the moral shamelessness of Gentile society. Compare the origin of the term 'cynics' in Greek, applied initially for exactly the same reason.

who is playing false to his own deepest convictions; the Judaizers are doing the same thing, whether they realize it or not.

F. DEATH AND THE NEW LIFE (2:17–21)

'But if, at the very moment when we are desiring to be justified through Christ, we prove to be sinners ourselves, does that mean that Christ is only causing us to sin? Perish the very thought. I say this because, if I try to build up again what I once pulled down, I only prove myself to be a law-breaker. For I, through law, "died" as far as law was concerned, so that I might "live" as far as God is concerned.

'I shared Christ's cross. It is no longer I who live, but Christ who lives in me. I live my present earthly life in commitment to God's Son, the one who loved me, and surrendered himself for me. No, I am not going to declare God's gracious act invalid: I say this, because, if righteousness comes through the law, then after all Christ died to no purpose.'

17. The passage 2:17–19 is again not easy to interpret. Here the problem is not disjointed thought and language, but rather some ambiguities in the first sentence. The question centres on the exact meaning of *heurethēmen hamartōloi, found to be sinners,* translated above as 'prove to be sinners' (NIV has 'it becomes evident that we ourselves are sinners'). In view of the later development of the argument, NEB mg. is probably right with 'we no less than the Gentiles have accepted the position of sinners'. In either case, *hamartōloi, sinners,* is to be understood with reference to our position in the eyes of God rather than our direct moral condition, although it is the same word used above for 'Gentile sinners', and this can hardly be an accident, since a different word is used below. Those who have thought that the word referred to actual sin see here a direct reference to the charge made by the Judaizers that Paul preached 'antinomianism'. To the Jew, Paul's gospel of salvation by free grace through faith in Christ would remove all incentive for moral effort and all desire to avoid sin. In their eyes, such a doctrine would lead to a

lower moral standard than under the law of Moses. Therefore, even Christ would have only become *hamartias diakonos, an agent of sin*, or 'an abettor of sin' (NEB), one who 'promotes sin' (NIV). Paul rightly recoils from such a blasphemy with horror. As often, his first reaction to this sort of charge is not theological argument, but a strong statement that this is utterly inconsistent with the revealed nature of God. There is no need for him to show in detail at this stage how utterly false such a charge would be. In the third and last section of the letter ('The argument from results', 5:2 – 6:18), Paul will develop this thought further.

If the first sentence had been standing by itself, unquestionably the above would have been the simplest interpretation. But in view of what follows, it may be better to understand it something like the following: 'If, at the very moment when we say that we ourselves are justified by faith alone, we turn out to be preaching to others that "faith alone" is inadequate, but that they must keep the law as well, does that not mean that trusting in Christ is only leading them into sin? for it is teaching them not to trust the law.'

The exact meaning of *dikaioumai*, translated conventionally 'be justified', need not be discussed in detail, since the dispute here is not over what 'justification' is, but how it is to be obtained. In general terms, it means to be put in right relation with God. BAGD therefore translates the verb as, 'to be acquitted, be pronounced and treated as righteous, and thereby become *dikaios* (righteous), receive the divine gift of *dikaiosynē* (righteousness)'. This reflects the modern swing from a purely forensic understanding of the verb (which could, at extremes, resemble a legal fiction) to the understanding that it is fundamentally a 'salvation-word', closely connected with the biblical concept of grace. Without in any way obliterating the biblical distinction between justification and sanctification, it is important to realize that being 'put right' with God involves and issues in a subsequent total change in our moral behaviour, though this in itself could never commend us to God.

18. This verse is plain sailing, especially if the interpretation of verse 17, which has been suggested here, is correct. The

Judaizers, with their reintroduction of law-keeping as an essential of salvation, are painfully rebuilding the very structure of
human 'merit' that, for Paul, had come crashing in ruins on the
Damascus road. At best all Paul can do through trying to keep
the law is to show that he is a *parabatēs, a transgressor*, or a
'law-breaker' (NIV). Paul will explain elsewhere that this convict-
ing task is the whole function of the law of Moses, but there is
clearly no path to salvation lying in that direction, although
there may well be a preparation for salvation.

19. For Paul, the 'once-for-allness' of his conversion experience will allow no return to the past. Perhaps he remembers
those three days of darkness and agony of mind in Straight
Street before Ananias came and the light streamed in. The law
had brought him to the gates of death; he was in despair, a
condemned criminal, with no hope. So be it; he accepted 'death'
as far as the law was concerned. He would never again turn to
it, hoping to find a path of life. But he had turned from the law
as a way of self-commendation to God only in order that he
might find the path of life offered by God in Christ.

20. Calmer water has been reached now. Paul will try to
explain more clearly this spiritual experience of his which has
involved such a revulsion from the law, to which he had after all
devoted the best years of his life. Judaism could think of a rabbi
as wedded to the Torah, in much the same way as a medieval
churchman might regard a bishop as wedded to the church.
What strange unfaithfulness is this, to leave the Torah, and seek
a new bride? In Romans, Paul will use this 'marriage' metaphor
to great effect (Rom. 7:3). Here, although Galatians may be in
many respects the 'rough draft' of Romans,[1] he does not
actually use the marriage analogy, although he uses the concept
of death breaking the relationship, as in Romans. But the
psychological problem is still the same. How can he explain this
total change, this complete revulsion?

[1]As often pointed out, however, we must not explain Galatians in the light of Romans,
but in its own light. There are many different emphases in Romans, even where the
vocabulary is similar: see Bruce. Perhaps the fact that Romans is a later letter is partly
responsible for this.

In many ways, this is one of the central passages of Galatians. It is, indeed, a text frequently used by preachers, but it is important to realize that it is not so much an exhortation to personal sanctification as a powerful argument for the total sufficiency and efficacy of the work of Christ. It is true that it deals with the great motives for Christian service, but the central thought is the complete breach with the old ways of thought and life which is demanded by faith-committal to Christ. The 'faith that justifies' is total, in extent if not in quantity: it is a radical faith, in this sense.

But what does Paul mean when he says *I have been crucified with Christ*, the verb form *synestaurōmai* giving the sense of past action issuing in a lasting result? Again, the context does not justify us in seeing this as an account of a mystical experience. There are certainly references to such experiences in Paul's writings (see 2 Cor. 12:2), but this is not one of them. This is initially a simple statement of Paul's relation to the law, which then becomes a statement of his relation to Christ. It stands for a complete change in his way of looking at all things, a 'reorientation of thought', to use modern jargon, which involves a total change of life. He means that, as the death of Christ marked a total change in the relationship of Christ to all things including, in this case, to the law of Moses, or even law, as a principle, in the wider sense, so it did for Paul himself. The cross was, for Christ, a complete break with this life. In one sense, every human death is just such a break, although there was a deeper sense in which it was true of Christ. He had perfectly fulfilled the law; we have utterly failed to keep it. But for both, law is now no more. Henceforth, Paul is dead to all claims of the law to be able to commend him to God.[1] Such appeals now fail to arouse him. He has long ago plumbed that agony and has reached the freedom on the other side. Those who spend all their lives in fear of death sometimes find a strange relief when death itself comes; there is nothing left now to fear. So it was with Paul; he had laboured all his life under the nagging fear that perhaps in spite of all his rigorous observance

[1]He is not of course dead to the moral demands of the law as such: but these are now fulfilled in the new 'law of Christ', the 'law of love', and they have no value for self-justification before God.

of the law, he might not be able after all to win God's favour. Now, as he sees the cross of Christ, and realizes the work of love and grace that was necessary to save him, he freely admits that this nagging fear of the past was fully justified. Not only is it possible that he may fail to commend himself to God; it is inevitable that he will fail. There go all his hopes for evermore. A lifetime of painstaking accumulation of 'merit' attained by 'works of the law' has been wasted. Paul must confess himself a sinner like any needy Gentile. That is the death of the 'old nature', the last killing blow to pride and self-esteem. There the old Paul dies, and who can assess the agony of that death for the proud self-righteous Pharisee? But likewise, who can tell the blessed peace and relief that has come to him, now that the fear of failing to win God's favour has been faced and acknowledged to be justified, or who can tell the new freedom and joy that comes from such spiritual release? We do well not to try to explain a spiritual experience in psychological terms alone, yet some understanding of our own psychological 'make-up' will help us to enter into Paul's thought here. If we do enter into it at all, we shall understand that a return to the law, seen as a possible means of 'putting oneself in the right' in God's eyes, is an utter impossibility to Paul.

It is not Paul's way to sketch the negative side alone, though sometimes, as here, the exigencies of controversy may demand that he deals with the negative side of a question first. At once he moves on to the positive aspect, to describe the new release of spiritual life and power. *It is no longer I who live*. Live? Of course Paul lives, but it is Christ living in him now. As in the old days the law had filled his horizon and dominated his thought-life, so now it is Christ. Christ is the sole meaning of life for him (Phil. 1:21): every moment is passed in conscious dependence on Christ, to whom he looks for everything. This is Christian faith; and it is intensely personal, both as regards subject and object, if these terms are allowed. It is *faith in the Son of God* (thus linking the cross with the will of the Father) *who loved* Paul, and *gave himself* (NEB has 'sacrificed himself' in its first edition of 1961) for Paul.

21. After this impassioned outburst, verse 21 is a calmer summary of the whole passage. An attitude like that of Paul's shows a full appreciation of *the grace of God* shown in Christ. But to act like the Judaizers is to declare this grace invalid or to *nullify* it. Obviously this is so: for if they are preaching a return to law-keeping, it can only be because they consider that what God did through Christ on the cross was inadequate or ineffectual. Furthermore, if this had been true, *then Christ died to no purpose*, his death was gratuitous; he died 'for nothing' (NIV): he might as well not have died. The reason and sheer logic of this is incontrovertible: not even the Judaizers should have been able to deny it. Paul is therefore free to return to a fresh argument.

II. THE ARGUMENT FROM THEOLOGY (3:1 – 5:1)

Paul could well have closed his letter at the end of chapter 2. The storm has passed into a calm and his point has already been made. But, as he thinks of what has happened in Galatia, his feelings overwhelm him just as they did in 1:6, and he returns to the charge for the second time. So, instead of the letter ending at 2:21, chapter 3 introduces a whole new section of his argument, that from theology or, more exactly, from Scripture. This may simply be because it was natural to a Jew, particularly one with Paul's rabbinic training, to turn to the Scriptures for proof in an argument. But it may also be because Paul knows that his Judaizing opponents will already have made great play of the Scriptures to prove their case. Whatever the reason, it should not surprise us if Paul's use of the Old Testament Scriptures is, at times, more 'rabbinic' than we would find natural. The nature of his opponents' training make this inevitable: he is meeting them on their ground, and using language which they can understand and must admit. But such a 'rabbinic approach' extends only to the manner of citing and treating the Scriptures, not to the Scriptures themselves. The great theological principles to which Paul appeals are as valid today as in first-century Galatia, although we might express them in different terminology. Much study has recently been devoted to Paul's own rabbinic background, and its possible influence on his exegesis, if not on his theology. Those who have dealt with this Jewish background (Davies, Daube, Schoeps and Munck) are particularly helpful here, although we must beware of over-emphasizing this aspect of Pauline thought: whatever his background, he is not a first-century rabbi, but a first-century Christian.

Hitherto, Paul has argued from his own spiritual experience, and the facts of Christian history. Now he will show that such experience is not subjective and illusory, but grounded upon the eternal purposes of God as revealed in his Word. But before he does that, in a short opening section, he will appeal briefly to the spiritual experience of the very Galatians to whom he writes and link it to the similar experience of Abraham. This has a twofold object. First, Paul wishes to show the Galatians that their present attitude is a contradiction not only of his spiritual history, but also of their own. Paul's spiritual pilgrimage is not therefore seen as reserved for great saints; it is and should be normative for every Christian, however humble. Secondly, he wants to show them that this common pilgrimage, both his and theirs, had been also that of Abraham; otherwise, to quote to the Galatians the example of Abraham would be utterly irrelevant. As it is, we find with a shock that Abraham's problems are our problems, even though the outward circumstances are so dissimilar. From that, Paul moves to the point where we see that Abraham's solution to the problem can also be our solution, since Abraham's God is still our God.

Paul has yet another crowning argument which he will use later. Abraham himself is, after all, a Gentile, as the Galatians are. He is no Jew, though he may have become the ancestor of the Jews. He knew nothing of the law of Moses (although later rabbis might claim that he kept it), nothing of the Temple, nothing of later food laws, nothing even of circumcision in his early days, for he had been accepted by God long before he was circumcised (Rom. 4:11) – decades earlier, in fact. He was not ancestor of the Jews alone: all the Gentile desert peoples of the Negev, the 'Southland', also traced their ancestry to him. Moreover, in God's gracious promise to Abraham, Gentiles found special mention. Judaizers might quote Moses to prove their point; Paul will quote Abraham to prove his. Let Judaizers quote law; Paul will quote promise. If they appeal to centuries of tradition and the proud history of the law and covenant of Moses, he will appeal to the tradition of the even grander 'covenant with Abraham', older by centuries still.

While Paul will pursue these arguments at greater length in Romans, they are present in outline and essence in Galatians. Indeed, one of the most striking proofs that Paul was correct when he said in earlier chapters that his gospel was independent of outside influence (especially from Jerusalem) is not only that his gospel is so distinctive in its Old Testament setting, but also that this aspect of his gospel shows little sign of 'development' over the years. No doubt this was the way in which Paul had come to terms with the gospel and with its Old Testament context during those early days in Arabia: the broad pattern was set then and it would not change.

A. INTRODUCTION (3:1–6)

'You stupid Galatians, who hoodwinked you? The message of Jesus, as a Messiah who died on a cross, was plastered up on the bill-boards before your very eyes. This is the one thing that I want to find out from you. Did you receive the Spirit by doing what the law demands, or by believing the message that you heard? Can you be as stupid as that? Are you trying to finish by natural means some process that began supernaturally? Have you been through so much, and all for nothing? – that is, if it should turn out to be all for nothing. God is continually providing you with the Spirit as a free gift and continually working deeds of power among you. Does he do it because you do what the law commands or because you believe the message that you hear? That was exactly Abraham's position; he believed God, and his belief was regarded as righteousness.'

1. Again, a loose paraphrase of the whole passage is the best introduction to a commentary upon it, for all through this central part of Galatians the interpretation of the part depends on the interpretation of the whole. Paul does not accuse the Galatians of desperate sin; he does however accuse them of being *anoētoi, foolish*, 'stupid'. After the Second World War, a group of pastors in Europe were lamenting that they had been misled by 'demonic forces', when a senior pastor present brought them back from near hysteria to sober reality by saying drily: 'Gentlemen, we have all been very foolish.' Paul never denies the reality of the spiritual battle for the souls of men. No-one believes more firmly than he in the existence and operation of demonic forces (see, for example, Eph. 6:12), but he will not, just because of this, allow the Galatians to shift the blame from themselves. A sheer lack of logical reasoning has led them into this theological inconsistency. As we read Paul's close argument here, it seems so simple and obvious that we wonder why we never saw it so before. But that is the mark of Paul the trained theologian, as well as the man filled by the Spirit. Paul never condemns the human intellect as such. In fallen humanity, it shares the fall; it must be brought under Christ's rule, like every other part (see 2 Cor. 10:5). After that has taken place, Paul is as anxious as any other theologian that we should serve God with our intellect as well as 'spiritually' (see 1 Cor. 14:14ff.). While it is true that, for Paul, spiritual things are spiritually discerned (1 Cor. 2:14), it is equally true (to enlarge a famous definition) that theology for him is nothing more than the ordinary rules of grammar and logic applied to the text of Scripture.

Some scholars have seen significance in the use of the word *Galatians* here as having bearing on the geographic destination of the letter: see the Introduction, pp. 18ff. It was addressed (1:2), to 'the Christian congregations of Galatia'. Most have felt that while this initial address must refer to an area, possibly an administrative area, yet it gives no clue as to race, and therefore no clue as to whether the recipients were the Celtic tribes of the north of the province or the mixed population of the southern cities. But if Paul here actually describes the recipients of the letter as 'Galatians', would this not prove that they are Galatians by race? If so, they must have been the Celtic folk of the northern plateau. Yet if Paul could call the whole area 'Galatia' (as he seems to do), then there is no reason why he should not have called all the inhabitants of the area 'Galatians', whether or not the term was applicable in the strict sense.

It is most unlikely that Paul is using the word as a term of abuse, as though he were saying 'You foolish country bumpkins', though it is true that occasionally in Hellenistic literature the *Galatai* are described as *aphrones*, another word for 'stupid'. But this is only a casual description in passing: the Galatians are never a 'stock figure' of Roman comedy. Paul may abuse his Judaizing enemies roundly: he is hardly likely to be directly insulting to his own converts, especially as he is trying to get them to see his point. Similarly, it would be foolish to try to settle the original destination of the letter by examining assumed racial characteristics of Celts, and comparing them with the known situation in Galatia. Luther thought, from this same reasoning, that the Galatians were Germans, because of the similarities to the situation in his own days. Perhaps the best interpretation is to say that the Galatians are everybody; in that sense Luther was right, for fickleness of this type is part of human nature. That, indeed is why this letter is universally applicable; it speaks to all Christians everywhere at all times. Otherwise, it would be a mere historical document, of archaeological interest only.

But Paul does not lay all the blame on the Galatians, whoever they were. *Who has bewitched you?* he asks.[1] The word *ebaskanen* is the same root as the English 'fascinated', which is derived from the Latin cognate of this Greek verb. We can imagine the fascination with which these simple Christians must have listened to the glib-tongued teachers from Jerusalem. But Paul will not waste time condemning the deceivers; they must give account of themselves before God, who alone can judge the hearts (1 Cor.4:5). Some have felt that the singular form used here, *tis, who*, supports the earlier reading of the singular in 1:8–9. In that case, it would refer to the 'arch-Judaizer', whoever he is. They would also say that this verse proves Paul's ignorance of his identity, but this is not necessarily so. The stress here is more on the verb *bewitched*. Paul is not really interested here in the idle question as to who the person is, or even whether the singular merely stands for a class. After such a clear presentation of the gospel by Paul, the Galatians must surely have been bewitched

---

[1]Of course, 'bewitched' is only a vivid metaphor. It is a mistake, with Schlier, to see a reference to magical spells (Betz). Paul faced magic as an enemy in Ephesus, not in Galatia, so far as we know, and he deals with the problem by theology, not by exorcism.

to forget its one salient point so soon. This in itself shows that the alternative possible translation, 'Who envied you?', is unlikely. Perhaps the Judaizers did secretly envy the Galatians their Christian freedom, but, if so, that is not the point here.

The Galatians are those *before whose eyes Jesus Christ was publicly* [NIV, 'clearly'] *portrayed as crucified*, or 'openly displayed upon his cross' (NEB). Presumably this refers to the content of the preaching of Paul during the initial evangelism of Galatia. 1 Corinthians 2:2 shows us that such total domination of all Pauline theology by the fact of the cross was no accident; it came of deliberate and set purpose of mind. The word *proegraphē, publicly portrayed*, may mean either 'portrayed' or 'placarded', like some notice of civic interest. The huge hoardings that carry advertisements by roadsides today would be the best parallel in the modern world. There was no missing such an announcement. The other possible translation 'set forth in a public proclamation' is given in BAGD: this would be a more direct reference to Paul's public preaching and proclamation of Christ. It is a New Testament commonplace to see the preacher as God's herald, God's town-crier (1 Tim. 2:7), though the verb is far more common than the noun.

The word *estaurōmenos, crucified*, is interesting because of its tense; it is the perfect passive participle, which usually expresses a past fact leading to a continuing result. So NEB translates 'upon his cross'; so we might render it 'Jesus, a crucified Messiah'. That one phrase cuts the ground from under all Judaizers, if only they understood it; and yet it is thoroughly Hebraic in every word.

2. One simple question will now be enough to convict the Galatians of the folly of their attitude. How did their Christian life begin? Or, as Paul puts it here: *Did you receive the Spirit by works of the law?* No: clearly the Spirit is not a prize to be won by trying to obey the law's demands; the Spirit is God's free gift. Then how was the Spirit received? By hearing the good news of the gospel, and by accepting the promised gift in simple faith; that is, to use Paul's words here, *by hearing with faith*, by hearing and believing. Of course, the Galatians knew that this had been just as true for them as for Paul. It was equally true of the

Judaizers themselves, if they were Christians at all; but Paul is not addressing them at the moment.

There are several possible translations of the phrase *ex akoēs pisteōs, by hearing with faith*, paraphrased by NIV as 'by believing what you heard': NEB mg. suggests as alternatives either 'by the message of faith' or 'by hearing and believing'. The last of these seems the best, but the difference is not great in any case. The opposition is to *ex ergōn nomou, by works of the law*, which really means 'by keeping the law' (NEB). To Paul, this *hearing* is very important: faith comes by hearing, and that is why to preach God's word is so essential (Rom. 10:14–17). For the importance of first hearing about the promise of the Spirit so that we may then enjoy the gift of the Spirit, we might perhaps compare the puzzled 'Spirit-less' disciples of Ephesus (Acts 19:1–7). There is no suggestion here that any subsequent ceremony or new experience had anything to do with the gift of the Spirit to the Galatians; it is associated directly with belief in the gospel and the initial response of faith. After the early chapters of Acts, we have no clear reference associating the gift of the Spirit with any outward ceremony, for it is quite uncertain whether 1 Timothy 4:14 refers to a later 'confirmation' or 'ordination', to use modern terms which may be completely inappropriate. Even in the account in Acts, the coming of the Spirit sometimes antedated the apostolic laying-on of hands, as in Acts 10:44, where it even antedates baptism. It seems, therefore, better to regard the action in those instances as having an evidential and symbolic value. Whether or not Paul continued the custom in the churches which he founded, we cannot say. In any case, as he was not one of the original twelve, the Jerusalem group would no doubt have regarded such action on Paul's part as highly irregular, if not invalid.

3. Paul often contrasts the beginning and end of a process; here, he uses the contrasting pair of words *pneumati, Spirit*, and *sarki, flesh*. It would be impossible in a book of this size to examine the full meaning of either word.[1] It is the less necessary

---

[1] There is a full discussion of both words in BAGD, with good book lists.

to discuss them as yet (see, however, the Commentary on 4:23 on p. 179) as they do not carry any great theological weight in this context except as a pair of opposites, corresponding to the only alternatives now open to the Galatians after such a gospelling as they had had. Fairly enough, therefore, NEB translates the terms as 'the spiritual' and 'the material'. There is, of course, a slight play on the word 'Spirit', in that the Christian life of the Galatians has indeed begun by the reception of the Spirit. What Paul means is that the whole Christian way is 'supernatural' from start to finish; but the Jewish path (whatever it might have been in design and origin) has become thoroughly 'naturalistic'. The adherents of every religion try to earn their own salvation by their own efforts, as do those following Judaism as a faith; the only difference is that the pagan has not such clear knowledge as the Jew. From this angle, Judaism is just 'another religion', although, seen from another angle, it has an eternal value as God's preparation for the gospel of Christ (3:24).

4. There is a slight ambiguity in *tosauta epathete, did you experience* [NIV, 'have you suffered'] *so many things?* If we take 'suffer' as the meaning, it could refer to the physical persecution that the Galatians had already suffered from their fellow countrymen. If the 'Galatians' are to be identified with the inhabitants of the south of Galatia, then we have sufficient evidence in Acts 14:19 of the sort of treatment that the early converts may have received, both from Jews and from the local countryfolk, to understand the meaning of the phrase.

But possibly the meaning could be paraphrased as 'Have you had such wonderful spiritual experiences all to no purpose?' (*cf.* NEB). This would fit the context better, with its references to the gift of the Spirit and the subsequent miraculous manifestations (v. 5). Again, Acts 14:10 would be an example of such experiences, if the churches were in the South Galatian region; but doubtless there were also many unrecorded instances of similar happenings.[1] Paul is loath even to admit the possibility of such

---

[1]Betz concludes that, for the Galatians, 'receiving the Spirit' meant an enthusiast's or ecstatic experience, citing 4:6 (the cry of 'Abba') and 6:1 (the title 'pneumatics' or 'spiritual'), as evidence. While not necessarily agreeing completely with Betz (for Paul normally

experiences being all *eikē, in vain*. For, if the Galatians slip back from the gospel into the twilight of a half-Jewish faith, it will mean not only the end of all such manifestations of the Spirit. It will also mean that they might as well never have had the experience at all, for all the good that it did them. Christ would have died to no purpose as far as they were concerned; the Spirit would have been given them to no purpose also.

5. The word used for the giving of the Spirit, *epichorēgōn, supplies*, has an interesting history in classical Greek. By Hellenistic days, however, its main two fields of meaning are either 'give', 'grant freely', or 'support', 'help' (so BAGD). Either of these would suit to describe the gift by God of the Paraclete to the Christian. For *works miracles*, see Käsemann, quoted by Cousar: 'Christianity cannot entirely do without enthusiasm . . . A Christianity in which there are no signs and mighty works, no visible charismata, is no longer heard,' although not all would agree with Käsemann's sweeping judgment here. This legitimate emphasis is however very fairly balanced in its context: see the Introduction (pp. 55ff.) for discussion of this aspect.

6. Having already linked the experience of the Galatians with his own, in a final flourish, which will introduce the main matter of this section, Paul further links it to the experience of Abraham. 'Why, that is exactly what Abraham did', he says in essence. Abraham, like the Galatians, had *believed God*, trusted God's word; God in turn had accepted that faith, that trust, as though it were that 'right standing with God' which Abraham manifestly could never win by his own efforts. Indeed, *it was reckoned to him as righteousness*. In other words, Abraham entered into his particular blessing by realizing that he could do nothing himself, by confessing that fact to God, and by throwing himself on God, counting on God to do that which he could not. That is the paradox of faith, as true for us as for Abraham. It was by ceasing to try to do anything for himself, and by accepting this position of humble and utter dependence, that Abraham was

---

emphasizes fruit of the Spirit rather than gifts of the Spirit), we may note that supernatural manifestations of some kind are clearly implied here.

'justified'. Nor was this a 'legal fiction', as sometimes claimed. This attitude alone is 'right standing' with God; any other attitude is stubborn pride and self-righteousness, which God opposes (Jas. 4:6).

B. ABRAHAM'S FAITH (3:7–9)

Having laid down his basic principle, Paul now needs to show to the Galatians the relevance to them of the experience of Abraham, and this he does by close exegesis of the Genesis texts. It is doubtful whether his Gentile converts were as familiar with the Old Testament as Paul was. But in South Galatia at least, there were considerable Jewish settlements (as the presence of the half-Jew Timothy shows), and we may perhaps assume a Jewish and proselyte element in the local church. In any case, whether the Galatians were familiar with it or not, the Old Testament, and the Old Testament alone, was the Bible of the New Testament church. If preachers like Paul used 'texts', it was from the Old Testament that they chose them, adding no doubt sayings and incidents from the life of Jesus to show how he fulfilled these Old Testament scriptures. Besides, as already noted, it was from these scriptures and especially from the law of Moses, that the Judaizers reasoned. The Old Testament, therefore, must be the battleground.

'I suppose you realize that those who have faith are Abraham's descendants. For the Scriptures, foreseeing that God is one who justifies the Gentiles as a result of their trust, preached the gospel in advance to Abraham when it said, "All the Gentiles will be blessed through you." So then those who believe do enjoy blessing along with believing Abraham.'

7. Modern scholars sometimes lose patience with what they describe as Paul's 'rabbinic' exegesis, but a little patience will nearly always show that underneath it lie relevant theological principles. In this case, there is nothing forced, and no real difficulty. Perhaps *hoi ek pisteōs, men of faith,* could be translated 'the faith party', as opposed to *hoi ek peritomēs,* 'the circumcision party' in 2:12. In any case, the term clearly means those who,

like Abraham, are trusting God to do what they have abandoned trying to do for themselves, namely, to commend themselves to God as worthy by their own efforts. These, says Paul, are truly *the sons of Abraham*; they bear the family likeness to Abraham in the shape of this saving faith. It is always possible that we should translate *hyioi Abraam*, not as *sons* [*i.e.* descendants] *of Abraham* but 'real, true Abrahams'. This would be following the normal Semitic practice by which, for instance, the wicked are called 'descendants of Belial'. But as physical descent from Abraham was regularly stressed by the Jews (*cf.* Jn. 8:33), and spiritual descent from Abraham is here stressed by Paul, it seems more appropriate to hold to the traditional translation here.

8. When Paul says 'Scripture says', or as here, *scripture, foreseeing*, he is not crediting the Bible with existence, knowledge, or activity independent of God; he is simply using a normal Hebraic form of speech. For Paul, as in the Gospels, 'Scripture says' (*e.g.* Jn. 19:37) is the equivalent of saying 'The Lord of Scripture says'. Here, therefore, Paul's meaning is that the wording of Scripture is appropriate and corresponds to what God will do long afterwards in the gospel of Christ. Nor is this correspondence, to Paul, an accident; it arises from the deliberate overruling by God of the content of Scripture. Any study of the Pauline doctrine of inspiration and revelation must take this into account.

The word *dikaioi, would justify*, is probably not to be taken in a future sense, as 'would yet, in the future, justify', although it is true that, in colloquial New Testament Greek, the present tense frequently has a future meaning, as it does in colloquial English. It is better to see in it a continuous present, and to translate it as 'justifies'. God is 'the Gentile-justifier', the one whose way it is to justify the Gentiles purely on the ground of their faith, their helpless committal to him in trust. Indeed, this is what God was doing at that very moment in the case of Abraham. The only difference between Abraham and us is that the reason for the possibility of such a process of justification is now made plain to us in Jesus Christ: the 'justification' itself is still exactly the same principle in either case.

This also helps to explain the verb *proeuēngelisato, preached the gospel beforehand*, where Scripture is the formal subject, but God is the actual subject. In one sense, the Christian cannot speak of the gospel being preached before Calvary. In another sense, here is an anticipation of the gospel. Indeed, it is far more than an anticipation, for it comes close to an identity with it, in that God's ways of dealing with humanity are eternally the same. It was a commonplace of Hebrew thought that Abraham was a prophet (Gn. 20:7, with Jn. 8:56). The exact meaning of the Hebrew word lying behind the Greek *eneulogēthēsontai* is disputed. It could be translated 'bless themselves' rather than *be blessed*. In that case it would mean that, when Gentiles wished to invoke blessing on one another, they would say, 'May the God of Abraham bless you', because they could conceive of no higher blessing to use. Genesis 18:18 could perhaps be translated thus, whatever may be the case with Genesis 12:3. But the traditional Jewish exegesis was the straight passive, and Paul clearly takes it as a direct passive here.

9. Paul can now round off the whole passage triumphantly by showing that, as a plain matter of fact, the 'faith people' are indeed at this moment enjoying the blessing of God, just as much as 'trusty' Abraham is. The word *pistō, who had faith*, is clearly active in sense here, meaning 'believing', rather than the passive 'trusted', although both meanings are linguistically possible. The Roman Catholic use of the term 'the faithful', to describe Christians, preserves this ambiguity, inherent in the Hebrew.

C. WHO IS UNDER THE CURSE? (3:10–14)

Paul must now swing around at once to meet a flank attack, real or expected. The Judaizers will have been fuming with impatience all this time. Why talk about Abraham, they will say, when the real question is the law? Abraham stood at the very beginning of God's revelatory process. Centuries later, God crowned the whole process by giving the law of Moses. It is by keeping this law that Israel looks for salvation. If God in his mercy used some other system in the days of Abraham, that was because there was as yet no law to keep. True, some rabbis wasted much ingenuity in trying to prove that the patriarchs, particularly Abraham, had in fact kept the law, though it had not yet been revealed (Kidd. 4:14). But that was necessary only to maintain the respectability of Abraham, not to uphold the cohesiveness of their own self-contained system. What the Judaizers were preaching to the Galatians was the utter necessity of keeping the law of Moses (in part at least) as essential for salvation. To them therefore all this talk about Abraham was quite irrelevant to the issue (unless they seriously believed that he had indeed kept the whole law) while to Paul, as we have seen, it was fundamental.

The common opinion of the Jewish scholar of Paul's day was that the vulgar *am hāāretz*, 'the people of the land', the common folk who had neither knowledge of, nor interest in, the law, were already under God's curse: see John 7:49, which could be paralleled by much stronger language outside the Bible. Now Paul turns the tables on them; it is the Jewish scholar, not the Gentile sinner, who is clearly under the curse. The details of the meaning of this curse will be given below. At the moment, the sole question is the curse's location, and Paul is clear on that question. Verses 10 and 11 may be paraphrased as follows:

'All of those who hunt for acceptance with God on the grounds of doing what the law commands are under the curse of God. That is clear from Scripture which says, "Everyone who fails to stand fast by everything written in the lawbook, and to do it, is under the curse of God." It is perfectly clear that no-one obtains right standing with God by law, for Scripture says, "The one who obtains right standing through faith will win life."'

10. Only a loose paraphrase such as the above can hope to bring out the meaning here. Paul is deliberately contrasting *hoi ek pisteōs*, 'men of faith', with *hosoi ex ergōn nomou, all who rely on works of the law*. In general terms, of course, the first correspond to the Christian and the second to the Jew. But for Paul, the categories are more inclusive still, for they correspond to the only two ways in which it is possible to approach God. Either we approach God completely without merit of our own, on the ground of his grace alone, or we approach him on the grounds of our own merits. In this sense Abraham 'pioneers' the first group while the Judaizers, in spite of their assertion that they too put their trust in Christ, support the second.

But what does *hypo kataran, under a curse,* mean? There are times in the New Testament when Paul almost seems to give *orgē* (wrath) and *katarā* (curse) independent existence. Indeed, in Romans we could enlarge this by adding abstract nouns like sin, death, law and others. But this is not so much a theological concept of hostile powers warring against God, or of abstract forces that, once unleashed by God, must find fulfilment. Instead, this is a purely Jewish form of expression; and in many cases, the reason for the apparent 'abstraction' can be found in some passage from the Old Testament. In the case of the abstract noun *katarā, curse,* there is a long history, beginning with Genesis 3:14–19, and ending with Malachi 2:2.[1] An examination of Genesis 3:14–19, for instance, or the similar passage in Genesis 4:11–12, will show how closely 'the curse' is related to the personal reaction of God to human sin. Nothing could be further from the concept of a blind depersonalized force.

'But this is all before the giving of the law,' the Jew might well say. So Paul comes at once to the period after the giving of the Torah. He quotes Deuteronomy 27:26 to show that failure to keep and do the law brings this same 'curse'. Now it is quite true that the Hebrew Bible does not have the word 'all' in this particular verse; it simply says, 'Cursed be he who does not confirm the words of this law by doing them', to which all the people add their 'Amen', thus accepting the justice of the pronouncement. But the 'all' appears in the next verse, 'being careful to do all his commandments' (Dt. 28:1). In his usual way, therefore, Paul is probably fusing two quotations into one.[2] Now since it was manifestly impossible to keep all the commandments of the law, that meant that, willy-nilly, all those who tried to keep the law came under this curse. The rabbis

[1] In every case, the abstract *katarā*, 'curse', is seen as distinct from *anathema*, translated in 1 Cor. 16:22 'accursed' (NIV, 'a curse be on him'), although both ultimately indicate the objects of God's wrath, so that there is an underlying unity of thought.

[2] Sometimes indeed he also fuses his own interpretation with the text: this is typical of rabbinic exegesis, and it is done to make the meaning more clear. A modern editor would use footnotes for the same purpose.

realized this; Paul himself knew it from his own experience before conversion. But there seemed to the rabbis to be no way out except by clinging to the 'merits of the Fathers' and to the merits of Abraham in particular. That was why the Jews clung so insistently to the reassuring thought of physical descent from Abraham, and the bearing in their body of the physical mark of circumcision that assured them of God's covenant with Abraham. The average Jew believed whole-heartedly that no circumcised son of Abraham would go to Gehenna. We cannot afford to smile at them when we remember how superstitiously some today can look on 'membership' of a church, or even the mere physical reception of water-baptism, or some other rite.

11. But now Paul wants to go further and prove that it is utterly impossible for anyone to be 'put in the right' with God by 'keeping the law'. To Paul, the fact that no-one can win 'life' through the law is perfectly clear, apart altogether from the rueful conclusion of the rabbis or his own religious experience. Scripture would not have offered another way of obtaining true 'life', if there had already been a possible way through keeping the law. He expresses all this in compressed form here,[1] but elsewhere he shows at length that this is part of his understanding of Scripture. The Scripture that Paul uses is Habakkuk 2:4, quoted as *he who through faith is righteous shall live*, or *the righteous shall live by faith* (RSV mg.).

Now this is a key verse for Paul's great doctrine of 'justification by faith'. Romans 1:17 is another place where he uses it with great effect, and in Hebrews 10:38 the unknown author employs it yet again. The question is often asked nowadays: is Paul being fair to the verse in Habakkuk by this exegesis, or is he 'reading in' a different meaning? Such a question can be answered only in the light of Paul's whole attitude to, and use of, the Old Testament.[2] No-one doubts what Paul's spiritual experience had been: none would doubt that this was his

---

[1] This in itself causes many of the exegetical problems of Galatians, since, as compared with Romans, it is written in 'theological shorthand'.

[2] See especially E. E. Ellis, *Paul's Use of the Old Testament* (Edinburgh: Oliver and Boyd, 1957), as well as more general books on the subject (Davies, Daube, Schoeps and Munck are examples).

interpretation of the verse. Some would say that, in view of his double quotation of it, this verse may have been the key which unlocked this new spiritual truth to him. But was it a correct exegesis?[1]

The brief answer to such a question is, first, that Paul does not even try to prove his doctrine of 'justification by faith' from this verse; he only illustrates it. He actually proves it from God's ways of dealing with Abraham. This verse is nothing more than a handy peg upon which to hang a spiritual truth which is made abundantly clear elsewhere in Scripture. Secondly, it is by no means certain that Paul is doing violence to the verse in Habakkuk, especially if we translate his quotation, as in RSV, *He who through faith is righteous shall live*, or even 'he shall gain life who is justified through faith' with NEB (NIV follows the older translations with 'The righteous will live by faith'). Even in the Old Testament, the line between 'trusty' and 'trusting' is a slender one, and we have already seen the ambiguity in the two meanings of the New Testament word *pistoi* as being either 'faithful' or 'believing'.

From now on the argument moves rapidly and easily. We may paraphrase verses 12–14 as follows:

'Now the law is certainly not "through faith" (*i.e.* the law has nothing to do with the notion of receiving "right standing" as a gracious gift from God, as a result of trust in him); for Scripture says, "He who performs these things will obtain life as a result of them." Christ bought us out from the sphere of the curse of the law by becoming accursed for us. The proof that he became "accursed" is seen in the Scripture, "Every man hanged upon a gallows is under a curse" (and Christ was hanged upon such a gallows). The positive purpose of all this was so that the "blessing", mentioned in the Abraham story as applying to non-Jewish peoples, should come to them through Jesus Christ, so that, through our trust in him, we might receive the promised gift of the Spirit.'

---

[1] See Betz for discussion of Paul's exegesis of this verse, and the relation of this exegesis to the MT and LXX.

12. Again, by inserting the missing steps in the argument, as here, we can see more clearly the flow of Paul's thought. When he says that *the law does not rest on faith*, he is not referring to the law itself, but the law seen as a supposed means of obtaining God's favour by winning 'merit'.[1] Later in this letter, Paul will make perfectly clear that he has no objection to the law as such. It is important to remember this, for it is an aspect of the Pauline theology which the Judaizers did not appreciate and which a casual reading of Paul's words might not make plain. Of course, the law itself lays down in many places the necessity of observing its commands. Paul is here summarizing Leviticus 18:5; 'You shall therefore keep my statutes and my ordinances, by doing which a man shall live.' Every Jew would agree that the law was concerned with 'doing'. That was axiomatic; there was no need for Paul to prove it, although he does quote this verse. Every system of 'natural religion' depends on 'doing'; therefore, as far as this aspect is concerned, Mosaic Judaism had become a thoroughly 'natural' system, whatever its original aim and object.

13. The word *exēgorasen, redeemed*, 'bought back' (this meaning is supported by Deissmann, as quoted in BAGD),[2] opens up with its ransom-metaphor a whole new area of understanding of the atonement. This is used to great effect elsewhere in the New Testament, notably 1 Peter 1:18–19, and by Paul himself in contexts such as that of Acts 20:28. But since, in this passage, Paul is not stressing the mechanics of redemption, we may pass it by with a brief notice. When Paul says that Christ 'bought us out' (as a soldier might formerly 'buy himself out' of the army) from the curse brought on us by our failure to keep the law, he uses the bold phrase *having become a curse for us*. This may be a simple use of the noun for the adjective, as assumed above in the paraphrase; or NEB may be right in translating as 'by

[1]Although Paul does not actually use the word 'merit', this seems to be what he means by 'works of the law', *i.e.* 'performance of the law'. When a modern Jew uses the phrase *'ōseh mitzvāh*, 'doing a commandment', it has the same overtone.

[2]But it is unlikely that Paul is thinking exclusively here of the formal sale in the Hellenistic world of a slave to a pagan god, in order that the slave might then be set free. The OT provides a rich background of explanation of 'ransom' quite independent of this.

becoming for our sake an accursed thing', in which case one noun would be used for another. Perhaps the use of *hamartia*, 'sin', in 2 Corinthians 5:21 where Christ is similarly described as 'becoming sin'[1] for us, is a parallel, although most modern commentators understand the word rather in the sense of 'sin-offering' in that context. It is interesting to refer back to 1:8, where Paul says that those who preach anything other than the true gospel are 'accursed'. It is true that the Greek word used there is *anathema*, something 'devoted to doom', not *katarā*, *curse*, as here,[2] but the two words come very close in their area of meaning, as mentioned above. That which the Judaizers deserve to be, Christ willingly accepted for our salvation as the place for himself. Verse 13 echoes verse 10 with *kataratos, cursed*.

Here Paul quotes from Deuteronomy: *Cursed be every one who hangs on a tree* (or 'a hanged man is accursed by God', Dt. 21:23). He does not mean that a man is cursed by God just because he is hanged, but that death by hanging was the outward sign in Israel of being cursed by God. A criminal was, in fact, hanged because he had broken the law, and this law-breaking brought both curse and punishment. So to Paul, or any other Jew, there was a peculiar appropriateness in the manner of the death that Christ endured. The cross was not only a death of shame to Jew and Gentile alike (the death of a slave, or a criminal), but, for the Christian, it also symbolized the fact that the one who hung there was willingly enduring 'the curse' for us. It is true that the later and hated Roman punishment of crucifixion (adopted by the bloody Alexander Jannaeus to deal with his Pharisee enemies) differed in many respects from the earlier Jewish custom of exposing the dead bodies of criminals on stakes; but it was sufficiently close to point the moral. (That crucifixion was not unknown among Jews is shown by Hengel.[3]) Christ was not 'cursed' simply because the manner of his death was the cross. Nevertheless, this death on the cross was to Paul yet another of

---

[1] 'Becoming sin' may well be simply a short way of saying 'becoming a sin offering', since Hebrew *hattath* could bear both meanings. But there is no similar ambiguity in the case of 'becoming a curse'.

[2] The words are discussed in BAGD: both have, in origin, a religious, not a secular, meaning.

[3] See Martin Hengel, *Crucifixion* (ET, Philadelphia: Fortress Press, 1977).

those correspondences of Scripture with later events which are too numerous to be accidental. To him, this was a 'fulfilment', the giving of a fuller, richer meaning at deeper level. Yet, to his Jewish opponents, this very death of Jesus on the cross, under God's curse, was the supreme proof that Jesus therefore could not be God's Messiah. Paul was meeting his enemies head on, as usual.

14. Paul now shows the positive purpose of God in all this: it was the way which God had chosen to fulfil the 'promise' made to Abraham, of blessing for the Gentiles. The two words *ethnē, Gentiles*, and *eulogia, blessing,* could well be put in inverted commas on this occasion, for both are a deliberate reminiscence of 3:8. To Paul, the promise to Abraham is understandable only in terms of Jesus Christ and his work, where alone it finds fulfilment. For a moment, Paul now groups himself with the Gentiles in order to show more vividly the content of this promise, unless his use of *we* is an admission that Jew and Gentile stand together here. The promise to Abraham is nothing less than the gift of the Spirit, the distinguishing mark of the child of God. That is why Paul speaks so much of the Spirit in this letter, for the Spirit is not peripheral, but central to his argument.

D. DOES LAW ANNUL PROMISE? (3:15–18)

But surely, someone might argue, even if this were so, the later law would have annulled any such earlier 'arrangements' with Abraham. Here is Paul, the ecclesiastical lawyer, at his best. He swoops like a hawk at his possible or real opponent.

'Fellow Christians, here is an ordinary human illustration. Even if it is only a last will and testament that has been ratified, no-one can set it aside or add a codicil. The promises were made to Abraham "and his posterity". Scripture does not say "and to his posterities", as though referring to more than one person, but, as though referring to one person only, "and to your posterity". This refers to Christ. But my real point is this: once a will and testament has been already ratified by God, no law coming four hundred and thirty years later can annul it and make void the promise which it contained. I say this because, if the inheritance of salvation comes through the law, then it has ceased to be in fulfilment of a promise. But God gave it, once and for all, as a gracious gift to Abraham, by promise.' The suppressed apodosis is: 'Therefore the law could not possibly change the conditions of salvation, from being the undeserving reception of a promise to being the merited reception of desert or "wages".'

15. Paul now offers *a human example* and refers to *a man's will*. In his writing he frequently appeals to analogies from ordinary life familiar to the lay person in order to illustrate, if not prove, a spiritual point.[1] Another good example is his use in Romans 7:1–3 of contemporary marriage laws to illustrate the possibility of a new union with Christ for those who have previously been 'wedded' to the law. This approach corresponds to the Lord's practice of appealing to the knowledge and instincts of ordinary people against the theological prejudice of the theologians (*cf.* Lk. 13:15 and 14:5). When Paul has illustrated his point at the human level, then he will apply it to the spiritual problem using the argument 'How much more . . .' Luke 11:13 shows the Lord using exactly the same process of argument, of the gift of the Spirit.

In English, part of the play on words here is lost because 'covenant' and 'will' (in the sense of a document) are two different words. But the Greek word *diathēkē* can be used in the New Testament in both senses, as BAGD points out. Something of this ambiguity can be kept by consistently translating it as 'last will and testament', if we continually remember the English use of the term exemplified in 'Old Testament' and 'New Testament'. This ambiguity exists only in biblical Greek, and has a long history in the LXX, where *diathēkē* is consistently used to translate the Hebrew *berīth*, 'covenant'. For the secular Gentile

---

[1]There are problems with this particular analogy, for which see Betz. By Greek and Roman law, a 'will' could be changed at any time, although there were certain types of Hebrew testamentary transactions which could not be altered, such as the so-called *mattenat barī'*. But clearly, unless there was some such situation widely known, Paul would not have appealed to it so confidently, nor would his hearers have acknowledged it.

reader, *diathēkē* meant 'will' and nothing more, although in classical times it had also had the sense of 'contract' (so BAGD). *Synthēkē*, the more common Greek word for 'covenant', does not occur in the New Testament. Of course, to the Gentile convert, certain difficulties arose when God was said to make a *diathēkē*, or 'will'. Such a will could be valid only after the death of the testator, and God could not be said to die. But Hebrews 9:11–21 shows the way in which early Christian apologetic could meet this difficulty triumphantly, by pointing to the death of Christ.

If we follow the argument in Hebrews as normative to New Testament thought, then, to Paul, the will and testament of God would have been *ratified* to Abraham by the blood shed at the covenant sacrifice. A death has already taken place: henceforward, not even a codicil can be added to the will. It certainly cannot be set aside by the Torah given to Moses centuries later. In verse 17, Paul plays on the two words *prokekyrōmenēn*, 'previously ratified', and *akyroi*, 'annul', in a way hard to reproduce in English. Both are linked closely with the word *kekyrōmenēn*, *ratified*, or perhaps, 'executed', used here in verse 15, and the result is to tie Paul's argument very closely together. The use of *epidiatassetai, adds to it*, translated in NEB 'add a codicil', is interesting. Presumably, Paul refers to those places in the Old Testament where it says, in anthropomorphic language, that God 'repented' of some proposed course of action. But nothing of this sort is ever recorded as having taken place in the case of Abraham. Here Jewish and Christian theology were at one, however strongly the Jews might feel about the Torah.

It is beside the point to argue whether, under either Hebrew or Graeco-Roman law, wills could be altered by the testator. Paul's argument is that, after the testator's death, his will must be carried out.

16. This verse is a highly compressed 'inset' which somewhat complicates the argument, but may be temporarily omitted without weakening it. Paul is simply concerned to make two points, elsewhere elaborated. First, such a 'will' (necessarily involving a promise for the future, as all wills must do) was in fact made, with Abraham as a beneficiary. Secondly, his 'offspring' was named as a further beneficiary, and this 'offspring', understood at the deepest level, was Jesus Christ. The second point is not really necessary here, but is a help in understanding the 'suppressed member' of Paul's argument. Paul knows as well as any other Hebrew scholar that *sperma*, *offspring*, literally, 'seed', can have a collective sense even when in the singular. There would have been no need to use the plural form to cover the meaning 'descendants'. Paul is saying, in typically Jewish fashion, that there is an appropriateness in the use of the singular form here, in that the true fulfilment came only in connection with one person, Christ. Here all must agree: and some at least will agree with Paul that such 'appropriateness' is not without the controlling guidance of the Holy Spirit.[1] Later, Paul himself will use *sperma*, 'offspring', in its collective sense, to cover a multitude of descendants.

17. The *four hundred and thirty years* between Abraham and the Torah is taken from Exodus 12:40 (MT) and is actually the figure given there for the duration of the stay in Egypt. Versions vary greatly in the duration of the stay, for numbers are notoriously difficult to transmit in ancient manuscripts. But the round figure has no special importance in itself, except to show the lateness of the Torah as compared with Abraham's covenant. Whether the Mosaic covenant is later than the Abrahamic covenant by one century or four, there is no contradicting the order in which they occurred.

18. The word *klēronomia*, *inheritance*, translated in the paraphrase as 'inheritance of salvation' (BAGD supports this meaning), means the actual 'enjoyment' of the benefits already promised under the will. Paul will return to this concept in 4:1, where the Christian is *klēronomos*, 'heir'. In Scripture, the *klēronomia* or 'inheritance' is inseparable from the gift of the Spirit, the *arrabōn*, 'the guarantee' or 'pledge', of our inheritance (Eph. 1:14). Similarly, when Paul speaks of *epangelia, promise*, he is undoubtedly thinking here in the first place of God's great promise to Abraham. But it is hard to avoid the conclusion that

---

[1]There are many excellent discussions of this 'generic singular', showing the rabbinic parallels for such arguments: the point is always theological, not linguistic.

147

he is also thinking, in a specifically New Testament sense, of the gift of the Spirit, as in verse 14. Similarly, when he used *kecharistai, gave*, or better still, 'gave freely', to describe God's attitude to Abraham, Paul is thinking of the deeper connotation of *charis*, 'grace', to the Christian. For the believer, God's 'grace' is personified in Christ. Paul's use of the perfect tense in this verb is probably deliberate. He wants to stress the 'once-for-all-ness' of God's grace; no later system of law can alter such an abiding gift to mankind.

E. WHAT IS THE PURPOSE OF THE LAW? (3:19–29)

Paul has now proved his point, certainly to his own satisfaction; perhaps even the Galatian converts are convinced by now. But he may have proved too much: it looks as if there is no place left for the law at all. Doubtless, this would not have troubled the Galatians, though it would ultimately have made any understanding with the Jerusalem church quite impossible. But the Judaizers would have pounced on this weak point at once. Not only would Paul's evangel have been antinomian in practice: it would have been antinomian even in theory. This was the charge that was already circulating in Jewish-Christian circles at Jerusalem, and to which James refers in Acts 21:21. Further, Paul's own understanding of God's plan demanded that he give the law of Moses its rightful place in God's historical plan. He was never more truly a Jew than when he had become a Christian (Rom. 9:1–5). In chapters 5 and 6, he will show that 'justification by faith' cannot possibly lead to antinomianism; it is instead the door to holy living. Elsewhere, he will show that the law has a present value in the life of the Christian; but there is no need to do this at the moment in Galatia, where its place is already being overstressed. All he needs to do here, in order to clear himself of false charges and also to show the consistency of God, is to demonstrate the place of the Torah in God's plan of salvation.

'Why then the law? It was added as a supplement because of sins – valid until the "posterity" arrived to whom the promise had been made in the will. Yes, it was negotiated through angels; yes, it was done through a middleman; but the very presence of a middleman implies more than one party, and our creed is that "God is one". Does that mean that the law is directly opposed to the promises? An impossible thought. If the kind of law had been given which could give "life", then it would have been true that right standing with God came from law. But the Scripture (*i.e.* the Torah) groups everything under the general heading of "sin", so that the promise, attendant on faith in Jesus Christ, might be given to those who believe.'

19. The little phrase *tōn parabaseōn charin* is not easy to interpret, although the grammatical meaning *because of transgressions* or 'sins' is plain. Paul may mean 'to restrain fallen human nature'. In that sense the law would have a temporary moral value, but it would be in a sense negative. Until Christ had come, humanity had neither the moral incentive nor the moral pattern that alone would make freedom from law something different from libertinism. The NEB, however, takes a stronger approach by paraphrasing 'to make wrongdoing a legal offence', which may well be correct. It would link with Paul's words in verse 22, 'consigned all things to sin', and his own moral experience depicted in Romans 7:7–25. Indeed, there are times when Paul boldly says that the function of law is to teach us the moral bankruptcy of fallen humanity. He does not mean that the law makes us sinners, but that it shows us to be sinners.

It was ordained by angels. The later Jewish belief in the angelic mediation of the law of Moses, perhaps based on Exodus 23:20, is shown in Stephen's speech (see Acts 7:53). Here Paul, like Stephen, is following strict Jewish orthodoxy. Like the author of the letter to the Hebrews, he will admit the claim before showing how such claims for the superiority of the law are transcended in Christ.

Through an intermediary (NIV, 'a mediator', is better). Paul is likewise prepared to accept this claim on behalf of Moses: this too was strict orthodoxy.

20. Having admitted the mediatorial work of Moses, Paul seems to be here claiming that this is a weakness, rather than a strength, of the law. His thought seems to be that, in his promise, God has dealt directly with Abraham and so with all mankind.[1] It is true that there is, in Christian thought, 'one mediator between God and men' (1 Tim. 2:5). But Christ is God as well as man, and so, in Christ, God is still dealing directly with humanity. In the *Theos heis estin, God is one*, Paul is appealing to Israel's age-old credal proclamation; no Jew would dare to dispute this for a moment.[2]

21. He has proved that the law cannot *annul* the promise of God. But is law even in opposition to, or *against the promises*? Paul's brief dismissal of the idea with the words *mē genoito*, *certainly not*, 'may it never be so', shows that such a thought to him comes near blasphemy, for it would imply an inner conflict within the mind of God. Promise is from God; law is equally from God. It remains only to relate them in one coherent system. Clearly the purpose of the law was not to *make alive*, not to give that eschatological 'life' which is one of the many biblical words for 'salvation'. If the Torah had been able to do that, then there might indeed have been some opposition between law and promise. But as it is, the function of the Torah was to bring to humanity a clearer knowledge of the character and demands of God which would, in its turn, bring a deeper consciousness of sin. Revelation to God's chosen people is therefore not favouritism; it is a heavy burden of responsibility. Paul never says that Gentiles knew nothing of God's law (see Rom 1:19–20), but he does claim that the Jew has a far deeper insight into God's will through their possession of the law of Moses (Rom. 2:17–18), and that this only condemns the Jew the more.

22. So it is that the law *synekleisen, consigned*, better 'grouped' (or perhaps 'imprisoned'), everything within the frontiers of acknowledged sin. We are all, Jew or Gentile, on the same

[1]God himself made his covenant directly with Abraham: no intermediary is there mentioned, angelic or otherwise. But, at Sinai, Israel was afraid to meet God directly (Ex. 20:18–19), and therefore demanded Moses as a mediator to stand between them and God. God dealt directly with Moses, indirectly with Israel.

[2]See Betz for the relevance of this Jewish credal statement to Paul's main argument here: literally hundreds of different explanations have been given. The main point seems to be that any concept of a mediator diminishes the oneness of God, and thus is automatically inferior.

footing now. When Paul says *hē graphē*, 'the Scripture' here, he is almost certainly thinking of the scriptures of the Law, and the phrase has been so translated in the paraphrase on page 149.[1] In Romans 3:9–20 he will prove the same truth from the other two divisions of the Hebrew Bible, the 'Prophets' and the 'Writings'; but Paul has a particular concern with the law of Moses at the moment, because of the nature of the Galatian controversy. The NIV has a happy translation here, 'declares . . . a prisoner'.

In recent years there has been much study of the phrase *ta panta*, *all things*, or 'everything', especially in connection with Paul's concept of 'cosmic redemption', as in Ephesians 1:22. But here Paul's meaning is probably only 'all people', referring to sin's universality, rather than 'all things' referring to its cosmic aspect.

Were Paul to stop with this negative aspect of the place and purpose of the law, we should indeed be in a terrible plight. But to Paul the purpose of classifying us all as 'sinners', and bringing us to see the justice of this classification, is solely so that we may be eligible for salvation. The righteous have no claim on Christ; it was to save sinners that he came (Mt. 9:12–13). Seen from this angle, even the condemnatory function of the law is all of grace; and this is what Paul has already insisted in the second half of verse 22. He will now expand his meaning in verses 23–26.

'Before Christian faith had entered the scene,[2] we were held under arrest by law, kept in gaol, awaiting the divine revelation of that faith that was to come. Seen in this light, the law was our "escort" to lead us to Christ so that we might be justified by trust. But once faith has come we are no longer under the authority of our "escort"; for we are all God's children, through trust in Christ Jesus.'

This passage is full of semi-personifications (vv. 23–26). The phrase *ho nomos*, with the definite article, should be translated as

---

[1]With deference, Betz (following Schlier) is probably incorrect in seeing here a contrast between 'scripture' and 'law': to the Jew, the law was scripture in the deepest sense.

[2]To Paul, Christ's coming divides religious history decisively (Acts 17:30–31). This applies equally to the position of Judaism and of pagan religions: after the coming of Christ, their respective roles were decisively changed. This is not of course to deny that Judaism had a peculiar place and purpose in this earlier period, as Paul now outlines.

'the law', with specific reference to the law of Moses; *nomos*, without the article, would usually be 'law' seen as a general principle, as here. But the use of the definite article with *pistis*, translated here by 'faith', is more ambiguous. Does Paul mean 'faith' as a principle, or 'the faith of Abraham', or 'the Christian faith', which is possible only to those who have heard and accepted the 'good news' as it is in Christ? Probably in Paul's mind there would be no contradiction between the three, and so we may translate it here as 'the (Christian) faith', in the sense in which the word is used later (*e.g.* 1 Tim. 4:1). Alternatively, we may regard the definite article as purely generic, and translate (as RSV) by *'faith'*, seen as a principle of God's operation.

23. The word *ephrouroumetha, confined*, is translated by NEB as 'in the custody of' (NIV, 'held prisoners'). In itself the word has the idea of 'guarding' in a good sense as much as that of 'confining' in a bad sense; perhaps therefore 'in protective custody' would give the sense better. The word *synkleiomenoi, kept under restraint*, or 'locked up' in NIV (NEB, 'we were close prisoners'), makes plain that some form of restrictive confinement is intended. It is a deliberate echo of *synekleisen* in verse 22. But, even taking all this together, the law is no grim captor, particularly in view of the fact that we are only being held in protective custody pending the arrival of a pardon. It is typical of Paul that he sees the need for God's revelation to us in connection with this gift of faith. The word *apokalyphthēnai, be revealed*, expresses the same truth as 1:12. Without a prior act of God, we cannot even believe in him. That is why not even faith itself is meritorious in Paul's eyes (Eph. 2:8).

24. Paul himself apparently feels it necessary to correct the possible idea that the law is a surly gaoler, and so, by a quick shift of metaphor, he transforms the law into a *paidagōgos*, a *custodian* or *escort for children*. Those who can remember the stern, old-fashioned 'governess' of a past generation will have a fair idea of the position and duties of the trusty, elderly slave who conducted his young charge to and from school.[1] The only

---

[1] A full study of the word *paidagōgos* is given in BAGD, with the literature there quoted: the meaning suggested in the text seems basic, to judge from this.

ambiguity lies in the two words *eis Christon, until Christ came.* The other possible translation is well expressed in the NIV, 'to lead us to Christ'. In view of the function of the 'tutor' in the ancient world, perhaps the second is preferable.[1] The law, Paul is saying, was designed to teach us the great truth that only through faith in Christ could we be justified, although its part in this process was negative, not positive. So far from the law being contradictory to 'the promise', or even irrelevant to it, Paul has shown that the law was indispensable to the promise, for it prepared the way for its reception.

25. But, like the child's escort, the law had its definite place in history. Once the faith-principle is operative, there is no room for the principle of law as a means of justification. The two cannot co-exist at the same time (as the Judaizers want) since the function of law is essentially preparatory. To return to Paul's human analogy; once the child has grown up, it is no longer under the control of the slave escort. Faith in Christ has given us full sonship of God, and the constraining patterns of the past are gone. It is possible that Paul may have been thinking of the respect traditionally due to the 'tutor', even after the child has attained his majority. Some such thought is clearly present in 1 Corinthians 4:15, but it is not actually expressed here. Such respect the Christian would always have for the law, both because of its place in the history of salvation and because of the abiding witness that it gives to the character of God. Because of this last point, law still has a place in the life of the Christian, even if it has now become the law of love or the law of Christ (6:2).

26. It is uncertain whether we should translate this with RSV and NIV as *sons of God, through faith (in Christ Jesus)*, or 'faith-children of God in the corporate whole that is the Body of Christ'. NEB favours the latter, with 'sons of God in union with Christ Jesus'. The grammar would favour the first, but the subsequent train of thought would favour the second.

---

[1]However, Betz seems incorrect in denying any 'positive educational developments' by which the law prepared for us the way to Christ. Paul's whole argument seems to demand this interpretation.

Strictly, this choice is more a matter of theological interpretation than linguistics; it hinges on the meaning of the great Pauline phrase *en Christō, in Christ*; the phrase is discussed in BAGD, with relevant literature quoted there.[1] Briefly, this is the Pauline (and Johannine) expression to denote the closeness of the relation of the individual to Christ. The phrase implies a closeness of communion which is neither absorption nor complete identification (see note on 2:20); for, while human personality may be changed by the new relationship, it is not obliterated. Thereafter, the collective whole of all Christians can be called 'the body of Christ', not just the individual who is *in Christ*, part of his body. John describes this continual and total dependence on Christ as 'remaining' in Christ (see Jn. 15:4).

Paul now develops this thought of our sonship of God, through faith in Christ.

'For all those of you who have been baptized into Jesus Christ have clothed yourselves with Christ. In him, there is no such distinction as Jew and non-Jew, slave and freeman, male and female. You are all an entity in Christ Jesus. But if you are joined to Christ (lit. "if you are Christ's"), then you are collectively the "posterity of Abraham" already mentioned; you are the beneficiaries of the promise in the will.'

27. It is presumably the relationship summed up in the words 'in Christ' (see note on verse 26) to which Paul here refers in the phrase *baptized into Christ*. Baptism, with its picture of death and new life symbolized by the passing of the 'waters of judgment' over the sinner, visibly and outwardly seals the ending of an old relationship and the beginning of a new. Ideally, baptism should coincide with, and correspond to, the dawn of new life in the heart of the believer. But even in the pages of the New Testament, we find the Spirit coming sometimes before baptism, sometimes during baptism, sometimes after baptism, and sometimes not coming at all (see the accounts of the baptized Ananias

---

[1]It is not fair, with older commentators, to dismiss this simply as 'Pauline Christmysticism'. In the first place, it is not 'mysticism' to Paul, but description of a theological and spiritual position, and only subsequently of an experience. In the second place, it is

and Simon Magus, Acts 5:1–11; 8:9–24). Not only does baptism fitly express visibly the establishment of a new personal relationship with Christ; it is also the outward means by which we enter that collective whole which is the church, the body of Christ.[1] So closely does Paul associate the outward sign with the inward grace that there are times when he uses expressions in connection with the outward symbol which are, theologically speaking, more properly applied to the spiritual reality. But this is a common phenomenon in the Bible and does not necessarily mean that he identified the two. Here Paul juxtaposes two verbs, the one strictly descriptive of a physical experience, the other of a spiritual experience, without any consciousness of incongruity. We who were baptized *have put on Christ*, like a garment. The word *enedysasthe, put on*, is discussed in BAGD. The metaphor probably comes from the Old Testament where, for instance, the Spirit 'clothes himself' with Gideon, and so 'puts on' Gideon, as it were (Jdg. 6:34). The word has a rich metaphorical use both in and outside the New Testament, especially in connection with moral qualities. Bold though this figure is, it can be paralleled almost exactly in pagan literature in the sense of 'assume the role of', although the Christian usage means far more than this. The use of 'stripping' and 'putting on' may derive, in Christian circles, from the undressing before baptism, and the subsequent dressing in clean white clothing. But the metaphor is peculiarly appropriate as describing a situation where certain habits and qualities have to be laid aside for ever, and a new set assumed. It is interesting that this is the only reference to baptism in the whole letter, and that even here it is introduced almost casually.

28. In the New Testament *eni* stands for *enesti, there is*; but it seems always to be used with the negative. In the collective whole which is 'the body of Christ', there is no longer any place for the traditional distinctions that divide mankind – cultural,

---

common to most if not all of the New Testament writers, even if at times it is phrased differently.

[1]This, however, does not necessarily mean that we are dealing here with an early Christian baptismal liturgy in the verses that follow, in spite of Betz. The letter is probably too early to assume such fixed formulations, which undoubtedly followed later.

linguistic, religious (for *Greek*, opposed to *Jew*, conveys all of these) or even sexual. Some have seen here another thrust at the Judaizers.[1] The Jewish male gave regular thanks to God in the liturgy that he was not born a Gentile or a woman. Paul would then be pointing out that, in Christ, all the old 'dividing walls' that were accepted and even extolled, in Judaism had been broken down (Eph. 2:14). But it may simply be that these were types of human division familiar to his hearers, and that he uses them to symbolize all such human divisions.

Paul bases his strong position (the total transcending of such distinctions) on the grounds that all are now *heis, one* (or 'an entity'), *in Christ Jesus*. (The NEB actually translates as 'one person', thus making the meaning doubly clear.) Here again is the concept of the collective whole of the Christian church. It is a short step from this to the use of the 'body concept' which sees the totality of believers as the body of Christ.

29. That the use of the *heis* ('one person') in verse 28 rather than the neuter *hen* ('one thing') is no accident is shown by this verse. Grammatically, it says *if you are Christ's*, but the meaning is stronger than this. We might almost paraphrase 'if you are part of Christ's body'. Paul is going to apply to the collective whole of the Christian church that which he has previously predicated of Christ in person, that is, the inheritance of the Abrahamic promise. Those who in this way are Christ's are (collectively) the 'offspring' (singular again) mentioned in the famous passage in Genesis, and so the 'heirs' (plural, for we severally enjoy the benefits) in fulfilment of God's promise. This in itself will show that Paul's insistence on the use of the

[1]This is the only place in Paul's writings where he actually states that men and women are 'one', *i.e.* that sexual difference has been transcended in Christ, although the same doctrine could perhaps be inferred from other passages. Does he state it here because of the Judaizing push for circumcision, which in itself differentiated the sexes in religion, in a way which Christian baptism did not? Even in the Temple at Jerusalem, women could enter only the 'Court of the Women' and no further: they were barred from the 'Court of Israel'. However (unlike the Gnostics), Paul never says that the gender distinction between man and woman has been abolished. Indeed (however we regard their relevance today), he bases certain of his regulations for church order upon this distinction (*e.g.* 1 Cor. 14:34). Some commentators regard this Corinthian passage as inconsistent with 3:28, but obviously Paul cannot have viewed it so.

singular in 3:16 is more an exegetic device than anything else. Once we see that the primary reference is to Christ, Paul is prepared to allow that there is a secondary and collective reference to all Christians, as being 'in Christ'.

F. THE DIFFERENCE BETWEEN SON AND INFANT (4:1–11)

There are certain pictures which captured Paul's imagination and which he therefore tended to use again and again: human birth and growth was one of them. Here he uses the image with reference to mental and intellectual development rather than to physical growth. If we are to look for a link with the argument of chapter 3, it is probably to be found in the thought of the child's being led to and from school by the *paidagōgos*, but only while still in his minority.

'What I am saying is this: as long as the heir is a minor, he is no better than a slave, even though he is the owner of all; he is under guardians and administrators until the time that his father has fixed (*i.e.* fixed in his last will and testament). So too, we, when we were "minors", were kept in slavery to the ABC of the universe. But when the time had fully passed, God sent out his own Son, woman-born, under the conditions of law, so, that he might "buy out" those who were under the conditions of law, in order that ours might be the privilege of adoption. Because you are children, God has sent his Son's spirit into your hearts. It is that Spirit who cries within us "my father". So that makes you, not a slave, but a child; and, as surely as you are a child, you are an heir by God's gift.'

1. The word *nēpios*, 'child', should in classical Greek mean 'baby', and there are places where Paul uses it in this sense. For example, in 1 Corinthians 3:1, the *nēpios* is a baby who is still on 'milk', unable to face the 'solid food' of Christian doctrine. Here, however, NEB is possibly correct in translating as 'a minor'; for the main point is that the child is not yet old enough to fulfil the terms of his father's will. But if *stoicheia*, 'elements', in verse 3 does indeed mean 'ABC' ('basic principles', NIV), then perhaps Paul is thinking of a child of kindergarten age. Such a young child is *no better than a slave: diapherei* usually has this sense of 'surpassing', not merely 'being different from'.

2. Paul does not re-introduce the concept of the *paidagōgos*, 'custodian', here, for he is not thinking so much of the child's education as of the administration of the estate which, though belonging to the child by right, is not yet his to manage. Otherwise, the phrase *epitropous kai oikonomous*, 'guardians and trustees'[1] answer fairly closely to the 'tutor' in 3:25 above. It is probably fanciful to see any theological distinction here. The law was certainly stated to be our *paidagōgos*, 'custodian', but that does not necessarily mean that something other than the Torah was our *epitropos* or *oikonomos*, 'guardian' or 'trustee'. Both of these words could equally correspond to the law in its other functions. Again, much hinges on the meaning of *stoicheia tou kosmou, elemental spirits of the universe*, in the next verse, and whether this phrase applies to the Jewish law or not.[2] It is just conceivable that Paul does make a slight distinction in his mind, and thinks of the 'guardians' and 'administrators' as those who taught the law, rather than as the law which was taught. In that case, the two words could well stand for the Judaizers in their proselytizing activity in Galatia. Paul would then be saying: in the past you may well have been under the authority of such people, but not now.

For *prothesmia, date set*, or 'time appointed', BAGD quotes literature referring to the father's legal right to fix the day when his heir would 'come of age', for the purpose of inheriting the father's property. For Paul, this is connected with the concept of *plērōma tou chronou*, 'the time had fully come', found in verse 4. To Paul, this moment is when, in the plan of God, all mankind attains its majority in the coming of Christ. The use of the word *plērōma* may be connected with the Jewish teaching being given in Galatia at the time, if, as is possible, it was tinged with

---

[1] It is unnecessary to see here any exact correspondence to particular recognized officials of the Roman world: Paul is speaking in a general way.

[2] Betz well points out that, whatever the exact meaning, the words convey the basic thought of 'the slave holders' or 'the slave masters' in this context, as distinct from those held in slavery by them.

pre-gnostic ideas. The later Jewish Gnostics made great play with the word in their theological systems, and Paul seems to counter this particular heresy with his Christological teaching in the later letters of Ephesians and Colossians. But it is not necessary to see an anti-gnostic undercurrent in the present passage, where Paul's thoughts are still directed to the legal illustration of a minor coming into an inheritance. In any case, it is probably too early for such a supposition, since Gnosticism was not a full-blown heresy till the second century.

3. Much will therefore depend on the meaning of *stoicheia tou kosmou, the elemental spirits of the universe*. But, in earlier Greek, *stoicheia* can mean 'elementary principles', or even 'alphabet', and so it has been translated in the paraphrase above on p. 157. This, or something similar, must be the meaning in Hebrews 5:12, and is probably the meaning in the present passage and might even be the meaning in Colossians 2:8 and 20. In that case, Paul is referring to the elementary stages of religious experience (whether Jewish or Gentile) through which the Galatians have gone in the past, but which are now all alike equally outdated by Christ.[1] There have been great names in support of this interpretation, as pointed out in the footnote to the relevant article in BAGD. The advantage is that this interpretation is equally applicable to Jew and Gentile. If the Galatians had been Gentile pagans before they were converted, they could scarcely have been said to have been in slavery to the Jewish law, no matter from what angle it is considered, but they could have been considered as in slavery to the elementary principles of universal moral law. To that extent at least, Jew and Gentile were alike in being *children*. The NEB mg. takes this view, cautiously, translating 'elementary ideas belonging to this world': NIV too has 'basic principles of the world'.

Most modern commentators, however, prefer to translate either as *elemental spirits of the universe*, or more fancifully as 'signs of the zodiac', which often represented such spirits in popular belief. Earth, air, fire, water ('the elements') and the

---

[1] This does not of course mean that Judaism is ever equated by Paul with paganism: it is only in their 'outmoded' nature that the two are now similar.

stars were often linked in the human mind with vague spiritual forces, as they are in astrology even today. In view of verse 10, with its apparent reference to careful observation of a 'calendar', some have felt that such an interpretation would suit the strange syncretistic Judaism that we know to have existed at the time, especially in Asia Minor. This was the soil from which later Jewish Gnosticism (as distinct from purely pagan Gnosticism) was to grow. On the other hand, if the Judaizers were strictly orthodox Jews from Jerusalem (as Acts seem to suggest), they would abhor this syncretism as much as Paul did. Every orthodox Jew believed fervently that the Exile had been due to the 'star worship' of Manasseh and others like him (*cf.* Je. 15:4). Admittedly, if the Galatians had been pagans before conversion, then such astrological speculation could well have formed part of their religious system, whatever deity they might actually have worshipped: but it is very hard to see how this sort of description could ever have been applied to the law of Moses, particularly by Paul.

In verse 9, Paul calls these same 'elements' *asthenē kai ptōcha*, 'weak and beggarly'. This does not really help us to fix the meaning more precisely; it merely gives Paul's opinion as to their comparative worthlessness.[1] The later references in Colossians 2:8 and 20 seem to represent a developed use of the word which may not, therefore, have exactly the same meaning as here: see O'Brien, *Colossians*, for both passages. Here, the word is associated closely with 'philosophy' and 'tradition', which at once suggests some esoteric system rather than a legal frame. However, in both Colossian references, these 'elements', *stoicheia*, are contrasted sharply with Christ, as they are in the Galatians passage.[2]

4. In the statement that God *exapesteilen, sent forth* ['sent on a mission'] *his Son*, it is tempting to see an allusion to the title *apostolos*, 'apostle', over which there had apparently been controversy between the Jerusalem church and Paul. It is

---

[1] It does, however, rule out any concept of 'demonic forces' (see Betz) in this context. It is their imperfection, not their power, which is stressed here.

[2] In addition to the standard Bible dictionaries and wordbooks, the thoughtful excursus in Burton should be consulted.

noteworthy that, after the admission of 1:17 (where Paul includes himself in the number), he does not in this letter use the title 'apostle' of the leaders at Jerusalem. The application of the term 'apostle' to Christ would not, of course, be isolated: Hebrews 3:1 applies the noun to him directly as God's unique 'messenger' or 'delegate'.[1]

When Christ is described as *genomenon ek gynaikos, born of woman*, the reference is probably to his full humanity, rather than to the virgin birth, though this could well be included. That Paul does not deal with this doctrine directly does not prove that he was not cognizant with it. If Luke, the author of the Gospel, was also the author of Acts and the travel companion of Paul, it is inconceivable that Paul should have been ignorant of the birth stories recorded in Luke 1 and 2. For any Jew, whether it be Paul or a Judaizer, the chief relevance of such a phrase would be its correspondence with Genesis 3:15. Here at last is the promised 'seed' of the woman who will crush the serpent's head. Paul was no doubt also thinking of the promise of Isaiah 7:14 concerning the bearing of Immanuel by the 'young woman' mentioned there.

But not only was Christ born as human; he was born *under* [conditions of] *law*. This is probably a reference to his birth in the Jewish race, although, as *nomos* has no article, it could be argued that this is simply another general reference to his status as human, and so under 'law' as a principle. To Paul, all are under *nomos*, 'law' of some kind; only Jews, however, are under *ho nomos*, 'the law of Moses' (although sometimes even *nomos* without the article is used in this special sense). Elsewhere the New Testament develops the twin concepts that Christ came to fulfil the law, and that Christ perfectly kept the law. Here Paul mentions only Christ's 'status', as it were. His real reason for mentioning it at all is that it introduces the next clause.

5. Christ was born under conditions of law so that he might ransom those who were themselves under such conditions. In 3:13 it was from the 'curse of the law', the curse which the law brings on law-breakers, that we were redeemed; here the figure

---

[1] See the appendix in Burton dealing with this topic.

is even bolder. We are redeemed from the law itself, seen of course as a system of attempted self-justification. Whether *apolabōmen, receive*, has anything of the sense of 'get back' is uncertain; it may simply be 'attain' with no thought of the privileges lost by the fall. *Huiothesian* is a fully legal term, *adoption as sons*, though in the New Testament it is only used in a religious sense. The idea, although not the word, comes from the Old Testament, referring to the new status given to Israel by God and the new relationship into which she had been called. It is, however, not such an abstract word as 'adoption' in English; perhaps, therefore, the NEB translation 'the status of sons' is preferable (NIV, 'full rights'). The use of the definite article with the noun, *tēn huiothesian*, literally, 'the adoption', may just be to mark it as an abstract noun. On the other hand, it may mean 'the famous adoption, of which Scripture speaks'.

6. Now the action quickens. It is because you are sons, says Paul, that *God has sent the Spirit of his Son into our hearts.* If it were possible to isolate stages in what is essentially one spiritual process, we should say that this gift was necessary to turn adoptive children into true-born children. For it is by the presence of the Spirit in our hearts that we are asssured of our sonship of God (*cf.* Rom. 8:16) and so are enabled to pray with confidence.[1]

Exactly the same word (*exapesteilen*) is used here in verse 6 of God's action in sending the Spirit as has already been used in verse 4 of God sending his Son. It is not strange, therefore, that the Spirit is here described as *the Spirit of his Son*. This is no confusion of the two persons of the Trinity, but simply a recognition of the close link between the two which exists in Scripture. It is by the Spirit that Christ lives in our hearts (Eph. 3:16–17). Indeed, so close is the link that, without the Spirit, no-one can belong to Christ (Rom. 8:9). *Abba, father*, is one of the Aramaic linguistic 'fossils' of the New Testament, preserved even in the later Greek. It was the very word used by Christ in prayer as recorded in Mark 14:36. As such, it seems to have

---

[1] It is interesting that in the Romans context also the word *Abbā* recurs, suggesting a definite thought link between the two passages: the Spirit, sonship and prayer are inextricably connected.

passed into the prayer life of the primitive church, even when the language used was different. While it was the usual intimate name used by a child to its father within the home, it is certainly over-sentimentalizing, if not trivializing, to translate it as 'Daddy'.

7. Yet the use of this intimate word is, to Paul, the proof that we have the 'inner witness' of the Spirit within our hearts; that in itself convinces us that we are children, not slaves.[1] The Greek *ei, if,* does not imply any doubt; NIV is correct in translating 'since'. As surely as we are children, we are God's heirs by his own gift; the two concepts are inseparable to Paul.

Verses 8–10 are a further elaboration of the nature of the Galatian error, and interesting from that point of view. All we have gathered so far is that they were under pressure to be circumcised, and that Paul regarded this as bringing the obligation to keep the whole law. The passage represents, however, only a slight excursus, and does not itself lead the main argument any further.

'But in those days, when you were without knowledge of God, you were slaves to those things which by their very nature are no-gods. But now that you do know God – or rather, now that God knows you – how is it that you are continually harking back to these powerless and limited elementary practices? Do you want to be their slaves all over again? I am referring to the way in which you keep special days, and months, and seasons and years.[2] I am afraid that I may have wasted all my pains on you.'

8. The contrast between God and no-gods[3] is typically Jewish; this sort of word-play was very congenial to the Hebrew language. The use of *physei, by nature,* is interesting. Just as Paul

[1] Romans 8:26 further discusses the function of the Spirit in connection with our prayer life, and indeed with our whole relationship with God. It reads like a later handling of the same topic.

[2] It is uncertain as to how much emphasis we should put on the verbal correspondence here with Genesis 1:14. But it would equally apply whether these were Jewish or pagan festivals.

[3] It is useless to speculate whether these 'no-gods' were perhaps old Celtic gods (Betz):

had pointed out to Peter at Antioch that they too were Jews 'by birth', or 'naturally' (2:15), so here he points out that, by their very nature, these 'elements', whatever they are, could not be gods. Had he enlarged on this theme, it would doubtless have involved the Hebrew doctrine of creation. To Paul, the great sin of idolatry is to worship the created thing rather than the creator (Rom. 1:25); and whether it be the 'elements' or the 'heavenly bodies', all are alike the work of God's hand.

9. In the Bible *to know* has a far deeper meaning than the superficial concept of intellectual knowledge alone. That is why it can be used of the relation of God and humanity, and also of the peculiarly intimate relation of husband and wife. But it is typical of Paul's strong theological position that he is reluctant to speak of humans 'knowing' God; at once, he corrects it to the passive *to be known by God*. This transfers salvation altogether out of the possibly subjective and possibly illusory into the great objective reality of the will of God.

For the *elemental spirits*, see the comment on verse 3. The same interpretation should apply in both cases: but much will depend on whether we see verse 10 as applying to Jewish or pagan festivals.

Whose slaves you want to be once more: of course, the Judaizers do not consciously intend to 'enslave' the Galatians; nor do the Galatians consciously intend to re-enter the spiritual slavery from which they have only just emerged. But since this will be the inevitable consequence of their actions, Paul wishes to shock them into the realization of what, all unknowing, they are doing at the very moment.

10. It is not certain whether the 'elemental spirits' of verse 9 (or 'elements') are actually identified by Paul with these *months and seasons*, now being observed in Galatia, or whether such customs are only an example of slavery to these elements by 'returning to the infants' class' in the religious world, which seems preferable. The *days* and *months* and *years* could refer to

---

that would largely depend on the destination of the letter. If it was sent to South Galatia, then Zeus and Hermes are actually mentioned in Acts (Acts 14:12). Better (again with Betz) to see the phrase as a general reference to all such pagan cults.

the liturgical calendar of orthodox Judaism, with its sabbaths, 'new moons' and 'sabbatical years',[1] and in view of the situation in Galatia, this would suit best. They could equally well of course refer to the quasi-magical observances that we know to have been rife in Ephesus and, presumably, in other parts of Asia Minor too (Acts 19:19). Heterodox Jews as well as pagans certainly practised these arts, as we see from Acts 19:13. In inter-testamental days, the Jews displayed immense interest in the calendar, probably considered from this aspect of 'lucky days': pseudepigraphical books like Jubilees give examples. It is not essential to see Jewish influence in these observances, though it is likely; in all forms of paganism, there is some form of 'casting horoscopes', with consequent 'lucky' and 'unlucky' days. However, if there is a direct reference to the observance of Jewish festivals, then this is yet another demand made by the Judaizers, in addition to their insistence on circumcision. We have seen that 2:12 probably refers to insistence on the observance of food laws as well: that would make three demands.

11. With *eikē, in vain*, 'to no purpose', Paul is returning to the thought of 3:4. There, he asked whether the Galatians themselves had gone through such initial spiritual experiences to no purpose. Here, the thought is rather that Paul may have 'wasted my efforts' (NIV) in preaching to them. It is doubtful if these verses can be used, either way, to illustrate Paul's views on the question of Christian security after salvation. Even in 3:4 his desire to win back the Galatians will not allow him to consider their loss as a serious possibility ('if it really is in vain'), although that does not necessarily mean that his remark here is purely ironical, as Betz would have it.

The word *kekopiaka, I have laboured*, or 'toiled', implies hard work leading to real weariness; it is a favourite word with Paul to explain the toil and trials of the Christian ministry. If those to whom he writes are the inhabitants of the cities of South Galatia, then we know from Acts 13 and 14 something of the 'toil'

---

[1] An obvious and immediate application would be to the observance of the Jewish Sabbath, presumably now for the first time introduced as an obligation. Paul seems to be referring to this in Romans 14:5–6. The Sabbath was obviously not observed universally among the early Christians, outside of Palestine at least.

involved. This verb (which has a good sense) should be distinguished from the phrase *kopous parechetō*, 'give me trouble', in 6:17, where the root has a bad meaning.

G. A PERSONAL APPEAL FOR BETTER RELATIONS (4:12–20)

Perhaps it is the thought of all that he has endured on their behalf which now turns the letter in a more personal direction. On the whole (and in contrast with 2 Corinthians) the whole argument, while intensely emotional, has been so far strangely impersonal, but now there comes a rapid and complete change. One suspects that until now, Paul has been either intent on the theological problem or thinking of his Judaizing opponents rather than of the local Christians, with whom he had so many individual bonds. The strongest terms of affection that he has so far allowed himself in the whole letter is *adelphoi*; but 'brother' or 'sister' is a very general term within the Christian community. He will use the term again here; but he will go far beyond the general use in his reminiscence of the past.

'I ask you to imagine yourselves in my position, fellow Christians, just as I have imagined myself in yours. Your attitude to me was once quite correct. You know that in sickness of body I preached the good news to you before, and you neither made little of the bodily trials that I had, nor felt any revulsion from me because of it. You welcomed me as God's own messenger, like Jesus Christ himself. What has happened to the blessing that you enjoyed then? I can bear witness myself that, if you could have taken out your own eyes and given them to me, you would have done so. So now I have become your enemy merely by acting faithfully towards you, have I?

'These others are envious of you, and their envy has an evil aim. They want to exclude you (*i.e.* "from blessing" or "from my love") so that you may come to envy them their position. Envy in a good cause is always good, not only when I am with you, my dear spiritual children. I have all the pains of child-labour over again for you, until Christ takes shape in you. Only I do wish that I could be with you now, and change my tone; for I really do not know what to do in your case.'[1]

This passage bristles with difficulties, although fortunately none of them are of a serious nature and none of them raise major theological problems. If we knew more of the relations of Paul with these 'Galatians', doubtless much that is now obscure would be clear. As it is, those who favour a South Galatian destination scent references to the Acts account at every turn. True, if the letter was written to the Galatians of the north, we are completely without a clue as to the meaning of the references. But we are not even sure that the account in Acts represents the full story of the evangelization of the south, so that we are little better off either way. Fortunately, the Greek itself is fairly straightforward, and the manuscript variation insignificant. All turns on the exact interpretation: one suspects that the main problems are emotional, not theological, in this very disjointed passage.

12. The opening clause *become as I am* is the first real exegetic puzzle.[2] Literally it means 'Be like me, as I too (have become) like you.' The NEB is probably right in turning it, 'Put yourselves in my place . . . for I have put myself in yours.' That Paul does not, in point of fact, continue in this vein is no argument that he may not have started thus. On the other hand, he may simply mean, 'Be as frank and loving with me as I have always been with you.' Either way, it is clearly a personal appeal to the Galatians to resume their old friendly relations with Paul which have apparently been ruptured by the work of the Judaizers. The exact details need not detain us. We should not, however, neglect the suggestion that what he means is, 'I have become like a Gentile for your sake – are you now going to Judaize?' (Betz).

When Paul says *you did me no wrong*, is he stating a fact, or is he quoting in indignation, a presumed remark of the Galatians? 'Never wronged me, did you?' In support of his indignation he

---

[1]The above translation assumes that *zēloō* means 'to envy', and not 'to court the favour of'. See the detailed discussion in the text for the reasons for this view.

[2]Indeed, the whole section is full of minor problems, though the main sense is clear, as commentators admit. Most editors rightly see an erratic style and grammar, springing from violent emotion: Betz strives hard to see a rhetorical framework, but this is not convincing.

would then contrast their past behaviour with their present. It seems an undoubted fact that in the Corinthian correspondence Paul frequently uses this device of putting a sentence into the mouth of his opponents only to confute it. As there is no other instance of this device in Galatians, however, this is perhaps the less likely explanation of the two. Betz explains it on rhetorical grounds, but this seems a little artificial and forced.

13. Paul preached to these Galatians, *because of a bodily ailment, di' astheneian*, or perhaps, 'amid bodily weakness'. Much profitless argument has raged around these few words. Those who favour a South Galatian destination sometimes choose to see a reference to the stoning recorded in Acts 14, and some consequent physical debility. But the stoning itself was not a 'bodily weakness', and Scripture does not mention any such permanent result, though it is always possible. Again, on the supposition that the ailment was a fever of malarial type, much discussion has raged on whether the southern plateau was malarial, or the coastal belt through which the missionaries had just passed. Others have argued that the fresh breezes of the northern plateau were just what a sick man needed. But, unfortunately, the Bible does not tell us that Paul had any such fever. In fact, the passage before us suggests that it was instead some constitutional infirmity to which Paul was subject. As to its nature, we can do no more than guess. If the reference is general, then it is probably correct to translate neutrally as 'amid bodily weakness' (rather than NEB, 'it was bodily illness[1] that originally led to my bringing you the Gospel'). We have no reference in Acts to any occasion where sickness or infirmity led to a longer stay in Galatia by Paul than originally intended, with consequent opportunities for evangelism, while on the other hand, it does seem as though Paul was constantly plagued by ill-health. However, the list of Paul's hairbreadth escapes detailed in 2 Corinthians 11:23–29 warns us that the account in Acts is not complete, but a highly compressed and selective account of what are regarded as significant incidents, so that this omission of a

[1]To assume physical illness is a little unfair: the problem could just as well have been one which we would call psychological, such as nervous prostration or timidity or shrinking from the task.

reference may not be determinative. 2 Corinthians 12:7 seems to describe Paul as suffering from a constant or recurring affliction described as *skolops tē sarki*, 'a thorn . . . in the flesh', better 'a stake thrust into my body', which suggests intense pain.[1]

In the paraphrase above on page 166, *to proteron*, *at first*, has been translated neutrally as 'before', although the NEB mg. gives the classical meaning of the phrase with 'on the first of my two visits'. If this last translation were certain, it would have bearing both on the date and the destination of the letter (see the Introduction, pp. 18ff.). We might see, for instance, a reference to the two trips through South Galatia on the first missionary journey. If the letter was written to North Galatia, the date would be much later, and indeed to identify two such trips would give us considerable difficulty, since Acts does not specifically mention preaching or churches on either possible occasion (Acts 16:6 and 18:23). But since in Hellenistic Greek the word *proteron* has a greatly weakened meaning, probably 'formerly' (NIV, 'first') is quite sufficient. The same problem, in outline, arose in connection with *palin*, 'again', in 2:1, although many witnesses to the text omit the *palin* there.

14. *My condition was a trial to you.* Most scholars have taken *peirasmos*, *trial*, as being directly connected with Paul's 'thorn in the flesh' (2 Cor. 12:7). But there is strong manuscript evidence to suggest that the translation should rather be 'the trial that you endured through the condition of my body' (so Nestlé and UBS editions). This reading is more difficult, so it may well be right. The *peirasmos* would then be the temptation to despise Paul because of his physical ailment. If this ailment was not only incapacitating but also unsightly, the word would take on a deeper meaning. In that case, we should follow the NEB with 'you resisted any temptation to show scorn or disgust at the state of my poor body'. This is somewhat free, but it links the *trial* satisfactorily with the two verbs *exouthenēsate*, 'scorned', and *exeptysate*, 'spat in contempt', immediately below. But, attractive though this explanation is, the object of these two

[1]Those who believe that there should be divine healing for every sickness for every Christian on every occasion will not allow this interpretation, but it does seem to be the most natural one.

verbs is clearly *ton peirasmon*, 'the trial': therefore it is better to take the trial as a direct reference to Paul's bodily complaint, whatever it was. In that case, *exouthenēsate*, though nominally applied to Paul's condition, is really applied to Paul.[1] NIV boldly translates as 'illness', but not all would accept this, on theological grounds.

Since *diaptyo* can certainly mean 'reject contemptuously', it is likely that *ekptyo* is also used in a similar metaphorical sense here, with no memory of the literal meaning of 'spit out'.[2] On the grounds that the sight of a madman or an epileptic demanded 'prophylactic spitting' on the part of bystanders, some have claimed that Paul's affliction was epilepsy.[3] But this is not the letter of an epileptic, who in Jewish eyes would have been probably classed as demon-possessed. In any case, the evidence here is far too slender; no case can be based on it alone. A third interesting possibility is that Paul is harking back to the thought of 3:1, *tis ebaskanen*, 'who bewitched you?', or 'cast the evil eye on you'. The protective act against suspected 'evil eye' was to spit. Does Paul mean that, just as the Judaizers have 'bewitched' the Galatians, they might have had reason to feel that he had previously bewitched them? Or, perhaps over-fancifully, was there something about the 'piercing eyes' of Paul, described by tradition, that might have made the Galatians uneasy and afraid? If Paul suffered from some ailment of the eyes, perhaps his very appearance could have suggested the possession of such magical powers to superstitious people, such as we know the Lycaonians at least to have been. But, at best, this is all hypothetical; there is no real evidence that Paul's trouble was connected with his eyes (see on verse 15), apart from somewhat unreliable early tradition as to his appearance. In any case, the main sense of the passage is not affected by these detailed explanations.

[1] BAGD rightly points out that *exoutheneō* has quite a wide range of meaning, but the translation suggested above certainly comes within this range.

[2] Revelation 3:16 uses the similar verb, *emeō*, 'vomit out', which is much stronger in force, and more of the original sense is therefore kept.

[3] Ezekiel, of the Old Testament prophets, has also sometimes been claimed as an epileptic: see the commentators. But, even if this theory were true, some of the greatest religious figures in world history have been subject to epileptic fits. Epilepsy in itself would not deny the reality of religious experience.

Be that as it may, the Galatians had not yielded to any such temptations to judge the messenger, or the message that he bore, by outward appearances. Still less had they despised either him or the message. On the contrary, they received him for what he was, God's own messenger: indeed, they received him as they might have received Christ himself. When Paul says *hōs angelon Theou, as an angel of God*, it is just possible that he may be referring to the 'royal' treatment which he had received at first in Lycaonia (Acts 14:11ff.). It is the more appropriate in that, while the grave Barnabas was taken for the god Zeus, the volatile and loquacious Paul was taken for Hermes, messenger or 'angel' of the Greek gods. But this tentative suggestion would depend on a South Galatian destination for the letter; while this is possible, it is safer not to make the exegesis depend upon an unproven theory.

There may also be a back-reference to the 'angel from heaven' of 1:8. Paul sadly feels that in the early days the Galatians had treated him with the same exaggerated veneration which they now accord to the Judaizers. It might also refer to the constant reference that later Judaism made to the part that angels played in the mediation of the law. Paul has already referred to this in 3:19. Time was when the Galatians received Paul's gospel as being 'angel-mediated' too, as Israel received the law of Moses. Or the word might be used in a simple superlative sense, rather as we might say today 'a perfect angel'. That there is some sort of ascending scale we can see, from the addition of *as Christ Jesus* as a final clause. Here Paul is not going beyond the gospel: the Lord had said that he who received his messenger received him (Mt. 10:40).

There is always, however, the possibility that Paul is using *angelos* here purely in its neutral sense of 'messenger'; naturally, 'God's messenger' often is a supernatural being or *angel*, but unless some further qualifying phrase is actually added, we cannot be sure. As this is the more general sense, it is preferable. In 2 Corinthians 12:7, Paul's 'thorn in the flesh' is described as *angelos Satanā*, 'Satan's messenger', in just such a neutral sense: we are not to think of some personified evil spirit as identified with the affliction, whatever it was.

15. What Paul means by *makarismos, satisfaction*, is not quite clear. It is obviously something once enjoyed by the Galatians but now lost. BAGD comes down firmly on the side of 'blessing', but glosses as 'the frame of mind in which you blessed yourselves'. The NIV translates as 'joy': the NEB amplifies with 'how happy you thought yourselves in having me with you', which is undoubtedly the general thought. Perhaps 'your former happy state', or even 'your self-congratulation', is safest, leaving open the exact reason for their happiness.[1] That it had something to do with their attitude to Paul is clear from the illustration. They would have *plucked out* their very *eyes* to help him if they could. Those who see here a proof that Paul suffered from ophthalmia, or some similar eye-disease, are welcome to do so. Certainly with smoky fires, lack of chimneys, and oil lamps, one would expect a high incidence of eye-trouble in the first-century Mediterranean world. To one who had spent years poring over crabbed Hebrew tomes, the risk might well be greater. But again we have no proof. In most languages, the eye is a symbol of the most precious possession. Both Old Testament and New Testament alike use the metaphor (Dt. 32:10 and Mt. 18:9), so there is no need to see here more than the language of extravagant devotion of convert to teacher. On other evidence, Paul's trouble would seem to have more likely been some form of 'nervous prostration' rather than a direct physical handicap like ophthalmia (2 Cor. 1:9): perhaps migraine was a symptom of this strain, but again we are in the area of pure speculation.

16. So far Paul has been describing their former attitude to him. Now the Galatians act as though he has become their enemy. Why is it? What has he done? This change has been brought about purely through his *alētheuōn, by telling you the truth*, or 'by being honest with you'. There is an implied contrast here with the Judaizers, whose behaviour has been thoroughly dishonest, but he will speak more of them later.

---

[1]'Self-congratulation' would fit the bill best (Burton), without necessarily going into the reasons for this previous complacency of theirs. Perhaps they were congratulating themselves both on the salvation which they had received, and on the messenger (Paul) who had brought it.

17. *Make much of you*: in verses 17–20 the only problem centres around the translation of *zēlousin* and kindred words. In the paraphrase above on p. 166, they have been uniformly translated 'envy'. This is preferred by the NEB. It is at least as possible, however, that they should be translated 'be deeply concerned about' or 'court someone's favour'[1] (so BAGD). This is the translation favoured by the NEB mg. If taken in this sense, the word should be understood in the context of the marriage metaphor used in 2 Corinthians 11:2. Otherwise we shall not understand what Paul means by saying that there is a 'good kind' as well as a 'bad kind' of *zēlos*, a word which means 'zeal' as well as 'envy' or 'jealousy' (so NIV, 'zealous'). One of the difficulties in English is that 'jealousy' has not only a defined meaning, but also a bad sense. Neither of these were true of Hebrew, and it is doubtful if they were true of Greek. For instance, we find it hard to see how God can be described as a 'jealous God' in Exodus 20:5 and elsewhere. To make this intelligible to a modern English-speaking congregation, we often have to substitute 'zealous', which originally was merely an alternative spelling of the same word, and preserved in English the other and good sense of the word. Nevertheless, within marriage there is an exclusive relationship, and any breach of this relationship should arouse strong feelings of the type that Paul is describing.[2]

A very strong case, however, can be made out for the simple translation 'envy'. It is quite consonant with Paul's position to say that the true psychological reason for the onslaught of the Judaizers on the Galatians is that they secretly envy the Galatians both their freedom in Christ and their relations with Paul. The Judaizers want to 'cut them out' from both of these and to reduce the Galatians to the pitiable state of envying the religious position of the Judaizers themselves.[3] Whether or not this is their conscious motive makes no difference; this will be the

[1] Lightfoot favours the translation 'pay court to' and this, while loose, is quite possible. Luther prefers 'flatter', which is more vigorous.

[2] The *zēlotypos*, 'the jealous husband', according to the evidence of *A Greek-English Lexicon* by Liddell, Scott and Jones, was a typical character in the Graeco-Roman theatrical world, although unfortunately usually a comic one.

[3] Possibly we should translate as 'looking up to them', or even 'copying them': there are secular parallels for both meanings.

inevitable result of their preaching. It must be admitted that verse 18 is hard to explain purely in terms of 'envy' without also introducing the idea of 'pay court to'. But the answer is probably that the speaker of Greek was equally conscious of the two meanings side by side all the time, and could easily slip from one to the other. It is simply that the 'universe of meaning' of the word is wider in Greek than in English: the problem is purely linguistic.

When Paul says that the Judaizers *want to shut you out*, *ekkleisai*, or, with the NEB, 'to bar the door' (NIV, 'alienate') he is probably thinking back to the *synkleiō* of 3:22–23. The law deliberately *consigned* or 'herded them in' as sinners, so that they might find salvation; these Judaizers are 'bolting them out' lest they should enjoy both salvation and fellowship with Paul. There could be no greater contrast between the action of the Judaizers and the aim of the very law which they professed to teach.

18–20. The second half of verse 18 is highly compressed, a fact which makes a literal translation difficult, though the sense is not in dispute. Paul means that, when he is present, the Galatians show plenty of this 'zeal' (whatever the quality is); he only wishes that they showed it equally in his absence. That leads him to the thought that, if only he were with them now, he would not need to use such a severe tone with them. This is the probable meaning of *allaxai tēn phōnēn, change my tone*, in verse 20. BAGD supports this: but note also the NEB mg. translation 'could exchange words with you'. As it is, Paul confesses that he does not know what to make of them: *I am perplexed about you*. Not even Paul himself is sure that he had taken the wisest line with these lapsed Christians; he may well have done so, but he is still full of misgiving.

Now, for the first time in this letter, Paul breaks through the more formal title of *adelphoi*, 'brothers and sisters in Christ'. In verse 19 he calls the Galatians *tekna mou, my little children*; for so indeed they were, the fruit of his labour in Christ. No word could better express the closeness of the bond that often exists between a pioneer evangelist and the church which God has used him to build. No term is more frequently on the lips of Paul to describe his converts, whether it is said collectively to the Corinthians (*e.g.* 1 Cor. 4:14–15) or individually to those like Timothy, Titus and Philemon (*e.g.* Phm. 10), who are equally the products of his work. Paul never attempts to deny the importance of 'follow-up' work (1 Cor. 3:6), but he does assert that this earlier relationship created by evangelism is of a deeper and exclusive nature (1 Cor. 4:15). His converts are his joy and crown, as well as his 'letters of introduction'; that is why he cannot bear to see them subverted (1 Thes. 2:19), as is happening in Galatia.

But all his 'labour pains' are not over yet;[1] for, with a typical mixture of metaphor, Paul says he is in labour all over again *until Christ be formed in you*, or 'until you take the shape of Christ' (NEB). No-one doubts his meaning: it is the agony of the pastor, watching for signs of Christian growth in his flock. Paul tells us in 2 Corinthians 11:28 that this was the heaviest burden which he had to bear. It is therefore inadequate to think of Paul merely as the prince of evangelists; he was also the prince of pastors, and nowhere is this more clearly seen than in passages like this.

The NEB translation quoted above may make admirable sense, and it undoubtedly rescues Paul from a difficulty: but it does not seem to be what he wrote. The *morphōthē, be formed*, or 'shaped', has *Christos* as its subject. The literal meaning can only be *until Christ be formed in you*, as in BAGD, which quotes Galen and others to show the use of this verb to describe the formation of the embryo in the womb before birth. If we say that this is an impossible mixture of metaphors, the answer is that, impossible or not, Paul has used it, and we all understand his meaning. He is not giving us a lecture on embryology, but an illustration of two things: first, his own care and anxiety on behalf of his converts, and second, the need for growth 'in Christ' to attain Christ-likeness. The thought is neither mystic nor gnostic: it is not a doctrine of a new 'incarnation', in spite of Calvin. Honesty

[1]This is the only place where Paul speaks of himself as a 'mother' of his spiritual children: usually 'father' is the metaphor used (Betz). He may be thinking of Old Testament passages like Is. 49:15, where God's love to Israel is compared to a mother's love. In 1 Thes. 2:7 Paul compares his gentleness towards his converts to the gentleness of 'a nurse taking care of her children': this, although not identical, is a close parallel. If NIV (similarly GNB and JB) is correct in translating 'a mother caring for her little children' (see Leon Morris, *1 and 2 Thessalonians*, TNTC [Leicester: Inter-Varsity Press, 1985]), the parallelism is complete.

compels us to admit that some of Paul's illustrations from seed-sowing and grafting are equally 'impossible' in the real horticultural world.[1] But that does not mean that they cease to be effective illustrations. It is unnecessary to take a Barthian theological position and say that Paul used these illustrations just because they were impossible, and therefore the only fit pictures of the working of the God of the impossible. It is enough to say that Paul was not a gardener or an embryologist: he was a theologian, and these are only intended as illustrations, not proofs.

H. AN ARGUMENT FROM RABBINICS (4:21 – 5:1)

Paul now uses a typically rabbinic argument. We have already seen certain rabbinic elements in his use of the wording of the promise made 'to Abraham's offspring' in 3:16; but this goes much further. Again, Ellis, *Paul's Use of the Old Testament*, may be consulted for the whole question.[2] There are several possible reasons for his use of this type of rabbinic argument here. It may be an argument addressed strictly to the audience which he expects to listen to it, whether Judaizers or Galatian sympathizers. The opening words suggest this strongly. The Galatians are fascinated by the typically rabbinic exegesis of the law employed by their new teachers, are they? Good; here then is an argument that, on their own terms, they must accept. At times Paul certainly uses the 'language of accommodation' in theological controversy; that is, for the sake of argument, he will use his opponents' terms, and sometimes even temporarily adopt their position, just to show that it is untenable. Of course, he may always be thinking of the Judaizers rather than the Galatians.

---

[1] See commentators on Rom. 11:17–19 for illustrations of this point. Exactly the same is true of some of Paul's arguments about the way in which death dissolves a marriage. The fact is incontrovertible, but if we were to follow Paul logically, we would find that the wrong marriage 'partner' had died, if we wished to produce the result which he wants. But all this is hypercriticism: it is only an illustration, and should be treated as such.

[2] It is arguable that what Paul is using here is not allegory but merely typology (Betz). The only trouble is that Isaac should represent the Jews, and Ishmael the Gentiles: but Paul turns this upside down (4:28), by making Isaac stand for believing Jew and believing Gentile alike.

Although addressed directly to his erring converts, this argument would be even more telling as far as their new teachers were concerned.

The other possibility is that Paul, from his long and thorough training under Gamaliel, was so steeped in rabbinics that this style of thought was congenial, and indeed natural, to him. But this is scarcely fair to Paul. It is true that he carries over into his Christian days many of the habits of thought of old Jewish days; but this was the divine preparation for his task. Moreover, such a strongly rabbinic flavour is not generally characteristic of Paul's exegesis, which has the same new freshness and directness as the rest of the new Christian 'school'. That suggests that there is a special reason for its use here, and a Judaizing or Judaized audience is as good a guess as any. If the South Galatian theory be followed, then a not inconsiderable part of the church could have had either a Jewish or proselyte background, and such arguments would have double interest for them. In any case, it is purely the manner, not the matter, of Paul's argument which is rabbinic;[1] the great scriptural principles remain true, however applied. Cousar may well be right in seeing the passage as a 'midrash', or typical Jewish commentary, on Genesis 21:9–12.

'Tell me, do you not listen to what the law says – you who want to be under law as a system? Scripture says that Abraham had two sons, one by the slave-wife and the other by the freeborn wife. The slave-wife's son was born perfectly naturally, but the son of the freeborn wife was born in fulfilment of God's promise. All this can be seen as a symbolic picture, for these women could represent two covenants. The first (*i.e.* the slave-wife) could stand for the covenant made at Mount Sinai; all her children (*i.e.* those under that covenant) are in spiritual bondage. That is Hagar for you. So the scriptural character "Hagar" could also stand for Mount Sinai in Arabia. Sinai stands in the same category as the Jerusalem that we know, for she is certainly in slavery, along with her "children". But the heavenly Jerusalem stands for the freeborn wife – and she is our "mother". For Scripture says:

---

[1] Some commentators will not allow that even the manner (let alone the matter) of Paul's

"Be glad, you woman who is not in childbirth;
Break into a shout of triumph, you who are not in labour;
For the abandoned wife has more children
Than the wife who has her husband."

'Now you, my fellow Christians, are children born in fulfilment of God's promise, like Isaac was. But just as in those days
the son born in the course of nature used to bully the son born
supernaturally, so it is today. But what does Scripture say to
that? "Expel the slave-wife and her son; for the slave-wife's son
is certainly not going to share the inheritance with the freeborn
wife's son." And so my summing-up is this: We Christians are
not children of the slave-wife, but of the freeborn wife. Christ
has given us our freedom; stand firm, and do not allow yourselves to be harnessed again to the yoke that spells slavery.'[1]

21–22. To Paul's apparently innocent enquiry as to whether
they were prepared to hear and obey the law, no doubt the
Galatians, especially after listening to the Judaizers, would have
given an indignant 'yes'. After Paul's stress on their newfound
desire to come 'under law', they could hardly say otherwise.

Paul now turns to the law with something of his old relish as a
student of Gamaliel. He begins with the time-honoured Jewish
formula of citation, taken over by Christians, *gegraptai gar, for it
is written*, traditionally introducing the vital proof text.[2] But
Paul's use of the law will surprise these Galatians, and possibly
their teachers as well. For, within that law, Paul will again
appeal to Abraham, not to Moses. It is sometimes forgotten by
Gentiles today that, when a Jew refers to the law, he includes

---

argument here is rabbinic, but this seems to ignore the plain evidence of the text. However,
whatever the evidence from rabbinic literature, Paul's exegesis is certainly not allegorical in
the extreme sense of the exegesis of Philo, who is no rabbi; for Philo, Sarah stands for
'philosophy' and Hagar for 'lower education' (Betz).

[1] It is a disputed point whether 5:1 belongs to this earlier section, as a concluding verse or
to the next chapter, as an introduction to Paul's expostulation as to the folly of Christians
accepting circumcision. As it is clearly a 'bridge verse', however, the question is not
important, and it is more convenient to take it with what precedes rather than with what
follows.

[2] The phrase *gegrammenon estin*, 'it stands written', is another such formula to introduce
proof texts. Mt. 4:10 shows the first form; Jn. 2:17 shows the second, but there are also other
similar phrases to be found in the New Testament, like *kathōs gegraptai*, 'as it stands written'
(Mt. 26:24).

Genesis as much as Leviticus or Deuteronomy, and so of course does Paul. If the 'Torah' is the 'instruction' of God to his people, then history, the story of the saving acts of God, has just as much place in the Torah as legislation. For the same reason, later historical books were classed among the Prophets. Undoubtedly, however, the Judaizers had laid more stress in Galatia on the ritualistic and legalistic aspects of the law. This then would be a flank attack by Paul.

23. As with all the stories of Genesis, there was much Jewish speculation in connection with the two sons of Abraham and the details of the story of Sarah and Hagar. This need not detain us, except to note that Paul is not choosing some obscure passage, but one which was a familiar battleground for Jewish exegesis. First, Paul runs quickly over the details of the story, with which the Galatians may not have been as familiar as he. When he says that Ishmael was born *kata sarka, according to the flesh*, he probably limits his meaning to 'in the ordinary course of events'.[1] What he means is that no miracle was necessary, and no special promise of God was involved. Whether he is blaming Abraham for taking this secondary wife, out of lack of faith, is not certain; there is certainly a contrast between the birth 'by natural means', as we would say, and the birth of Isaac *through promise*. But even if he had blamed Abraham for this, no Jew would object to Paul doing so: some rabbis so taught, and *kata sarka* could have the nuance of 'sinfully'.

24. So far, not the most ardent Judaizer could disagree with Paul, not even when he says that these things are *allēgoroumena, an allegory*, in the corresponding English form of the word. Most Jews were quite ready to treat the Old Testament in this way. Philo was the extreme example. The only question is, What do these two women stand for allegorically? There is plenty of evidence in pagan literature for the use of this verb in the sense of 'to speak allegorically' (so BAGD). It is doubtful if Paul is using allegory in any highly technical sense to distinguish it

---

[1] At times *sarx*, 'flesh', is used in a euphemistic sense in connection with physical generation, or the organs connected with it, rather like the Hebrew *bāsar*, 'flesh'. Here, the first meaning is appropriate.

from other types of 'simple' exegesis known to Jews, and later amplified by Christians. If he were doing so, such finesse would probably have been wasted on the Galatians. Nor does he wish to deny the literal truth of the story, as some allegorists might do. His sole concern is to show the Galatians that, behind the plain meaning of the words, there is to be found the exemplification of a great spiritual truth. This truth, this divine principle or 'type', he finds demonstrated on a larger scale elsewhere in God's dealing with his people; and he proceeds to show where and how this is. A little reflection will show that, since God is changeless, and since these spiritual principles are therefore also changeless, this is not an arbitrary form of interpretation. What Paul is offering is again more an illustration than a proof, as is usual with him in such cases.

Some might object that the chief actor in the Genesis story is not God, but Abraham, and that Paul, by using this illustration, is thus arguing, not 'from God to God' (as we might say), which would have been quite legitimate, but 'from Abraham to God', which is illegitimate. In reply, it could be said that Abraham, in his life, exemplifies the only two possible human attitudes towards God, faith and unbelief. This is the main point of the allegory, and if this is kept central, all else will fall into place. After all, illustrations have no fixed rules governing their form. Unbelief and faith; natural and spiritual; earthly and heavenly; below and above; slavish and free: there are many pairs of opposites used in the passage, but all have this one root. It is only when Paul applies the same distinction to the *two covenants* that the Jews would sharply disagree; indeed, to the latter, the very concept of *two covenants* was abhorrent: there was only God's eternal covenant with his people, one and the same (Ezk. 37:26). The 'new covenant' to them was something eschatological, still to come, belonging to the age of the Messiah (Je. 31:31). What they could not believe was that this day had already come without their noticing it (*cf.* Lk. 11:20, with its use of *ephthasen*, 'come unexpectedly upon you').

Now if we follow this line of reasoning, we can see why the Jews are compared by Paul to Ishmael and his descendants, not to Isaac and his seed, as any rabbi would have compared them. Certainly they are 'children of the covenant' (their own proud claim), but they are children of the covenant made on Mount Sinai, not of that made with Abraham, which foreshadows the covenant of Christ. Paul has already shown that to try to win salvation by keeping the law is to enter a hopeless and fruitless bondage. Yet this is the bondage inevitable to the Jew. That is why this covenant is described here as *bearing children for slavery*. This was doubly appropriate in the ancient world, for the children of a slave-wife were themselves slaves, unless the husband and master acknowledged them as true sons. Of course, it was not inevitable that the Jews should serve in this 'slavish' way. They were 'Abraham's seed' and therefore children of the covenant with Abraham as truly as they were children of the covenant with Moses.[1] But as long as they looked on the law as a possible means of salvation, such 'slavery' to the law was inevitable. This reasoning is theologically impeccable, but it must have been a bitter pill for any Jew, all the more so because Jews prided themselves not only as being Abraham's seed but on being Isaac's offspring, not 'Ishmaelite' like the despised desert-dwellers of the Negev. The argument is unanswerable, and the tables have been turned completely on Paul's adversaries.

25. There has been much discussion on the first three words *to de Agar, now Hagar*. It is possible that they ought to be omitted altogether, as an explanatory 'gloss' on the text (so RSV mg.). But this conjecture is not borne out by the majority of ancient witnesses. If the clause is kept, it is best explained simply as a further back-reference to Hagar the slave-wife, introduced because Paul is anxious to keep us reminded of the 'corresponding terms' of the analogy. Much ingenuity has been expended by commentators, ancient and modern, in finding here a reference to some generic or specific name for an actual mountain in 'Arabia'.[2] However, if the explanation above is correct, this is

[1] In every case, 'children' is used in the idiomatic Hebrew sense of 'sharers in' the covenant; but Paul plays on the literal sense of the word as well here.

[2] See Betz for discussion of this point. Paul was not a philologist, and probably did not speak Arabic: a rough correspondence in sound, even an approximate pun, would have been sufficient for him to use in this argument. It is true that there is an Arabic word somewhat similar in sound to 'Hagar' which means 'a rock', and it is geographically correct that there is a mountain in Paul's 'Arabia' bearing this name, but it is nowhere in the vicinity

quite unnecessary, even if, on the basis of Arabic, some such name could be postulated. Paul's only point is to sharpen the 'correspondence' between Hagar and the law which had been given on Mount Sinai.

One other reason that has made commentators of the past anxious to discover a local geographic reference here was the allusion in 1:17 to a time spent by Paul in 'Arabia' immediately after his conversion. But it is highly unlikely that this refers to anything other than the country areas in the immediate vicinity of Damascus, under the control of Aretas. There is no evidence in Scripture to suggest that Paul had any knowledge of the southern desert where Sinai was situated, or that he ever journeyed there, either immediately after his conversion or later. Besides, Paul's 'Hagar' experience was surely his spiritual experience before conversion, not after it.

The word *systoichei, corresponds to*, or literally, 'marches with', is used primarily of soldiers 'dressing ranks'. Hence it may be used of objects or ideas in 'similar categories'. Here it is not used in any highly technical sense; perhaps 'stands for' (NIV) might therefore be sufficient (NEB, 'represents'). In this passage Paul seems to use *estin, is*, of Hagar in the same sense of 'represents': for neither Sinai, nor the Sinaitic covenant, *is* Hagar, in the full sense of the predicate (compare the end of verse 24 with the beginning of verse 25).

26. When Paul contrasts 'the present Jerusalem' (v. 25) with the *Jerusalem above*, he is really mixing two pairs of opposites, but with no danger of misunderstanding. The exact contrast would be, first, between the present Jerusalem and the future Jerusalem, and secondly, between Jerusalem on earth below and Jerusalem in heaven above. The concept of a 'new Jerusalem' is very familiar from the Old Testament, especially in the days when the old, familiar earthly city had been burnt and ravaged (see, for example Zc. 8:1–8, to take a random instance). Naturally, since this 'new Jerusalem' was an eschatological concept, it tended to be contrasted, as future, with the miserable

---

of the traditional Mount Sinai, 'Jebel Musa', or 'Moses' Mountain'. This, difficulty, however, would not necessarily have deterred Paul in the midst of a heated argument.

Jerusalem of the present. Also, in view of passages like Ezekiel 48 and Isaiah 62, it was easy to speak of an ideal Jerusalem already existing in heaven in the mind and purpose of God, and one day destined to be established on earth by the act of God. All of these thoughts find full expression in Revelation 3:12 and 21:2; but these passages are really only a cento of quotations from the Old Testament. To Paul, 'the present Jerusalem', or 'the Jerusalem of today' (NEB), is not only the familiar city of his boyhood, with the Temple at its heart, but also the whole race of Israel.[1] Again, this was a familiar usage from the Old Testament, where 'Jerusalem' can stand for its inhabitants or even for the whole nation, especially in prophetic address. This heavenly Jerusalem *is our mother*.[2] To be her children is to have already entered this eschatological age of fulfilment of all of God's promises; and this the Christian has already done through trust in God's Messiah. This is the same stress as that in 4:4 and elsewhere, with its concept of 'the fullness of time': God's hour has struck.

27. The quotation from Isaiah 54 is appropriate here for many reasons, although there is no direct evidence in the original text that it was ever applied by the prophet to the barren Sarah. Its primary reference is to desolate Israel, and secondarily to the city of Jerusalem (witness the architectural metaphors in Isaiah 54:11ff.). Since in this passage Israel is seen as the 'bride' of God, the thought finds a ready echo in Revelation. Because the Christian church is also seen in the New Testament as the 'bride of Christ' (see 2 Cor. 11:2 for this Pauline use), a whole system of identifications comes into operation at once. To the Jew, it was long familiar from prophecy that the Gentiles would one day turn to God in multitudes. What was a stumbling-block (or 'staggering') in this new Christian interpretation was that these Gentiles did not need to become Jews first. Even for an 'orthodox' Jewish Christian of the time of Paul, it must have

[1]Betz rightly understands 'the present Jerusalem' as 'the political religious institution of Judaism for which the Holy City stands as a symbol': but, in view of the physical location of the Temple there, it is much more than a symbol.

[2]But, in contrast to some 'traditional' commentators, Paul never equates the heavenly Jerusalem with the church, however understood (Betz).

come as a shock to realize that Gentile Christians already far outnumbered Jewish Christians, a fact which we accept without thinking today. Stranger still, the time would come when the Gentile Christian church would far outnumber unbelieving Jewry. Then indeed the words of this prophecy would find fulfilment: *the desolate* will have more children than *her that is married* (literally, 'has a husband'). We, who live in an age where the axis of world Christianity has ceased to be the traditional 'Western' lands, and become the 'third world', can imagine something of the psychological shock and consequent necessary change in thinking demanded.

28–29. After all this, it was easy for the Christians to see that they, *like Isaac, are children of promise*. They knew that there was nothing 'natural' about their spiritual re-birth (*cf.* Jn. 1:13). But they may also have ruefully wondered why, if all this could be shown so clearly from the Torah, their Jewish 'kinsfolk' should persecute them so in Galatia. Paul has an answer to that too, again drawn from the traditional rabbinic exegesis of Genesis 21:9, where 'playing with' Isaac was traditionally interpreted as 'mocking at' him (*cf.* AV).[1] To Paul this is not only an illustration of Ishmael's traditional attitude towards Isaac; it was also the actual attitude of Judaism to the church in his own day. More, it is the inevitable reaction of all 'natural' religion to 'supernatural' religion. Acts 14:19 shows the sort of experience that Paul at least had already had at the hands of the Jews of Asia Minor, as indeed had the 'South Galatians'. The irony is that Paul the persecutor had now become Paul the persecuted, for the sake of the same Messiah.

30. Does that mean, then, that Jew by religion and Christian by religion are together co-heirs of God's grace?[2] No: only in

[1]There is no need to explore the various ways (sometimes far fetched) in which rabbis tried to deduce this from the text. The sole relevant points are: first, that Paul's theological adversaries would have agreed with him on this exegesis of the passage, and secondly, that the Christians were, in some areas at least, actually suffering persecution at the hand of Jewish extremists at the time.

[2]This is a favourite view in a modern ecumenical age, but it finds no basis whatsoever in Scripture. True Israel may yet turn to Christ (Rom. 11:25–26), but that is another matter: until she turns, a 'hardening' (of heart), or possibly 'blindness', holds her captive.

Christ can heirship be enjoyed, says Paul, returning again to his illustration of Sarah and Hagar. The reason why all 'natural' religious systems are bound to come into conflict with Christianity, the 'supernatural' system, is because they cannot co-exist as parallel paths to the same goal. That is why the 'persecution' mentioned above is inevitable. Christianity is in this sense inevitably 'narrow-minded'. That is an unpopular doctrine today when open-ended 'conversation' with non-Christian faiths is often suggested, rather than preaching the gospel. But this is the 'severity' of God that co-exists for Paul along with his goodness (Rom. 11:22); and it is nowhere exhibited more clearly than in God's dealings with Israel and the church respectively. Ishmael cannot inherit along with Isaac. Jew and Gentile may and will co-exist in the Christian church: that is the crowning glory of the gospel, but they co-exist only as 'Isaac', not as 'Ishmael'. Unbelieving Israel is excluded from blessing, as unbelieving Gentiles are excluded, and for the same reason.

31. After all the above, *dio, so,* or 'therefore' (NIV), is only a summary of the whole argument. It would be weakening Paul's position to take the word in any stronger sense, as though Paul were saying, 'Because Ishmael's fate is so terrible, we must determine to follow Isaac.' The thought of warning may well be in his mind; it may indeed be one reason why he tells the story at all. But it is not expressed here. So we may legitimately translate with the NEB, 'You see, then': Paul is summing up and rounding off his whole argument so far.

5:1. This verse, part of the same summary, is thoroughly Hebraic in grammatical form, with its *for freedom Christ has set us free,* though Deissmann claims it as the Hellenistic formula for 'sacral' manumission of slaves. In translation, an emphasis of voice would be sufficient to bring out the force of the repetition, a common Semitic grammatical device. It is also possible that we should understand the dative *eleutheriā, for freedom,* as the goal or object: 'with a view to enjoying freedom, Christ set us free.' The emphatic position of the word might support this (Betz therefore takes it in this way), but, in view of Semitic syntax, it is not necessary.

III. THE ARGUMENT FROM RESULTS (5:2 – 6:18)

Paul has three great lines of argument, any one of which would be in itself incontrovertible. The combination of the three is overpowering. First, he has argued in chapters 1 and 2 from past history, from what all knew to have taken place. His own experience and the experience of the Galatians were known to all, however some might try to explain them away. Paul's relations with the Jerusalem church were also an open book which all might read. Even had Paul been capable of attempting to falsify such evidence, it would have been an impossible task. There were too many Christians still alive who could have contradicted him, and the Judaizers would have been the very first to seize upon any such inconsistency or inaccuracy.

Secondly, he has argued in chapters 3 and 4 from theology, or rather from Scripture. Both by 'general' and by 'special' (*i.e.* rabbinic) exegesis, he has shown the utter inconsistency of the theological position of the Judaizers and of their Galatian followers. He has established beyond doubt that such retrograde teaching is contradicted by the very Torah which they claimed to teach. Promise and fulfilment meet in the Christian church, in the cross of Christ, not in the law of Moses, and the covenant with Abraham had been the great prototype and preparation for this.

But there still remains one very powerful argument – some would say, the most powerful argument of all. This is the argument from results, the appeal to the total inward moral change brought about by the 'freedom' of the gospel, combined with the gift of the Spirit, a change in character which all the restraints or 'bondage' of the Jewish law had utterly failed to produce.[1] In these last two chapters Paul will hammer this home in order to clinch the matter. But he does not merely have the Judaizers in mind when he stresses the moral obligations and fruits of the gospel; he also does it lest his preaching of 'freedom' be misinterpreted as 'antinomianism' by the Gentile

---

[1] Indeed, we could therefore call this 'the argument from the Spirit', although sometimes Paul expresses it in terms of the indwelling Christ. In this sense, there is no difference between the work of Christ and the work of the Spirit in the human heart.

Galatians. If liberty becomes licence, then the worst suspicions of the Judaizers would be true and the last state of the Galatians would indeed be worse than the first.[1] From every point of view, therefore, these chapters are the crown of the whole book.

A. THE GOAL OF THE GOSPEL (5:2–6)

At first sight, this short section may look like a simple attack on the Judaizers for their preaching of circumcision, but it goes far beyond that. It is an exposition of the true end and goal of law and gospel alike,[2] and of the impotence of any outward observance to effect that which can only be achieved by the inward working of the Spirit. The true centre of gravity of the passage lies in the last clause. But Cousar may also be right in regarding it as an attempt to tone down any frantic activism, whether 'religious' or 'enthusiastic', on the part of the Galatians.

'Look, I Paul, in person, tell you this: if you should now accept circumcision, Christ will be no good to you. I affirm solemnly again to everyone who accepts circumcision that he is thereby accepting an obligation to carry out the whole of the law. Seeing that you are trying to obtain right standing with God through obeying the law, you have already broken the bond (*i.e.* "of faith") that united you to Christ; you have slipped from the level where grace operates. For we Christians wait eagerly for that righteousness which we expect as a result of faith; and all is the Spirit's doing. Once faith is placed in Christ, neither circumcision nor uncircumcision is any good; the only thing that counts is faith, working out in love' (*cf.* NEB mg., 'faith inspired by love').

2. When Paul bursts into this passionate personal testimony, one wonders whether he has not already taken the stylus from

[1] Some commentators hold that this had already happened in Galatia, and hence the letter: see the list of 'works of the flesh' in 5:19–21. But, unlike the letter to the Corinthians, this letter does not actually charge the Galatians with any specific sins, except perhaps that of quarrelsomeness (see 5:15).

[2] For Paul does not, even in Galatians, attribute an exclusively negative significance to the law: it is its powerlessness, because of human sin, that he attacks. For a positive assessment of the law on a wider scale, see Romans.

the hand of the scribe and is writing it in his own handwriting, as he does in 6:11. It resembles the opening formula with which he introduces autograph passages elsewhere (as in 1 Cor. 16:21). 2 Thessalonians 3:17 tells us that this autographing of letters was apparently Paul's invariable practice to guard against forgery. So we may assume that wherever 'the grace' occurs at the end of a letter, it at least was originally in autograph, even if not specifically stated in the context. But there is no specific reference here to Paul's handwriting; for that, we must wait until 6:11. It therefore seems unlikely that Paul picked up the pen so early in the letter unless, as is always possible, he wrote this particular letter without the aid of an amanuensis, since none is mentioned (contrast Romans 16:22). That would make the reference in 6:11 to the size and shape of the letters more understandable; for Paul does not normally write more than 'the grace' in his own hand, and this will not come until 6:18. What exactly, then, is the force of the *I, Paul*? Perhaps it is only to lend force to the solemn affirmation which follows. When Paul says, in the next verse, *martyromai*, 'I testify', his words take on the character of a formal declaration under oath in a court of law. Paul's lawyer's training, apart altogether from his Jewish background, would not allow him to use such a phrase lightly. Normally in his letters such an introduction marks a point of more than usual weight and moment.

That may well be the explanation of the phrase here. But it is also possible that the words are pregnant with deeper meaning. Even Paul, the circumcised Jew, proud of all his background and traditions (*cf.* Phil. 3:4–6), tells them that circumcision is of no avail. Who more than he should know its value? Yet he had counted it as 'debit', as 'refuse', in comparison with Christ. Paul is never anti-Jewish even when he is in his most controversial moods. Although he does not develop in Galatians the argument for the positive values and abiding contribution of Judaism, Romans 9 – 11 shows his general position in this area clearly. Israel never had a member who loved her more dearly than Paul. Yet even such a Jewish patriot sees clearly the comparative unimportance of circumcision now; it is *of no advantage* to the Galatians.

The tenses of the verbs are very important in this passage.

Paul says to the Galatians *if you receive circumcision, ean peritem-nesthe*, in the present tense, not the past tense. This implies that they have not already taken the step, but are only considering it. It also means that Paul is in no way condemning those Jewish Christians who are in any case already circumcised. He does not say 'if you are already in the position of being circumcised', a meaning which would normally require the perfect passive of the verb. To such, Paul's advice is quite clear in 1 Corinthians 7:17–20, where it is set in a wider context. If God's call came to a man while he was a Jew, and therefore circumcised, then 'let him not seek to remove the marks of circumcision' (1 Cor. 7:18a; some had tried to do this in time of persecution, *cf.* 1 Macc. 1:15). If the call came while he was a Gentile, and therefore uncircumcised, then 'let him not seek circumcision' (1 Cor. 7:18b). Paul in no way condemned the Jewish usages of the Jerusalem church. That is an important point, for he was often accused by his Judaizing foes of doing this very thing (*e.g.* Acts 21:21). What Paul did condemn was the attitude of mind that saw such historic practices as necessary to salvation and which tried to force them on Gentile churches as the price of fellowship at the Lord's Table. This is an attitude of mind that the church of the twentieth century has not yet outgrown. We cannot afford to smile at the Judaizers if we 'Judaize' in our attitude to other Christians with different customs from our own.

That this force of the verb is not imaginary is shown by *peritemnomenō*, in verse 3, 'becoming circumcised at this very moment', where the present tense is likewise used. It would not be unfair to translate this as 'trying to be circumcised' or 'wanting to be circumcised', although there are places in the New Testament where the present participle may have either of these nuances.[1] Hence the urgency of this letter. Paul may be able to stop the Galatians from what in his opinion would be an irrecoverable and retrograde step. It is beside the point to say that Abraham was circumcised, and that he indeed circumcised his 'Gentile' son, Ishmael, as well as his 'Jewish' son, Isaac (Gn. 17:23). This was a sign of God's covenant of promise with

---

[1] This is the so-called 'conative use' of the present: see Bruce, always a safe guide on grammatical matters.

Abraham, not the covenant of law under Moses, and so is irrelevant here.

To say *Christ will be of no advantage to you, ouden ophelēsei,*[1] is to use a very strong expression. But, once again, Paul wants to shock the Galatians into a full realization of what they might have done. He will explain what he means in the following verses. Meanwhile, we may note the untranslatable pun in the Greek between *ophelēsei,* 'be of advantage', and *opheiletēs, bound,* or 'a debtor', in the next verse. It is somewhat of a bitter pun, but it heightens the contrast. We might attempt to bring out some of the force by saying, 'So far from Christ helping you, you yourself will be helpless in law's clutches.'

3-4. Paul's point is now quite clear. If the Galatians accept circumcision, it can only be because they consider that circumcision is necessary to salvation. This would mean that they consider that Christ's death was not enough; they are no longer trusting Christ to save them. Rather, they are hoping to save themselves by what they do. So they have in fact left the region where grace is operative; as he says, *tēs charitos exepesate, you have fallen away from grace,* where 'fallen out of the realm of grace' would be a better translation. No-one can be justified in two ways at once; we cannot be justified at the same time by faith in Christ and by our own efforts. It is 'all or nothing' as far as faith and grace are concerned.

Paul probably could have proved this point even if the Judaizers were limiting their demands to the one rite of circumcision. But 4:10 shows that the whole range of Jewish festivals was involved (including, of course, the Sabbath), and 2:12 makes it highly probable that the Jewish food laws were also included. For, while to Paul circumcision is primarily the 'seal' of God on the faith of Abraham (Ro. 4:11) and an assurance of that righteousness which was already his by faith, to the Jew of Paul's day circumcision was something fundamentally different. To him, it was the first act of obedience to that law which would henceforth, if he was a pious Jew, rule every tiny detail of his

---

[1] Betz sees the future ('will be of no advantage') as a reference to the last judgment, but the meaning seems to be rather that Christ will be of no advantage to them in the here and now. Naturally, there is no contradiction between the two.

life.[1] Through complete obedience to all its precepts he hoped to win merit in God's eyes, and so attain 'life'. Circumcision, in Jewish eyes, was therefore more closely associated with Moses and Sinai than with Abraham and the promised land: it introduced obligation, not promise. So Paul is right when he says that to accept circumcision as obligatory is to accept *the whole law* as obligatory. This is a word other than that of Christ and of grace, and the Galatians must accept the full consequences of their act in voluntarily entering it.

That is why he can say, *you are severed [katērgēthēte] from Christ.* The vital bond of faith in God's grace has been broken, and no other relationship with Christ is possible for the Christian. It is true that this Greek verb can also mean 'make ineffective, nullify' in a general sense (so BAGD). But Paul uses it in Romans 7:2 in the sense of 'be freed from a marriage bond', and that is a most suitable meaning here too. The NEB translates, 'your relation with Christ is completely severed': NIV has 'alienated from Christ', which gives the sense well.

5. As against this, we now find one of the clearest statements of 'justification by faith' in the whole letter. The *hēmeis, we,* is so strongly adversative that it may not be incorrect to interpret it as 'we Christians', as opposed to those who have *fallen away from grace.* It may well be that Paul uses the plural deliberately here, as though he wants to include the wavering Galatians along with himself. But the use of plural for singular, with no noticeable difference in meaning, is common enough throughout the whole New Testament. The intensive meaning 'eagerly wait for' seems established for *apekdechometha, we wait* (so BAGD); otherwise it would be tempting to translate 'receive payment in full', with a future reference. There is a future aspect in any case, implied not only by the verb but also by the phrase *elpida dikaiosynēs, the hope of righteousness.* This does not mean that, to Paul, 'justification' is something still to come, and therefore something uncertain as yet. He uses the past tense of the verb

[1] See Bruce for the way that this is brought out in the advice given by one strictly orthodox Jew to Izates, king of Adiabene, when contemplating becoming a proselyte. However, as another equally orthodox Jew gave exactly the opposite advice to the same king (according to Josephus), it only shows that Jewish opinion was divided.

'justified' too often to admit that.[1] Instead of *hope of righteousness* we should probably translate 'that righteousness which we confidently expect', for there is nothing uncertain about *elpis*, 'hope', in the Bible. In that case, Paul will either be referring to the continual attitude of the Christian, which is a buoyant expectation that God has in fact accepted the believer as 'in the right'; or there may be a slight eschatological flavour,[2] as though the Christian were waiting confidently for that 'right standing' to be finally manifest to all. It was a wise theologian who said that, in the Bible, salvation is at one and the same time past, present, and future. We have been saved, we are being saved, and we shall be saved: and yet there is no contradiction between these three. The future is the crown and consummation of the past, not something new: to talk of a 'double justification' is therefore incorrect (Betz).

But the weight of the verse, as far as Paul is concerned, does not fall on the second half, interesting though it may be to us. The whole stress is on the words that he has deliberately brought forward for emphasis: *pneumati, through the Spirit,* and *ek pisteōs, by faith.* These are the two aspects that distinguish the Christian hope from the Jewish, for here the two approaches to God are poles apart. If circumcision was anything, it would have been not *pneumati, through the Spirit,* but *sarki,* 'in the flesh'; and although Paul does not use the latter word here, it can hardly be absent from his mind. To the Christian, justification has nothing to do with anything 'fleshly' or 'natural'; all is of God, for all is 'the work of the Spirit' (NEB). Paul may simply wish to contrast a 'spiritual' (*through the Spirit*) with a 'natural' method of justification. Or, as the NEB translation suggests, he may be emphasizing that, from start to finish, it is due to the work of the Spirit. This need not have direct reference to the work of the Spirit in 'sanctification'. It is equally by the work of

---

[1] See Ro. 5:1, *etc.,* where *dikaiōthentes,* 'having been justified', by the aorist tense gives the sense of 'decisively, once for all'.

[2] Editors have pointed out that, in contrast with Thessalonians, this is almost the only eschatological expression in the whole letter. But that is natural: Paul is dealing with an urgent present problem, not a future hope.

the Spirit that we are convinced of the utter impossibility of commending ourselves to God by our own activities, whether it be by attempted obedience to the Jewish law, in the case of Jews, or attempted obedience to the dictates of conscience, in the case of Gentiles. Further, it is only by the work of the Spirit that we can see Christ as our Saviour. Indeed, it might almost be said that the gift of faith is the first gift of the Spirit to the newborn soul, the gift of grace from which all the other gifts and graces follow (Eph. 2:8).

After the explosive *pneumati, through the Spirit*, comes the almost equally emphatic *ek pisteōs*, by faith, or 'as a result of faith'. What this means to the Christian has already been shown in the letter. Here it is clearly and decisively contrasted with *en nomō*, 'by the law', in the verse immediately above. Between these two there can be no compromise: instead of *en nomō*, 'by the law', Paul could indeed have equally well written *en sarki*, 'by the flesh', since that is what 'trying to be justified by law' comes down to, at the last.

6. It is part of the greatness of Paul that even in the midst of controversy he is not one-sided. Just as in 1:18 he readily admits that he did actually go to Jerusalem 'to see Peter', although knowing that this admission might well weaken and damage his case, so here he is not content merely to prove that circumcision is not *of any avail* (NIV, 'has any value'), or 'does no good', or even 'makes no difference' (with the NEB). He readily admits that uncircumcision is equally valueless, a point often forgotten by those filled with reforming zeal, as it was probably forgotten by many a Gentile Christian. He will not allow the Gentile to boast of his uncircumcised state, any more than he will allow the Jew to boast of 'the sign of the covenant'. Both states are now totally irrelevant 'in Christ'; they have ceased to have either meaning or value.

This perspective might have saved the church many a quarrel, much heart-burning, and not a little mutual criticism. To him, these outward observances are all unimportant compared with *faith working through love* (NIV, 'expressing itself') unless the participle *energoumenē* is to be taken as fully passive, meaning 'worked', or 'produced', in which case the NEB mg. 'faith inspired by love' might possibly be correct.[1]

Either translation of *energoumenē*, 'working out' or 'being worked out', therefore makes good sense. For it is the love of Christ which moves our hearts to respond to him; so in that sense it is true to say that our faith is 'inspired by love' (NEB mg.). But it is more usual in the New Testament to say that Christ's love evokes a corresponding love in us (1 Jn. 4:19) than to say that it evokes faith. It seems then as if *faith working through love*, or 'expressing itself in love' (NIV) is nearer the mark. This would link with two favourite Pauline thoughts; first, that love is the fulfilment of the law (Rom. 13:10), and secondly, that Christian faith brings with it, as a necessary corollary, the 'fruit of the Spirit', with which Paul will deal shortly. The first is necessary to show that there is no opposition between the moral 'righteousness' which the law seeks vainly to produce and the righteousness which is the free gift of God in response to faith.[2] The second is necessary to show that the faith through which we are justified is not mere intellectual understanding, but a life-changing committal. Nobody soberly reading the rest of Galatians could seriously believe that there was any real conflict between James and Paul as to the nature of faith; any apparent contradiction is superficial and verbal only. Whether of course this was equally plain to James, we cannot tell; but certainly he recognized the Pauline gospel as the same as his own (2:6), when faced by it at Jerusalem.

B. A PERSONAL ASIDE (5:7–12)

Paul, by mentioning 'faith working through love', has set the tone for the whole of this last section of the letter. But in the next few verses he turns aside for another personal expostulation directed to the Galatians. It is not without interest, both because

[1] There has often been a major difference of exegesis here between 'reformed' and 'unreformed' commentators, but it is not necessary to enter into it, to understand Paul's main point.

[2] This goes far to bridge the theological gulf between those who press for the meaning 'declare righteous', for the Greek word *dikaioō*, and those who press for the meaning 'make righteous'. The one who is 'justified by faith' will in fact thereafter live a transformed life, if the change is real.

of the reference to the 'enemy' at Galatia, whether individual or collective, and also because of the reference to Paul's own personal position.

'You were running strongly: who was it who thwarted you, by stopping you from believing the truth? This sort of persuasiveness never came from the God who called you; as they say, "a little pinch of yeast sets the whole lump of dough in fermentation". But I have a Christian confidence as far as you are concerned that you will not change your outlook. This disturber of your peace will bear his judgment, no matter how high his position. But I ask you, fellow Christians, if I am one who proclaims the need of circumcision, why am I still being harried from place to place? The stumbling-block of the cross would be gone then. Oh, if only those who trouble you would go the whole way and mutilate themselves!'

7. The metaphor in *etrechete, you were running*, is taken from the athletic track, which, with the theatre and amphitheatre, dominated the Greek world. No orthodox Jew could or would join in such an exercise since it involved nudity as well as worship of heathen gods. The pictures that we draw of Paul watching athletic games at Tarsus as a boy are therefore probably figments of our imagination, unless Paul, like other naughty boys, disobeyed his parents. But the imagery of the arena fascinated him, and he often uses it as a metaphor of the Christian life. Perhaps there is a deliberate reminiscence of 2:2, where Paul explains to the Jerusalem elders the gospel that he preaches 'lest somehow I should be running or had run in vain'. The figurative use of this verb with reference to moral effort is very common throughout the whole New Testament.

If the track metaphor is still strongly felt, it is tempting to take *enekopsen*, 'hinder', as a reference to 'foul running' by rivals (NIV has the literal 'cut in on you') and translate 'edged you off the track' (*cf*. Philips, 'put you off the course'). But although meanings like 'knock in' are found for this verb, there is no evidence to justify such an interpretation.[1] It is probably better to take it

---

[1] Betz quotes a papyrus with an example of this very word *enkoptō*, meaning 'got in your way', which would suit very well.

simply as *hindered*, or 'obstructed', and assume that the force of the metaphor has weakened. When Paul says that the purpose (or perhaps result) of this 'hindering' was that the Galatians were *hindered from obeying the truth*, he uses the infinitive *peithesthai*, which means 'to be persuaded' as well as 'to obey'. The meaning is quite clear. This persuasive Judaizing approach has pushed the Galatians away from obeying the plain truth of the gospel, whether they know it or not.

8. The choice of this particular verb, *peithesthai*, allows him a play on words hard to reproduce in English, for the verb is now taken up by the rare cognate noun *peismonē, persuasion*, or 'persuasiveness', used to describe the activity of the Judaizers. While Paul does not actually say here that they are plausible deceivers (which he has already hinted in 4:17), this deduction is obvious. Those who translate *peismonē* as 'obedience', referring to the ready response of the Galatians rather than to the pros-elytizing activity of the Judaizers, must depart from the best text for the passage in order to do so (so BAGD). In either case, the play on words remains: and it is taken up by *pepoitha*, 'I have confidence', in verse 10. Perhaps, at the risk of clumsiness, we might paraphrase the three verses as: 'Who hindered you from being persuaded as to the truth? The sort of "persuasion" that they used is not from Christ. But I am still persuaded better things of you.' The effect is to give the whole passage a coherence that it lacks in an English translation. *Tou kalountos, him who calls you*, is always God or Christ in Pauline theology; it cannot be used of the human evangelist, who is summoning others to believe, necessary though that work may be. See also note on 1:15.

9. The NIV is almost certainly right in putting verse 9 in quotation marks. It seems to be an example of Paul's use of a proverbial saying,[1] which he also quotes in 1 Corinthians 5:6. BAGD remarks on the phrase, which 'serves to picture the influence of apparently insignificant factors in the moral and

---

[1] It is quite unnecessary to explain this Pauline use of proverbs, with some commentators (*e.g.* Betz), as a rhetorical feature, deliberately introduced here. Proverbs came very natur-ally to the Semitic mind, and are frequent in the Old Testament.

spiritual sphere'. *Zymē, leaven,* or 'yeast', is very frequently used in the Gospels, both as a symbol of the pervasiveness of evil, as it is here, and also of the pervasiveness of good, as in Matthew 13:33, though not all expositors are agreed there. A common Jewish proverbial source is sufficient to explain the similarities between gospels and letters. Such a proverb was particularly natural to Israel, for whom the use of 'leaven' or 'yeast' was forbidden in sacrifice (Ex 34:25). Not only so, but on certain ceremonial occasions, such as the Feast of Unleavened Bread (which immediately followed Passover), the removal of all leaven from the house had become a solemn ritual (1 Cor 5:7–8), which to the Jews was a symbol of the putting away of sin. It is probable that the reason for the prohibition of the use of leaven in sacrifice came from an analogy between the 'leavening' activity of yeast whereby the bread 'rises', and the natural process of putrefaction in meat or other foods. No carrion or decayed flesh might be offered to the Lord, just as no maimed or imperfect beast might be used in sacrifice (Lv. 22:21–25). Paul's point is that, unless checked, this Judaizing tendency, though small in itself, will permeate the whole Christian community in Galatia, and make self-offering to God both impossible and unacceptable.

The *phyrama, lump,* is the shapeless mass of the 'batch of dough' (NIV): it literally means 'that which is mixed or kneaded' (so BAGD). It can also be used as in Romans 9:21 of the formless lump of clay which the potter takes up in his hand to mould into a clay vessel, but this is not Paul's thought in Galatians.

10. Here we are faced with the usual questions as to the force and meaning of *en Kyriō, in the Lord,* which for the Christian was equivalent to *en Christō,* 'in Christ'. Without trying to go into the full theological implications of this expression, we may note that there are two main possibilities here. The first, and simpler, is that Paul means that this *confidence* of his is no human confidence, but one wrought in his heart by Jesus Christ.[1] This is a straightforward explanation which would suit both the context

---

[1] For Paul knows that there can be no such thing as confidence 'in the flesh' (Betz), whether it be confidence in himself or in the Galatians. Only God can bring about this miracle: so it can only be 'confidence in the Lord'.

in particular and Pauline theology in general. The second, perhaps more attractive, is to translate 'united with you in the Lord'
(SO NEB). This is part of the modern trend to translate *en Christō*,
'in Christ', as 'in union with Jesus Christ', whether this union is
seen as an individual or a collective relationship. It is possibly
because of this slight difficulty in interpretation that some early
witnesses to the text omit the words, *en Kyriō*, altogether. Paul's
confidence in the Galatians is that they will *take no other view,
ouden allo phronēsete*. There is no difficulty with the use of the
verb *phroneō*, perhaps best translated 'think': it is often used by
Paul of attitudes or habits of mind. But we may well ask the
meaning of *allo*, 'different'. Does it mean different from Paul's
gospel, or from their original attitude, or from what he has just
said? The answer is that, although the wording may be a trifle
loose, there is no real conflict: these three are one. The NEB interprets well as 'you will not take the wrong view', although this
goes beyond the Greek text.

Again, *ho tarassōn, he who is troubling you*, is the vague character behind the scenes, whether known or unknown to Paul, the
one referred to by the indignant interrogative *tis*, 'who?', in
verse 7 immediately above, which suggests that Paul was ignorant of his identity. The use of the singular for the plural may
only be a rhetorical device; on the other hand, even if there were
several Judaizers, there is almost certain to have been one
ringleader along them.[1] The verb *tarassō*, 'trouble', represents
the complete antithesis of that sense of peace, coming from right
relationships with God, which should be the characteristic mark
of the Christian, no matter what the outward circumstances.

Paul may not know who this ringleader is, but he seems to
suspect that he holds a high position, possibly in the Jerusalem
church. That is the meaning of *hostis ean ē, whoever he is*; it does
not so much refer to Paul's ignorance of the identity of the
troubler as allude to his status or rank. (NIV takes a more neutral
position with 'whoever he may be'.) Perhaps the use of *hopoioi*,
'no matter who', in 2:6 had a similar sense, though Paul is

[1] It is vain (with some commentators) to seek to establish the troublemaker's identity: we
are in the realm of pure speculation. It was certainly not an apostolic figure, and we know
few other names among the members of the Jerusalem church, and none at all among the
Pharisaic party there.

certainly not accusing in either passage any of the Jerusalem 'apostles' of having a direct hand in Galatian affairs.

Anyway, says Paul, such a one will *bear his judgment*. Because the Greek is *to krima*, 'the judgment', NEB is undoubtedly right in glossing as 'God's judgement'.[1] Paul is thinking, not of some council at Jerusalem, where indeed such troublers were condemned, but of the day when all evangelists and teachers alike must give account before God (*cf.* 1 Cor. 3:10–15). The word *bastasei, will bear*, is interesting. It is the very word used of Christ, carrying his cross to Golgotha (Jn. 19:17). The word is also used in Acts 15:10, in the impatient speech of Peter which turns the scale at the Jerusalem discussions. There the law is described as a *zygon*, 'yoke' (*cf.* Gal. 5:1), which no Jew, past or present, has been able 'to bear', *bastasai* (or possibly 'to endure'). If the letter to the Galatians was written after the Council, it is conceivable that Paul is referring to, or at least subconsciously remembering, Peter's strong words. However, if Paul is echoing Peter here, he is altering the sense. Do the Judaizers want to make the new converts carry the heavy burden and yoke of the law? Let them beware. In the day of judgment, they themselves will bear the far heavier burden of the wrath of God. But it is better to see both Peter and Paul referring to what were Christian 'commonplaces' rather than to see any direct or indirect dependence.

11. The great question here is whether anyone seriously claimed that Paul still advocated circumcision. If so, what did the claim mean? When he says, *if I . . . still preach circumcision*, Paul may mean only 'if I were advocating it, which everybody knows that I do not'. This is certainly the simplest explanation. It is made more likely by the use of *kēryssō, preach*, or 'herald abroad'. This, in Paul's writings, is the typical verb used for the initial preaching of the gospel (*cf.* 2:2). Nobody could possibly think that circumcision had any place in Paul's initial proclamation of Christ. As he says himself, if only he would allow circumcision to hold such a place, then the Judaizers would cease to harry him from pillar to post (*diōkomai, am persecuted*, is the very word

---

[1] This is really the same thing as saying that 'the troubler' is under God's curse (1:8–9).

199

that Paul used to describe his own bitter attacks on the church in his pre-Christian days; see 1:13). Indeed, as far as Judaism was concerned, a preaching of circumcision would remove the *skandalon*, the *stumbling block*, from the gospel. Few would mind 'Jesus the Messiah' being added to the law by some minor Messianic sect within Judaism: but the 'either/or' of Christian preaching was an impossible obstacle in their eyes.

Some ancient witnesses to the text omit the word *eti, still*. That would certainly make the sentence run more smoothly, reading, 'If I am a circumcision-preacher'. But such smoothness makes us suspicious that the difficult word was deliberately cut out. It may be that, if kept, *eti, still*, refers to Paul's pre-Christian days when he would most certainly have preached circumcision and the law with all his might to possible Gentile proselytes. 'I preached it then,' he says; 'but not now.' It can scarcely be claimed that in his early days of gospel preaching Paul found a greater place for the Jewish law and its observances than he did later, for we have seen that the lines of Paul's preaching had hardened very early. Besides, such behaviour would have meant an avoidance of conflict in those early days with Jew and Judaizer, and this we see from Acts not to have been the case. Jewish riots follow the path of Paul across Asia Minor like a trail of bushfires. There never seems to have been any such halcyonic period of good relations as that postulated by this theory. It may be, of course, that the Judaizers pointed back to a time when Paul had been willing to circumcise Timothy (Acts 16:3) and, just possibly, even to circumcise Titus (see discussion on 2:3). They may have told the Galatians that, in those days, Paul had preached circumcision. But, even if they said this, Paul's indignation in 2:1–5 shows that he himself would not admit for one moment the truth of such a charge. Whatever the meaning of the *still*, it cannot therefore be explained in this way. Probably it is to be taken in a weak sense as meaning 'at the present moment', with no sense of contrast with a past period when things were different.

The 'offence of the cross', *skandalon tou staurou*, 'the staggering nature of the cross', is a fundamental concept in Pauline theology and therefore demands consideration. In the Greek Old Testament, *skandalon* means a 'trap' or 'snare', and is used in parallelism with other words of the same meaning.[1] In the New Testament, the word is frequently used of a temptation to sin, that which causes a person to fall. But the typical New Testament use is when it means, as here, 'that which causes revulsion, arouses opposition' (BAGD). The very preaching of a crucified Messiah is of course a *stumbling block* to the religiously minded Jew (1 Cor. 1:23). There is a slight difference here in that Paul is not thinking of the fact of the Messiah dying a death under God's curse; rather, he is stressing that this way of salvation through the cross leaves no room for 'merit' to be acquired by outward observances such as circumcision or the law. Ultimately, of course, the two come to the same thing, for the nature of the Messiahship and the nature of the salvation that he brings are inextricably linked. Further, if salvation is to be altogether of grace, with nothing of merit, it is inevitable that both Gentile and Jew may find salvation in the same way: there is no longer a 'most favoured nation'. This was a bitter pill for Israel, even for the Jewish Christian. Circumcision separated Jew from Gentile: baptism made them one in Christ (3:27–28), as it made male and female one, again unlike circumcision, which separated them. No wonder that the failure to preach circumcision was the greatest stumbling block of the gospel. Only by the gift of God's Spirit can that which was once a stumbling block to Paul now become his greatest boast and glory (6:14). Paul once again uses here *katērgētai, has been removed*, better translated 'made ineffective' as in verse 4. In its different senses it is a favourite verb with him. The NEB, with 'is . . . no more', is hardly a strong enough translation: NIV, with 'has been abolished', hits the mark.

12. Here we have Paul's final rejoinder to the Judaizers. If they are so enthusiastic about circumcision, one 'mutilation' of the flesh, why not go the whole way and castrate themselves, as did the indigenous enunch priests of Asia Minor in honour of their strange, barbarous gods?[2] That is the only possible meaning of *apokopsontai, mutilate themselves*. The language is bitter, but

[1]More properly, *skandalon* means the small stick which, when touched, triggers off the snare: but, as often, the part is used for the whole.
[2]Since these eunuch priests or 'Corybantes' were sometimes called 'galli', Paul may even

it is not merely a 'coarse jest', as is sometimes said. It is designed to set circumcision in its true light as but one of the many ritual cuttings and markings practised in the ancient world. True, God had once used circumcision as the 'sign of the covenant' in Israel; but, since he was not now using it in the Christian church, it had no more relevance to the Gentile Christians than any other of these strange customs. Indeed, the eunuch priests of paganism undoubtedly thought that they were acquiring great 'merit' by their action. In this sense at least, therefore, there is a real comparison. Whether the Galatians lived in the north or in the south of the Roman province, they could not fail to be familiar with these barbaric cultic practices; the point would therefore not be lost on them. The fact that these priests were often called 'Galli' might possibly have given more point when Paul was writing to the Galatians, although there is no evidence that the two names were etymologically connected.

In Philippians 3:2 Paul uses very similar language, apparrently of these same Judaizers. They are 'dogs' in very truth (unlike the Gentiles whom they sometimes so describe); they are 'evil workers' in spite of all their reliance on 'good deeds'. They are seen as 'choppers', or 'mutilators': so he scornfully calls them *tēn katatomēn*, 'the mutilation', not *tēn peritomēn*, 'the circumcision', which is an honorable term for Jews.[1] It was probably because the Roman emperors confused the two practices of circumcision and ritual mutilation that they issued such stringent decrees later, forbidding Jewish circumcision. Paul would not have forbidden circumcision, but he would have agreed theologically with their judgment on its general nature.

C. THE TRUE USE OF FREEDOM (5:13–18)

In this letter, Paul has already dealt with the question of Christian freedom on several occasions (*cf.* 5:1). Now he will describe

---

intend by this allusion a pun on the name 'Galatians', although such priests were usually Phrygian in origin, and he was not likely to insult the Galatians in this way. If there is such an allusion, it would be to the 'mutilating' Judaizers, not to the sorely tempted Christians.

[1]This is a deliberate reversal of terms. Just as Gentiles had once been called by Jews in mockery *akrobustia*, a somewhat rude substitute for the proper word, *akroposthia*, both words

its right use and its limitations. This is partly to show, no doubt, how the new law of love, inextricably bound up with this freedom in Christ, is the true fulfilment of the law of Moses (v. 14). It is also, perhaps, partly to forestall the usual objections by the Judaizers as to the antinomian tendencies of Pauline teaching. But one suspects that another possible reason for its introduction here may be the state of local church life in Galatia. Paul seems to have had some accurate information as to the local church (4:10), and he may well have heard of a state of affairs that was anything but glorifying to Christian 'liberty'. It may even be that the church of Galatia was just as much divided by factions as that of Corinth (cf. 1 Cor. 1:10–13). True, we do not know of the names or natures of the factions in Galatia; but if we may hazard a guess from what we know from the letter, and also from the analogy of Corinth, there was probably a faithful 'Pauline' group. If there had not been, it is hard to see how Paul would have heard of the new tendencies there. Also there must clearly have been a majority that favoured the Judaizers; indeed, the assumed ringleader in this movement may not have come from outside the church at all, but from within. Then, to judge from the passage before us, there may even have been a third 'Gentile' circle, glorifying in their 'liberty', which to them was licence for unlimited self-indulgence. Even if there was no such circle, in any Gentile church there were bound to be such individuals. Paul did not want the support of such a group, and he may therefore have been fighting a three-cornered battle in Galatia as in other places.[1] In any case, whether this sort of 'libertine' group (prototype of one flank of the later Gnostic movement) existed or not, it is obvious that incipient 'party feeling' ran high in Galatia, and Paul would not condone that, not even in the name of gospel truth. If this third group existed, they may have accused Paul of 'Judaizing' tendencies, in their zeal for complete Christian emancipation: to such, Timothy's circumcision might have seemed a complete betrayal. It is

---

meaning 'uncircumcised', so Jews are now called in mockery *katatomē*, 'choppers', instead of *peritomē*, 'circumcisers'.

[1] Probably to think of full-blown theological 'parties' at this stage is an anachronism, in spite of Ropes and others: 'tendencies' would be a strong enough word to use.

therefore just possible that 5:11, 'if I . . . still preach circum-cision', might have some reference to their supposed position; but this again is pure hypothesis. Any theory that makes Paul himself a Judaizer is obviously wrong-headed, but all else is speculation.

'Yes, fellow Christians, you have been called by God with a view to freedom, only not a freedom which is a bridgehead for unredeemed human nature; instead, be willing slaves of one another for love's sake. For the whole of the law stands summed up in this one saying, "You are to love your fellow as you love yourself." But if you are continually snapping at one another and eating one another alive, take care that you do not annihilate each other. What I mean is this: let your way of life be Spirit-controlled, and you will not do that for which your natural self yearns. For the yearnings of the natural self are opposed to the Spirit, and the yearnings of the Spirit are opposed to the natural self. This is because the two are utterly opposed to each other, so that you cannot do the sort of things that you want to do. But if you are continually being guided by the Spirit, then you are not under law as a system.'

13. *You were called to freedom* reminds us of 5:1: 'for freedom Christ has set us free' (NEB mg., 'What Christ has done is to set us free'). True, says Paul; the goal of the divine calling (for *kaleō*, 'call', always implies this divine activity) is indeed freedom. But it must not become *aphormēn tē sarki, an opportunity for the flesh. Aphormē* means originally 'the starting point or base of opera-tions for an expedition' (so BAGD); hence 'bridgehead' or 'springboard' would be a possible translation. In 2 Corinthians 11:12 the word clearly means 'pretext', and perhaps that is the meaning here: those who shout 'liberty' loudest in Galatia may well have their tongues in their cheeks. It may, however, be quite neutral in meaning, as the RSV translates it here, with *opportunity*. Cousar thinks that Paul adds this whole section to balance his polemical presentation of *freedom* in the earlier chap-ters, and to avoid misunderstanding.

Paul's use of *sarx, flesh*, usually as opposed to *pneuma*, 'spirit', is important and characteristic. Many individual studies have been made of both words, as shown in any of the standard Bible wordbooks.[1] In brief, *sarx* begins by meaning the physical sub-stance 'flesh', like the Hebrew *bāsār*, the word which it translates in the Greek Old Testament (so Abbott-Smith). From that, it comes to mean either 'body', as substance, although the word for this is more properly *sōma*, or 'mortal', especially in the phrase 'flesh and blood'. From that, it is an easy transition to 'that which is natural to mortals' or 'human nature'. It could be argued that this is not necessarily sinful in itself, just as *sōma*, 'body', is certainly not sinful in itself. But there are two aspects in which *sarx* is inadequate, even if not actually sinful. The first is that, when we say 'human', we now must mean 'fallen human': this is inevitable, in a fallen world. Thus, in so far as *sarx* is the 'flesh' of fallen humanity, it is sinful.

Secondly, at a deeper level than this, even if we could concede that 'flesh' was once sinless and that its 'nature' was once 'unfallen nature', it is still grossly inadequate as 'flesh'. God is spirit, and not flesh (Is. 31:3); his thoughts and plans are as far above our thoughts as heaven is above earth (Is. 55:9). That is what Paul means by saying that his gospel is 'not . . . from any man' but 'by revelation' (1:12, NIV). As this aspect more properly falls under the heading of *pneuma*, 'spirit', it need not be further pursued here: Paul will take it up in verse 16 onwards.

When Paul says we must not use (or abuse) our Christian liberty as an opportunity for the flesh, or, as we might say, as a 'springboard for the flesh', he means 'you must not use this as an opportunity to show what you are really like as humans'. We may choose to translate it by 'lower nature' (NEB) or 'sinful nature' (NIV) to make the meaning clearer; but to Paul, all fallen human nature is by definition this 'lower nature'. We can see from the list of vices below that, while he certainly includes the grosser vices of the body in his purview – very necessary in a Gentile church – he also includes those subtler vices of the mind which we normally consider as 'respectable'. The law, of course, was equally realistic in its approach: it was designed to stop us from behaving in a 'natural' manner. The modern cult of 'self-expression' therefore finds little support in the Bible.

[1] Appendix 17 in Burton, entitled *'Pneuma and Sarx'*, is one of the most useful earlier treatments of 'spirit' and 'flesh'. The distinction is deeply rooted in the Old Testament (Is. 31:3), although not always in Paul's sense.

Paul uses the verb, *douleuete, be servants*, 'be slaves of (one another)' very effectively as a foil to *eleutheria*, the *freedom*, which they enjoy. This is part of the whole paradox by which Paul himself, freed by Jesus Christ from bondage to the Jewish law, becomes a *doulos*, 'slave', of Christ, for love's sake (see Rom. 1:1 'a servant' and, indeed, the opening of most other letters).[1] But such service is now voluntary; the only compulsion is that of love (2 Cor. 5:14). If we seek an Old Testament analogy, it is to be found in the 'freed' slave who refuses to leave the household of the master whom he loves, but chooses deliberately to remain a 'slave' for ever (Ex. 21:1–6). Indeed 6:17 may possibly even refer to the 'ear-marking' which was the Old Testament practice on such occasions. It is true that even in the Gentile world the 'freedman' still had certain obligations and duties towards his previous master; but this is not such a likely analogy, and certainly did not involve voluntary 'slavery'.

As in verse 6 faith worked itself out 'through love' (*di' agapēs*), so here the mutual service to which Christians are dedicated is also *through love*; the repetition must be intentional. Some early witnesses to the text read 'through the love of the Spirit'. This, although quite correct theologically, reads like a later explanatory addition, and was probably not part of the original text.

For *agapē*, 'love', see Burton, Appendix 21, among the earlier editors. There has been discussion in recent years of a possible distinction between *agapē*, seen as 'unselfish, self-giving, outgoing love', and *erōs*, seen as 'selfish, acquisitive, centripetal love'. As far as the New Testament itself is concerned, the discussion is purely academic; *erōs* is nowhere used, while even the 'love for the world' which is condemned in 1 John 2:15 is described by the verb *agapaō*. The probable truth is that *erōs* was archaic, and by now virtually displaced in *Koinē* Greek by the other word.[2] Yet, since for the Christian the norm of love is the

---

[1] Not only is Paul a 'slave of Christ'; he makes himself a 'slave' of other Christians (2 Cor. 4:5), which is a far deeper blow to human pride.

[2] There is a long article in BAGD, quoting an unquestionably pagan use of *agapē*, which cannot therefore be claimed as purely Christian usage. However, this pagan use is only from the third century AD (Leon Morris, *Testaments of Love* [Grand Rapids: Eerdmans, 1981], p. 124). Possibly the fact that *erōs* was also the name of a god of paganism may have led to its being dropped by Judaism and Christianity in favour of the other word.

love of God, and such love is free from all the human limitations mentioned above, we may justly interpret *agapē* in the New Testament as being love on a higher plane.

14. When Paul says that *the whole law is fulfilled, peplērōtai*, 'has reached its climax', 'has reached its end', he is probably punning upon two of the meanings of this Greek word. First, he means that the content of the whole law 'can be summed up' in the great words of Leviticus 19:18 commanding love to one's neighbour. This was a commonplace of Jewish theology, for which great rabbinic names could be quoted, and which the Lord had used in the Gospels (Mt. 22:39).

But, apart from the aspect of the command to love as being the sum of all the commandments of the law, Paul wants to show that Christian love is actually the practical 'carrying-out' of the law as well. This is the answer both to the criticisms of the Judaizers and the scandalous living of some of the Gentile converts, not to mention their present party spirit, which is apparently singularly lacking in love.

Nomos, law, is in this instance the Jewish Torah with which Paul and his opponents are most directly concerned. There are, as we have seen, many places where he uses it in a wider sense, of 'law' either as a general system of restraints, or as a possible means of commending ourselves to God: see Burton, Appendix 14. Because *tōrāh* in Hebrew and *nomos* in Greek are far wider in meaning than the English word 'law', we have tended to lose something of the richness of the concept. *Tōrāh*, roughly speaking, means 'instruction' in Hebrew, while *nomos* in Greek covers 'customary law', and even 'customs'. Nevertheless, in view of the list of virtues and vices which follows, Paul seems to be thinking of the law here in terms of a series of injunctions, which is the usual English understanding of the word. BAGD suggests 'Jewish religion' as a possible translation of *law*, whenever the definite article is used; this has much to commend it.

15. The word *daknete, bite*, is primarily used of snakes and animals. It can still be employed in this literal sense in Hellenistic Greek, but a more frequent use is in connection with various words meaning 'abuse'. The common Aramaic use of '*ekhal qartzē*, 'eat the pieces of',[1] meaning 'criticize', may have helped here, especially as Paul probably boasts of being Aramaic-speaking as a boy ('a Hebrew', Phil. 3:5). However, as *daknete* is used here in close connection with *katesthiete*, 'gulp down', perhaps Paul is still conscious of the original force of the metaphor as referring to conduct more fitting to wild animals than to brothers and sisters in Christ. The Old Testament, particularly the Psalter, makes free use of the 'ravenous beast' metaphor to describe the attitude of enemies of the people of God (Ps. 35:25, *etc.*). Probably the reference is to the savage, half-wild, scavenger dogs that still infest many a third-world city where they were once the only way of disposing of refuse. The NEB well translates, 'if you go on fighting one another, tooth and nail', which suggests a cat fight. Had it not been for the link with *daknete*, and the Old Testament references, we could have translated simply 'destroy', for the verb *katesthiō* often has this weakened metaphorical meaning. Whatever the origin of the metaphor, it certainly gives a lively picture of strife within the Galatian church. Paul will encourage resistance to the false gospel of the Judaizers, but never in the sense of party politics.

The word *analōthēte*, *consumed*, or 'annihilated', is often used of destruction by fire; the basic idea seems to be that nothing at all remains. Paul may be thinking here of beasts fighting to the death in the amphitheatre. He is of course speaking metaphorically: what he dreads is the virtual disappearance of all his work in Galatia. How far this was an actual danger, we cannot now say: if it was a real danger, it was certainly overcome, as we can see from the survival of the Galatian church, and indeed of this very letter.

16. To Paul, the answer to all such abuses lies in a way of life which is continually Spirit-controlled; then people will cease to act 'naturally', and so will cease to 'fulfil themselves'.[2] The use

---

[1] This typically vivid Aramaic usage is quoted in W. Jennings, *Lexicon to the Syriac New Testament* (Oxford: Clarendon Press, 1926), under the entry for these words: but compare also the Hebrew metaphorical usages mentioned here in the Commentary.

[2] This promise of deliverance from the 'flesh' is not automatic or magical. Failure to realize this has caused much disillusionment among young Christians, as perhaps it did also among the Galatians. Indeed, as suggested, it may have been one of the reasons for their lapse into

of *peripateite, walk,* in a moral sense is too common to need comment. When Paul says *pneumati, by the spirit,* or 'in spirit', it is not always clear whether he is referring directly to the Holy Spirit or simply means 'spiritually', as opposed to 'carnally'. We may, if we choose, paraphrase as 'a spiritual walk' to keep this linguistic ambiguity, although, in the light of what follows, the Holy Spirit seems to be meant here.[1]

17. Paul's use of *epithymia, desires,* or 'yearning', and the kindred verb, is probably connected with Genesis 4:7, and traditional Jewish interpretations of that verse, where sin's 'desire' is stated to be directed to Cain, although Cain must master it. Even if this is so, however, it is only for Paul a verbal similarity, a peg upon which to hang a great theological truth. This is the fact that by nature we do not find the leadings of the Spirit of God to be congenial; indeed, they are utterly repugnant to our own 'natural' inclinations (1 Cor. 2:14). Paul himself in Romans 7:5–25 shows that his knowledge of our inability to do what we desire springs from the inner religious experience of the proud Pharisee. In this sense, *ha ean thelete, what you would,* is only to be understood of moral strivings and yearnings, not baser impulses.

18. This verse seems best taken as a summary of all that has gone before rather than as any fresh advance in the argument. There seems to be a continuous force in the present tense of *agesthe, you are led,* as though Paul wished to say 'As long as you are being thus led'. *Hypo nomon,* in accordance with the principle enunciated above, is probably to be taken in the general sense of 'under law as a principle', rather than in the particular sense of 'under the law of Moses'. Of course, the difference is not great, for the one must include the other: if the Galatians (like all Spirit-led Christians) are not under law as a system, they obviously cannot be under any particular law, whether Jewish or Gentile.

---

legalism. As Betz well says, 'the promise depends upon the previous imperative – and its result'.

[1] See Additional Note on p. 210 on the meaning of *pneuma, Spirit*: there is always a potential ambiguity.

Additional Note: The meaning of 'pneuma' (5:16)

There is a very valuable article under *pneuma* in BAGD, which helpfully outlines the various meanings of this word. Like *ruach* in the Old Testament, it has travelled far from its original meaning of 'wind, breath'. From being the 'breath of life', the immaterial part that alone gives life to the *sarx*, 'flesh', it comes virtually to mean 'self'.[1] BAGD well says 'as the source and seat of insight, feeling, and will, generally as the representative part of the inner life of man'. This is where the above-mentioned ambiguity enters: for *pneumati*, or *en pneumati*, may thus at times mean simply 'inwardly', or, at most, 'spiritually', not 'by the Spirit'. This is especially so when there is a contrast, explicit or implied, with 'body' or 'flesh', while Romans 8:16, 'the Spirit himself bearing witness with our spirit' (or 'to our very spirit', following BAGD), shows the ambiguity. Since 'spirit' essentially means 'very self', or 'very nature', then it may be equally used either of humans or of God.

When so used of God, the noun 'spirit' usually has the definite article in Greek, and often the adjective 'holy' as well. When the word is thus differentiated, it presents no problems. This is God's Holy Spirit, sometimes in the New Testament called 'the Spirit of the Lord', or 'the Spirit of Christ', and even once 'the Spirit of Jesus' (Acts 16:7). In this sense, the Spirit is 'that which differentiates God from everything that is not God . . . All those who belong to God possess or receive this Spirit and hence have a share in his life. This Spirit also serves to distinguish the Christians from all unbelievers . . .' (BAGD under *pneuma*).

To Paul, possession of the Spirit is therefore at the same time the possession of 'the mind of Christ' (1 Cor. 2:16), which alone makes possible the understanding of spiritual truths. In Galatians, however, Paul is more concerned with the later fruits of the Spirit shown in Christ-like conduct than he is with the initial revelatory work of the Spirit. Christians are to 'walk by the Spirit' (5:16), to be 'led by the Spirit' (5:18), to 'keep in step with

[1] This meaning, however, is more often expressed by *psychē* in Greek, corresponding to *nephesh* in Hebrew. Abbott-Smith discusses both words and their corresponding Hebrew terms, which may influence the sense in Greek.

the Spirit' (5:25, NIV), to 'live by the Spirit' (5:25), to 'sow to the Spirit' (6:8). All these are varied metaphors for what is essentially one and the same thing, a life completely and continuously under the control and the direction of the Holy Spirit. What this means in practical terms of ethical conduct, Paul will now show in detail.

D. THE 'NATURAL RESULTS' OF HUMAN NATURE (5:19–21)

Paul now moves on to a detailed consideration of the differences produced in the human life by the presence of the Spirit. He has already given, in broad outline, the substance of his 'moral argument' which is the main theme of this section of the letter.[1] Now, in order to point his argument, he deals with the total contrast between the 'natural' life and the 'spiritual' life and does so in embarrassing detail, no doubt very appropriate to the situation in Galatia, as in any other pagan area. First he gives a list of some of the vices typical of the paganism of his day, as he does elsewhere in his letters (e.g. Rom. 1:29–31). Lest Paul be accused of taking an unduly pessimistic view of life, it is well to remember that pagan moralists were, if anything, more severe in their strictures; indeed, some have felt that Paul is drawing on a pagan philosopher's 'stock list' here. The one difference was that pagan moralists, while they also regarded these things with horror, yet regarded them as contrary to humanity's true nature; Paul however regarded them as 'natural' and inevitable results.[2] We can see from Corinthians how hard Paul had to fight against even the grossest of vices in the Gentile Christian churches which he founded. Indeed, it was just because of this floodtide of Gentile immorality that the Judaizers felt the observance of the law to be so necessary, a view which the despairing Galatians may have shared. Jewish Christian churches were not

[1] Paul's whole argument here is really the same as the proverbial 'by their fruits you will know them' (see Mt. 7:16): this is of course equally true of the works of the flesh and of the fruits of the Spirit.

[2] Elsewhere, Paul defines these same things as 'the works of darkness' (Rom. 13:12, noted by Betz). This may either imply their satanic origin, or simply be a description of their nature. But here he is concerned to show how 'naturally' they arise, not to seek a supernatural cause for them outside of humanity itself.

usually as exposed to gross vices of this sort (but see Rom. 2:22). Their typical 'spiritual' sins were subtler: pride, self-righteousness, hypocrisy and the like. It is therefore equally possible that Paul's list of vices comes from a Jewish source, designed to instruct Gentile proselytes in the elements of moral behaviour: Paul the Rabbi must have know such lists well.

'What the human nature produces is plain for all to see – things like unchastity, unnatural vice, sexual excess; idolatry, magic; hostile feelings, contentiousness, jealousy, temper tantrums, canvassing for position, dissentions, factions, envy; alcoholism, wild parties, and all that sort of behaviour. I tell you in advance (as I did before) that those who do things like that will never prove to be heirs of God's kingdom.'

The exact shade of meaning of each word is not easy to establish, although the general sense is that given here: many seem to be almost synonymous or variants on a common theme. Burton discusses them in detail, although his interpretation needs to be supplemented by more recent material, available since his time. The NEB, with others, tries to divide the vices into groups. First come three concerned with breaches of sexual law; then two concerned with 'ritual sins', idolatry and sorcery, which are usually linked in the Old Testament, as being so linked in pagan religions; then eight concerned with social life; then two dealing with strong drink. If, as suggested, this does indeed come from some 'Jewish missionary handbook', used in proselytism of Gentiles and familiar to Paul from pre-Christian days, such an orderly presentation is all the more likely. The fact that Paul ends the list with *ta homoia toutois*, 'and such like', shows us that it is by no means considered by him as exhaustive, but merely typical. If we had a complete list, we might well find that it corresponded to the ten commandments, or some other obvious division of the law.

It may be, of course, that what we have is simply the first sign of a Christian 'catalogue', soon to become standard through the catechetical work of the church. But the similarity of the description of pagan vices in various parts of the New Testament reads as though there had been some common original. And though the interpretation (and even the text) of the so-called 'decree of the Council of Jerusalem' is doubtful, there is a similar division into sections there (Acts 15:29). That this is part of a system of common 'types', no-one doubts; the only question is as to how far they are original with Christianity, and how far borrowed from earlier prototypes, constructed either by Jewish or by Gentile moralists. In any case, the uniqueness of the Christian understanding of sin as covering motivation as much as act (Mt. 5:28) has altered any original list beyond recognition, and made it far more searching.

19. It has been sometimes felt that there is an implied contrast in the text between *ta erga, the works* (of the flesh), laboriously produced, and *ho karpos*, 'the fruit' (of the Spirit), which is a spontaneous growth (v. 22), as though, for all its striving after good, this was the best of which natural humanity was capable.[1] The true answer may simply be that, while the metaphor of 'fruit-bearing' is still vivid in the case of the *pneuma*, 'Spirit', the original metaphor latent in *erga, works*, is so weakened as to be lost in the case of the *sarx, flesh*.

The general nature of the vices described will be plain from the paraphrase on p. 212 above where the definitions follow BAGD in the main, although the lines of demarcation between the vices are not always very clear. Indeed, if Paul was using some kind of traditional 'list', whatever its source, it may not always be necessary to look for such distinctions; it may be that the 'piling up' of nouns is largely for rhetorical effect. *Porneia*, for instance, usually translated *fornication*, seems in point of fact to cover most kinds of 'natural' sexual irregularities. Hence the deliberately vague word 'unchastity' used in the paraphrase. It is also used in the Old Testament to denote 'idolatry' in the sense of unfaithfulness to God, but it is not likely to have that metaphorical sense here, especially as *idolatry* appears as a separate item below. The two following words (*akatharsia* and *aselgeia*) probably describe some of the sexual perversions (such as the practice of homosexuality and lesbianism) which, as Paul reminds us in Romans 1:26–27, were common in the pagan

---

[1] Any such contrast seems over-exegesis: Paul's stress, in either case, is on the inevitable onflowing consequences. But it is true that, to Paul, *ta erga*, 'the works', tends to have a pejorative sense, perhaps because the phrase is so often used of 'the works of the law' in theological controversy.

world, and indeed often characterize the world of today. They have therefore been translated in the paraphrase as 'unnatural vice' and 'sexual excess', although their reference may well be broader. They seem to be deliberately vague, and are probably used as euphemisms here.

20. *Pharmakeia, sorcery,* had a special relevance for inhabitants of Asia Minor, as can be seen from the story in Acts 19:19 of the burning of the books containing 'Ephesian Letters', as such magic spells were called in the ancient world. If the Galatians had become entangled with some star-cult (4:10), the mention would be even more relevant here. The orthodox Jew regarded this sin with peculiar horror, as directly forbidden in the law (Ex. 22:18), and as, like sexual immorality, closely connected with *idolatry,* to which doubtless the Galatians had been enslaved. The word can also mean 'poisoning', from its etymological derivation. Both witchcraft and poisoning were apparently prevalent in the Roman world and severely dealt with by law.

Next come a group of sins which, in view of the reference to quarrels in verse 15, may possibly have had a particular relevance to the Galatian situation at the time. Here again the barriers between the vices are thin and it is not important to distinguish them sharply; it will perhaps be sufficient to single out a few of the important and characteristic words for detailed consideration. Several will recur in other such catalogues of vices elsewhere in the New Testament. For an attempted translation of each word, see the paraphrase on page 212. *Eris, strife,* for instance, is clearly something like 'a contentious temper' (so NEB). There seems no point to be made of the fact that the singular is used of this noun while many others in the list are quoted in the plural. By the usual Greek rule, the plural, if used in such cases, should mean 'acts of contention', although Paul uses the plural *erides* in 1 Corinthians 1:11 in substantially the same sense as the singular here. It would apply very well to the 'biting' and 'devouring' taking place in Galatia (v. 15).

It is hard to see the distinction between *zēlos, jealousy,* used here, and *phthonoi,* 'envy', in the next verse. Both have the same basic meaning. Perhaps Paul's use of *zēlos* goes back to his use of the cognate verb in 4:17–18, referring to the activity of the Judaizers. Clearly, the sense of *zēlos* is bad here, whatever we may decide about Paul's usage of it in the earlier context. For *phthonoi*, 'envy', some witnesses here read *phonoi*, 'murders': but that is less likely, as not being a parallel to *zēlos*. *Phthonoi* should mean 'acts of envy' or 'bursts of envy', usually aroused by the position or good fortune of others. The concept therefore comes close to covetousness.

Eritheiai, selfishness, is well expanded by the NEB as 'selfish ambitions', although it more properly denotes the unfair 'canvassing for office' which is prompted by such ambitions for power (so BAGD). Any linguistic connection with *eris, strife,* is very doubtful. Distinct from it is *haireseis, party spirit,* which, although giving the English word 'heresies', probably means 'factions', as in 1 Corinthians 11:19. The NEB translation, 'party intrigues', may be a little too strong, but conveys the right idea, and would suit the presumed Galatian situation.

21. *Methai* (lit. 'drunkennesses')[1] and *kōmoi,* 'carousings', probably refer primarily to the drunken orgies encouraged at festivals of the pagan gods, and secondarily to the general insobriety of pagan life. Wild parties would be the modern equivalents, not to mention drug abuse of various other kinds. We can see from 1 Corinthians 11:21 how easily such abuses could creep into Gentile churches even at the Lord's Supper; they were, after all, characteristic of pagan worship, and old religious habits die hard.

When Paul says *as I warned you before, proeipon,* we are faced with the same problem as in 1:9 where the perfect tense of the same verb (*proeirēkamen,* 'as we have said before') occurred. When had Paul delivered this previous warning? We cannot assume a mere 'epistolatory aorist', in view of the use in the context of the present tense as well, *I warn you,* in deliberate contrast. In this instance, it is difficult to find an earlier context in the same letter to justify the use; nor can we assume a 'lost' earlier letter to the Galatians as we might perhaps in the case of

[1] By the Greek grammatical rule, the plural normally means 'instances of' drunkenness, or whatever the particular vice may be: it transfers the idea from an abstract notion to practical instances, and so makes the whole more vivid.

Corinth. The only logical conclusion, therefore, is that Paul, in his initial evangelism of Galatia, was far from restricting himself to the 'simple gospel' as sometimes we erroneously suppose. He must also have given strong moral teaching verbally as well: he certainly includes it in writing in all his letters. This in itself gives the lie to the Jewish charge that Paul taught freedom from all moral restraints (Rom. 3:8). Admittedly, if the letter is regarded as being addressed to South Galatia, the narrative in Acts suggests too brief a period on the initial visit to allow much teaching (see Acts 13 and 14); but on the return journey, some such moral instruction is possible and suggested strongly by the *strengthening* and *exhorting* of Acts 14:22.

Inherit the kingdom of God; although Paul is emphatic that we cannot by 'doing' the works of the law enter our promised inheritance (3:12, 18), but that entry is by faith alone (3:11), yet he strongly asserts here that by 'doing' these very different things we can bar ourselves from the kingdom.[1] That is not the paradox that it seems to us at first sight. Paul's whole point is that *those who do such things* thereby show themselves to be without the transforming gift of faith which leads to the gift of the promised Spirit, which, in turn, leads to the fruits of the Spirit, the seal of our inheritance. To all these things the Christian has died already, as Paul will show below; therefore he or she shows the reality of the 'faith that justifies', and the reality of the new 'life in Christ' that is within, by a clear break with all these 'works of darkness', familiar though they may have been in the past. It comes as a shock when Paul, in 1 Corinthians 6:11, after a similar list of loathsome vices, says, 'Some of you were once like that', although he does hasten to reassure the Corinthians of their new standing in Christ. Paul only gives this 'black list' to remind the Galatians of what their past slavery to sin had been before the gospel brought them freedom in Christ.

The reference in what might be translated 'will never prove to be heirs',[2] *ou klēronomēsousin*, probably goes back to the discussion about Abraham and his 'offspring' in chapter 3. Paul has

---

[1]Betz sees the archaic and formal language of the quotation as showing that it was part of formal catechetical instruction. But it may simply indicate the solemnity of the warning.

[2]'The inheritance' seems usually associated in Paul with the gift of the Spirit, as here: that in itself marks the difference between the two lists.

shown in 4:7 that, if we are sons, then, by the same token, we are 'heirs', *klēronomoi*, or 'fellow heirs with Christ', as Rom. 8:17 has it. But chapter 4 had ended with the stern warning that the children of the slave-wife, themselves slaves, cannot share in God's promised wealth of glory; indeed, they are specifically excluded. So it is here: those who are 'slaves' to such passions show themselves to be no true-born children of God; such can never inherit the kingdom of God.

Additional Note: The 'kingdom of God' (5:21)

Paul's use of *basileian Theou*, 'the kingdom of God', is very interesting. The concept of the 'kingdom of God' is dominant in the Synoptic Gospels, especially perhaps in Matthew, who writes in a thoroughly Jewish milieu and as the heir to a long Old Testament tradition. However, the image is also used in the book of Acts. Indeed, Acts 14:22, if we are supporters of the South Galatian theory, shows us Paul teaching to these very Galatians 'that through many tribulations we must enter the kingdom of God'. Paul himself used the analogy more often than might be supposed; Romans 14:17 and 1 Corinthians 4:20 are two random instances out of some eight in all. Paul therefore seems to have employed the picture fairly consistently through his ministry, whether early or late, Jewish or Gentile. It is however true to say that, although present in Pauline theology, the kingdom of God is never a dominant concept. Paul prefers to speak in terms of 'gospel' and 'church', for instance, rather than 'kingdom'. This is not of course to identify these concepts completely, but merely to say that all three belong to the same realm of ideas, in the sense that they describe the relation of God to us. *Basileia*, 'kingdom', itself would actually be better translated as 'rule of God' rather than 'kingdom' (or, with Moffatt, 'realm of God') which in English suggests a spatial and temporal location.[1] If the recipients of the letter were ethnic Galatians of the north, and remembered the traditions of their

---

[1] For 'kingdom' as an eschatological concept, see especially the so-called 'parables of the kingdom' in Matthew 13.

own Celtic king Amyntas, before the Roman province was formed, the word might have even more relevance for them.

E. THE HARVEST OF THE SPIRIT (5:22–26)

Now comes a corresponding list of spiritual qualities. Although such a roll-call exists in other parts of the New Testament (as in 2 Pet. 1:5–7) there is no such close similarity between the lists as there is in the corresponding classification of the vices. The Petrine list of qualities, for instance, is in the reverse order, with *agapē*, 'love', as the climax. This suggests that no Hebrew proto-type existed here, but that these 'positive' lists are a Christian creation. It seems obvious that, while Judaism and Christianity might well agree on what were vices, their concept of spiritual virtues might be different.

'But, by contrast, the harvest[1] that the Spirit brings is love, joy, tranquillity, forbearance with others, kindness, generosity, reliability, humility, self-control in the realm of sex. There is no law against those who act like this. For those who belong to Christ Jesus have put their "flesh" to death, along with all its passionate desires. Now, as surely as we are living by the rule of the Spirit, let us walk by the rule of the Spirit. Let us, for instance, not be boastful, challenging and envying one another's position.'

For the reasons leading to the choice of these particular terms in translation, BAGD has been taken as a guide. Again, as in the case of the vices, the difficulty is to know where to draw the line of demarcation between one virtue and another. In most cases, the 'areas of meaning' overlap considerably. Also, without giving a very expanded paraphrase, it is not easy to cover all the shades of meaning conveyed; so an attempt has been made to select the one word which seems most central to the meaning as well as appropriate to this context and to the presumed actual position in Galatia.

---

[1]Betz, perhaps rightly, sees a contrast between the essential 'unity' of 'the fruit of the Spirit' and the unstructured list of unrelated vices.

22. The first three aspects of the Spirit's harvest need little comment; the second and third, *chara, joy,* and *eirēnē, peace,* are probably suggested by the typically Jewish-Christian greeting of 'grace and peace', *charis kai eirēnē,* of 1:3, although *charis* and *chara* are not directly connected. To the Christian, joy is something quite independent of outward circumstances, and its source is the Holy Spirit (see 1 Thes. 1:6 and Rom. 14:17). *Agapē* has been already considered; it is put first on the list as embracing all the others if rightly understood. Whether we are justified in bracketing these three as a 'triad' apart from the other virtues is uncertain. The list certainly does not fall into sections as readily as that of the vices did. See 1 Corinthians 13:13 for another but different triad: faith, hope, and love, with 'love' as the climax.

The use of *karpos, fruit,* as mentioned above, suggests that all these spiritual qualities, and many more, are the spontaneous product of the presence of the Spirit of Christ within the heart of the Christian. The metaphor is a very old one, natural to an agricultural people like Israel. While *karpos* means any kind of fruit, it is most frequently employed of the product of the fruit tree or vine. It was a principle enunciated by the Lord himself that a tree could be recognized by the fruit that it bore (Mt. 7:16); so, by the presence of these 'fruits', the presence of the Spirit in the hearts of the Galatians is proved. It is interesting that Paul does not here use the presence of spiritual gifts, equally coming from the Spirit, as a proof of spiritual life, although such gifts seem to have existed among the Galatians ('works miracles among you', 3:5). Perhaps it is because fruit of the Spirit cannot be simulated, while gifts of the Spirit can (Mt. 7:22).

Makrothymia, patience, is well paraphrased by Bruce by the coined word 'long tempered' as opposed to 'short tempered'; perhaps 'tolerance' would give the idea better in modern English. It is the quality of 'putting up with' other people, even when one's patience is sorely tried. It is interesting to speculate why Paul put this quality in such a lofty place in his list. Perhaps it was because in Galatia neither 'party' displayed much of this virtue. *Chrēstotēs, kindness,* also has the connotations of 'goodness' or 'generosity' (so BAGD), but these thoughts are already covered by other words in the list before us. The common slave-name *Chrēstos* comes from this root, so that the word must suggest some quality that was desired in the ideal servant, as indeed do all the other qualities listed here: it has been well said that they are a list of 'slave virtues'. If these are the qualities of the 'servant Messiah', on whom Christians are called to pattern themselves, this is not surprising. Indeed, there may even be a pun based on the similar pronunciation of *Christos*, the Messiah, and *Chrēstos*, the slave name. Did the wits of Antioch intend this pun when they called this 'reformed sect' of Judaism 'Christians', hinting at 'the goody-goodies' (Acts 11:26)? *Agathōsynē* has here probably more of its colloquial meaning of 'generosity' than its original meaning of *goodness* although both interpretations are possible: *prautēs, gentleness* (v. 23), would then mean something like 'humility'.

These qualities are basically manward rather than Godward in their aspect, and most, if not all, would be directly relevant to a state of party strife in a church, whether two-sided or three-sided. Most of them are qualities of restraint and humility, to be displayed by the victor to the vanquished. That in itself suggests that Paul may fear over-violent dealing with the erring Judaizers by a victorious 'orthodox party' in the Galatian church, should his appeal be successful. The apostle's exhortation in 6:1 concerning anyone 'overtaken in any trespass', bears this out. Once Paul has vanquished an opponent theologically, that person ceases, for Paul, to be an opponent and becomes instead an erring brother or sister in need of pastoral care (2 Cor. 2:5–8). But he knows human nature too well to expect that the Galatian reaction will necessarily be the same. Indeed, the more tempted the Galatians had been to succumb to the attack of the Judaizers, the more likely they would be to lead the 'heresy hunt' now, in order to justify themselves for their own past wavering.

Of the two remaining qualities, *pistis, faithfulness*, if translated 'faith', would be primarily directed to God; Paul does not speak of having 'faith' in fellow humans. However, it can equally well be translated, as here, 'faithfulness' (NEB, 'fidelity').[1] If this is the correct rendering, it could apply to the Christian's attitude

---

[1] Whenever a word from this root is applied to God elsewhere in the Bible, the meaning is clearly 'faithfulness' or 'constancy' (Rom. 3:3).

manwards as well as Godwards. It would then refer to the Galatians' lack of fidelity towards Paul, of which he had complained in 4:12–20.

23. The last quality, *enkrateia, self-control*, is neither Godward nor manward, but more properly 'selfward'. It is usually employed to describe self-control in sexual matters; if that is its meaning here, then it looks back to the grosser vices of the list above. If there was a 'libertine' group at Galatia, boasting of their antinomian 'freedom', then they sorely needed this gift. *Tōn toioutōn, such*, could be amplified, with NEB, as 'such things as these', and the sense would be excellent. No law forbids qualities like these; such virtues are in fact the 'keeping', or 'fulfilling', of the law. But, in view of the personal nature of the reference in verse 21, *hoi toiauta prassontes*, 'those who habitually behave thus', it is better to translate personally here too, as 'such people', not 'such things'. The phrase will then become 'The law was never meant for (or "was never directed against") people like this'. In either case, the main sense is the same,[1] though NIV prefers 'such things'.

24. Paul now gives the reason for the production of this rich spiritual harvest and for the freedom of the Christian from the law. Christians have already *crucified the flesh, tēn sarka estaurōsan*, 'put the old self to death'. As before, 'original nature' is perhaps a strong enough equivalent for *sarx*: to say 'lower nature' (with NEB) or 'sinful nature' (with NIV) is to suggest that unaided humanity is actually capable of 'higher' things, and this Paul will not allow. The point of *estaurōsan, crucified*, is to link this total change in attitude, and therefore change in conduct, with the death of Christ.[2] It is another way of expressing 2:20, 'I have been crucified with Christ' (see Commentary on pp. 124f.). There were many other words that Paul could have used, and indeed does use elsewhere, like 'put to death' or 'abolish',

---

[1] See Betz for a discussion of the issues involved: he sees Paul's motive as being to encourage ethical responsibility, which an external law could never do. This is true, but inadequate.

[2] As Betz well says, Paul is referring to the overwhelming presence of Christ, the crucified and resurrected Lord, living in them by his Spirit.

which would have conveyed his general meaning, but would not convey this direct connection with Christ's death.

The words *pathēmasin*, *passions*, and *epithymiais*, *desires*, are to be taken closely together; so to translate 'passionate longings' is not misleading. Hebrew was chary in the use of adjectives, as were many ancient languages. Often two nouns, juxtaposed, would serve the purpose as well. Either through the Greek translation of the Old Testament, or through the persistence of old speech-habits among Greek speakers whose mother-tongue was not Greek, the same tendency to avoid adjectives appears in the New Testament, though in reduced form. Like *pathos*, the word *pathēma* has a twofold meaning, either 'experience' or 'suffering' (in a neutral sense), or 'passion' (in a bad sense). The *epithymia*, 'longing' (of the flesh), is taken from verse 17 above, where the cognate verb occurs. However, 'passionate longings' should not be restricted to sexual matters: it means anything for which the natural self longs intensely.

25. The use of *pneumati*, *by the Spirit*, or 'in Spirit', has the same possible ambiguity as before, in that it may have a general or a specific reference. If general, we must translate 'spiritually'; if specific, we may follow the NEB with: 'If the Spirit is the source of our life, let the Spirit also direct our course.' A good colloquial translation of the latter phrase would be 'keep in step with the Spirit' (NIV). Again, the *ei*, *if*, does not express any sense of contingency or doubt when it is used with the indicative mood; rather it means 'since', as often in Paul.

26. *No self-conceit*: at first sight this verse might look as though its function was simply to sum up the humble and self-effacing fruits of the Spirit already mentioned. But it is more than that, if it is intended to lead to a particular application to the Galatian situation. *No provoking* (or challenging) *of one another*: this 'spiritual' way of life, says Paul, utterly forbids all forms of ambitious rivalry and envy. This does sound suspiciously as though there was party strife in the church of Galatia of the type familiar to us from Corinth. It may be, of course, that we need not seek for such a particular application. Paul was well acquainted with human nature, from the pastoral care of so many churches; he knew that this was a danger everywhere, and therefore cautioned them against it. The word *kenodoxoi* in the first part of this verse means either 'conceited' or 'boastful'. Perhaps the danger was that those who had not fallen to the Judaizing error were now boasting of their superior spiritual strength, while those who had given way were *phthonountes*, either 'full of envy' or 'jealous'. Alternatively, the trouble in Galatia may be a simple power struggle within the church; in that case, we may be wrong in looking for deeper motives, or seeing any reference to the Judaizing controversy.

F. HOW TO DEAL WITH AN OFFENDER (6:1–6)

Should the 'specific' rather than the 'general' interpretation suggested above be correct, then Paul is now turning to the question of how the church should deal with the repentant Judaizer, actual or imagined: compare again 2 Corinthians 2:5–11 for a similar case. The use of the singular may refer either to some known individual ringleader, probably inside the church, or may be used, with studied indifference, to describe a whole group. If it was one who claimed some special position for himself, then the application of verse 4 would be obvious, while, if the erring leader had actually been a 'teaching elder' in the Galatian church, then verse 6 would be full of local relevance. The great danger, however, in all New Testament exegesis is that of reading too much into the text, particularly when we are almost without knowledge as to the actual local background. However, if we do not adopt some such system of coherent interpretation, then we must assume that these closing sections are a mere theological 'portmanteau', into which Paul bundles a sequence of unrelated Christian injunctions. This is always possible; some of the remarks at the end of his major letters read suspiciously like such random postscripts, but it does not seem likely here.

Further, we do have the very close parallel to the situation depicted in the Corinthian correspondence, to which we have already made reference, where Paul speaks specifically of the duty of 'winning back' just such an erring member (2 Cor.

2:5–11). Certainly the existence of party strife in Galatia would be a close parallel to the situation at Corinth; but how far we can justifiably press the analogy is uncertain, since it is only a hypothesis.

'Fellow Christians, even if someone is caught doing something wrong, you who are "the spiritual party" must set that person to rights in a gentle, humble way. Watch yourself; you may be tested too. Carry heavy loads for one another; that is how you will observe Christ's law to the full. If anyone thinks himself to be a somebody (when he is really a nobody), all that he achieves is to hoodwink himself. Let each person carefully weigh up what he has actually achieved, and then he can have pride in his own work, not in someone else's. For each will have to shoulder his own pack. But the one who is being taught Christian doctrine ought to share with the teacher all the good things that he has.'

1. The word *prolēmphthē, is overtaken*, can mean either 'to be caught[1] (doing something wrong)' (so NEB mg.), or 'trapped', or in a more vivid sense 'should (do something wrong) on a sudden impulse'. The latter is more graphic, but does not suit the context so well if there is a reference to Judaizing. That could hardly be described as 'a sudden impulse'. The subject is the suitably vague *anthrōpos*, 'anybody'. Whether we regard the vagueness as deliberate or not will depend upon our interpretation of the whole situation. If this is the local ringleader in the Judaizing movement, then we must agree that the *tis*, 'somebody, anybody', of verse 3 is equally specific and pointed in its reference.

Who are the *pneumatikoi, you who are spiritual*, or the 'spiritually minded'? Paul may use the word at its face value as meaning, simply 'You who are walking by the rule of the Spirit'; that would certainly fit with the previous chapter. In that case it would be a straightforward appeal to the unfallen Galatians to assist the fallen. But in view of the suggested use of the word *pneumatikos* as the self-chosen title (almost a 'party title') of those

---

[1]It is not clear whether this means 'caught out' by other humans in the sense of 'found out', or 'caught out' by Satan. Probably Paul would not make the distinction: naturally, the second would always be true, the first only sometimes so.

who boasted themselves of a superior spiritual position, some have suspected a deeper meaning here. It is as though Paul were saying: 'You claim a superior spirituality? Prove it, then, by acting spiritually in this case.' The later gnostic associations of the word are probably irrelevant here. It is quite likely that one of the groups in Galatia used this as a title. 1 Corinthians 3:1, however, uses the word in a good sense as opposed to *sarkinoi*, 'earthly-minded Christians', and *nēpioi*, 'immature Christians'. So, even if it was a 'party name' in Galatia, there is no need to associate it as yet with the 'immoral' proto-gnostic group to whom some of Paul's later injunctions are directed. *Kartartizete*, *restore*, means either 'restore to its former condition' or 'complete'. The first of these meanings is highly suitable to describe the restoration of a Christian who has 'lapsed', whether by Judaizing or in any other way. The Gospels use the word of 'mending nets' (Mt. 4:21). In *skopōn*, *look*, 'keeping an eye on', Paul changes very vividly from the plural to the singular. It is as though he changes from the collective duty of the church to the individual duty of each member. *Skopōn*, while basically meaning *look*, has the colloquial sense of 'look out for', exactly like the corresponding verb in English.

2. This verse introduces yet another use of *bastazete*, *bear*, or 'shoulder'. In 5:10 it had been used of the chief Judaizer, who will have to 'bear' or 'endure' the heavy judgment of God. Here it is again used of shouldering a heavy burden; but this time the burden has a good sense, for it is a load of responsibility and care (unless with the NEB we translate 'Help one another to carry these heavy loads', where the thought is the burden of shame, of the guilty sinner). In verse 5, when the verb is used with *phortion*, 'burden', the meaning is lighter still, in the sense of 'shoulder a pack', as a porter or pedlar might do. The last use of the word in this letter will be the most significant of all: in 6:17, Paul will say *bastazō*, 'I "carry about" in my body the marks of the Lord Jesus'. The meaning of this is considered in the Commentary on pp. 237ff.

The phrase *ton nomon tou Christou*, *the law of Christ*, is arresting. This is the closest that Paul ever comes to setting

'Christ's law' over against 'Moses' law';[1] and had it not been in the context of the special problem facing the Galatians, he might not have put it so bluntly. Yet nevertheless, in the context, *anaplerōsate, fulfil,* takes on an even deeper meaning. The Galatians and their teachers had been eager to keep the law of Moses; but here was a higher way by which they might not keep it but fulfil it, by keeping the law of Christ.

3. The phrase *dokei tis einai,* means either *thinks he is something* or 'seems to be a somebody'. It reminds us of the threefold use of *hoi dokountes,* 'those who were of repute' in 2:2 and 6, describing the Jerusalem 'apostles'. Here the reference is probably entirely general; *dokei,* 'seems', is violently contrasted with *ōn,* 'actually being', and *tis,* 'a somebody', with *mēden,* 'a nothing'. A more crushing assessment could hardly be made of one who, at best, can have been nothing greater than a large frog in a small pond. But Paul is probably thinking more of the poor spiritual state of this Christian than of his real unimportance.

This is the sole use of the word *phrenapatā, deceives,* or 'hoodwinks', in the New Testament, although other similar words for 'deceive' abound. The cognate noun *phrenapatēs,* 'deceiver', occurs for instance in Titus 1:10 (again, of 'the circumcision party'). Perhaps Paul's choice of the word here is governed by the fact that such a person has been too clever. He has succeeded in taking himself in, although deceiving nobody else.

4. What Paul means by saying *let each one test his own work,* or 'scrutinize his own achievement', is not wholly clear. It depends upon whether we should translate strictly with the Galatian context in view, or whether we may use the presumably similar situations described in other Pauline letters as analogy. The NEB seems to translate in the first way with 'Each man should examine his own conduct for himself; then he can measure his achievement by comparing himself with himself and not with anyone else'. The second half of this translation perhaps deals a little too freely with the word *kauchēma, reason to boast,* or 'object

---

[1] Elsewhere, 'the law of Christ' can be phrased as 'the royal law' (Jas. 2:8), which is the law of love, to which all Christians are bound.

of boasting' (the usual meaning in Paul); but the first half is quite possible. In Paul's writings, however, *dokimazō*, *test*, and its cognates are often used of the scrutiny of God as applied to the work of the Christian evangelist or teacher; and this seems likely here too, especially in view of the general background of the letter. Paul may be therefore thinking at one and the same time of the *work* (NIV, 'actions') of the Judaizing teachers, which will not endure the divine scrutiny, and his own work, which will.[1] This would have the advantage of introducing as well the reason for this *kauchēma*, 'boasting'. The Galatians have been boasting in the 'work' of the Judaizers, shoddy though it was: Paul's boasting, as we shall see, is very different.

5. *Bear his own load*: Paul may mean that the Judaizers would do better not to 'count scalps', but to see where they stand themselves, in view of the coming judgment. For, on that day, each of us must be answerable for ourselves: as J. B. Phillips says, 'every man must "shoulder his own pack".' There is therefore no contradiction between this declaration of individual responsibility before the Lord and the general injunction given in verse 2, to *bear one another's burdens*, where the Greek word for *burdens* is *barē*, 'heavy loads'.

6. It is, as often, difficult to decide whether this is the final verse of this section or the opening verse of the next. As usual, it will be best to take it as a 'bridge verse', whichever group it is considered as falling under. The one who is *katēchoumenos ton logon*, *taught the word*, is clearly the one 'under Christian instruction': so it is quite legitimate to gloss the plain *word*, *logon*, as meaning 'the faith', with the NEB. Whether this implies as yet any highly developed catechetical system in the infant church is extremely doubtful.[2] We may therefore translate it in a general sense as describing the relation between 'teacher' and 'taught',

---

[1] 1 Cor. 3:12–15 is the classic passage dealing with God's judgment of the 'worker', on the basis of the lasting quality of the work done.

[2] Some see a technical sense in the use of *homologia*, 'confession', as well as of *katēcheō*, 'teach'. Scholars such as Hunter, Carrington and Cullmann are great names in favour of such a catechetical system: but, while by the days of the apostolic fathers we are probably justified in seeing such a formal system of teaching for converts, it is unlikely as early as the pages of the New Testament.

without assuming too set a pattern. If the one who led the Galatians astray had been a 'teaching elder' (1 Tim. 5:17), then this injunction would have special meaning; but it may of course be quite broad. When Paul says *koinōneito*, *share*, or 'have fellowship', it is a Christian euphemism for 'make a financial contribution'. To Paul, this phraseology is more than an exhibition of the duty of a pupil to a teacher; such Christian giving is the only fit expression of that *koinōnia*, 'sharing', 'fellowship', which marks the common life in Christ.[1] For the duty of supporting a teaching elder, see again 1 Tim. 5:17–18. Were the Galatians perhaps refusing financial support for an erring or even Judaizing pastor?

G. SOWING AND REAPING (6:7–10)

Paul now returns to the metaphor of 5:22, with its picture of 'fruit of the Spirit'. While *karpos*, as noted there, is more commonly used of 'fruits', it can also be used of 'grain', and the metaphor here is that of a grain harvest. This again is a very old biblical simile, used frequently in the Gospels, though principally with reference to the task of evangelism. The metaphor may have been suggested to Paul's mind by the mention of Christian giving in the verse immediately above. Paul sometimes sees 'charity' in terms of 'sowing'; 2 Corinthians 9:6 is a good example.

'Make no mistake about this: you cannot turn up your nose at God. A person will harvest exactly what he sows. I mean that the person who sows as his own nature bids him will reap a harvest of corruption from that nature; but the person who sows as the Spirit bids him will reap from that Spirit a harvest of life eternal. So let us never lose heart and give up doing what is good. When the right time comes we will reap a harvest[2] – if

[1] One of Paul's chief concerns among the Gentile churches was to encourage them to make just such a Christian gift to the church at Jerusalem (Rom. 15:27). It is however unlikely that there is any direct reference to this in the context.

[2] Betz is right in saying that this is an 'eschatological warning': all references to 'harvest' in Scripture seem to point to the last day. But Christian experience can be described as 'entered eschatology': the first fruits of this eschatological harvest of good or ill are reaped even in this life.

only we do not give up now, through weariness. Well then, whenever we have opportunity, let us work for the common good, especially for the good of those who are our blood-relatives in the Christian faith.'

7. The word *planāsthe* is one of the commonest words used in the New Testament for *deceived*. It does suggest, in its passive form here, that the Galatians have been 'led astray' in this matter by some from outside. The two clauses are sharply juxtaposed in what is really colloquial speech, not syntax: 'Do not be led astray – you cannot mock God.' The NEB translates *myktērizetai* as 'God is not to be fooled'. This gives the general sense, but if we can translate 'turn up the nose at', the original Greek meaning will be kept in English.[1]

This verse, both in view of its general rhythmic nature and in view of its constant recurrence in roughly similar forms, probably represents a proverb or folk saying.

8. When Paul says of a person *will from the flesh reap corruption*, he means more than that we must reap in this life the wild oats which we sow. To him, *phthoran, corruption*, is not only, or even primarily, moral decay. It is also that physical decay which inevitably awaits the human frame, whether this is described as *sōma*, 'body', or *sarx*, 'flesh', and reminds us of the fallen state of human nature (1 Cor. 15:42), only to be overcome by resurrection. Indeed, since to the Hebrew mind death was so closely connected with sin, it is doubtful if Paul would have made the sharp distinction between 'moral' and 'physical' corruption which we find so congenial to our modern thought-patterns. The physical death and decay in the world at large are to him only the consequences of the spiritual and moral death and decay that are present already. That is why in the New Testament the doctrine of resurrection is so closely connected with that of the new birth, which is itself life out of death (Eph. 2:5–6). Once the Christian is removed from the realm of sin, he or she is also removed from the realm of death, sin's grim ally. So here

---

[1] BAGD draws attention to the colloquial nature of this interesting word, with its vivid consequent imagery.

the opposite of *phthoran, corruption,* is *zoēn aiōnion, eternal life,* one of the many biblical expressions for salvation. To see 'salvation' in terms of 'life' is as old as the Old Testament (*e.g.* Ps. 16:11, to take a random example); but in the New Testament the concept takes on a new richness, as shown in an excellent article in BAGD, since 'life' is no longer merely, or even primarily, physical.

9-10. While Paul never wearies of telling folk that they cannot win God's favour by good deeds, he equally never wearies of telling them of their duty to *do good.* Twice in this short passage the idea recurs, with *to kalon poiountes, well-doing,* in verse 9, and *ergazōmetha to agathon, do good,* in verse 10. It is doubtful if there is any distinction intended between the two sets of words translated 'do' (*poiein* and *ergazesthai*) and translated 'good' (*kalos* and *agathos*); the only probable reason for the choice is a desire for variety. The NEB may be right, however, in translating the last phrase as 'Let us work for the good of all', rather than *do good to all men.* But this is only a minor point of interpretation, not affecting the main issue of the plain duty of a Christian.

There is only one danger that faces the 'spiritual farmer', for there is only one thing that can hinder this harvest. It is doubly expressed here as *mē enkakōmen, grow weary,* and *mē eklyomenoi, lose heart.* The word *enkakeō* is properly 'to despair'. 'Giving in to evil' or 'giving in to difficulty' seems to be the original idea; but it soon takes on the weaker sense 'to grow weary'. The word *eklyomai,* with very different etymology, finally comes to signify almost the same thing. It seems to mean originally the opposite of 'belt up'. As the Hebrew 'tightened his belt' to do work, so, when he 'loosened his belt', it meant he had abandoned effort. BAGD suggests 'become slack', which would preserve the metaphor in English; in the medical writers, when used in the passive, it means something like 'become limp', 'grow weary'. As describing a disheartened farmer the picture is very graphic; as describing the disheartened Galatians, who have found so much previous 'effort' vain, it is equally striking. The reason for the despair is the same in either case: it is the lack of observed results.

In due season: Paul plays in this context on the meaning of *kairos*, 'time'. In Greek, *chronos* is usually held to be 'time in the abstract', while *kairos* means 'the right time' for anything, and so both 'opportunity' and 'due season', although the distinction may not be absolute (so James Barr[1]). We shall therefore not reap our harvest until God's right time comes. Nevertheless, now is God's right time to do good to all, especially to our fellow Christians; we have a continual present opportunity to do good and we must not neglect it.

The words used here for 'fellow Christians', *oikeious tēs pisteōs*, *those who are of the household of faith*, mean in essence 'those who are related to us by a common faith', or 'those who are members of our household by faith'. This is a highly compressed way of saying that they, like us, have been born into God's family through their faith in Christ. Therefore, says Paul, they have a special family claim upon us,[2] although we are debtors to all men and women. Since *do good* almost certainly means 'give alms', there may possibly be an inner meaning here: Paul may be trying to promote his collection for the Jerusalem poor, though Betz thinks this a forced interpretation.

In spite of the views of Betz, there is much in the context to make this interpretation possible, if not actually to commend it. Paul has already expressed his concern for taking a collection to aid the 'poor saints'; if the atmosphere in Galatia is still too stormy to mention such a controversial matter directly, that need not surprise us. If this interpretation is correct, 'teacher' and 'taught' in verse 6 could then be Jewish Christian and Gentile Christian respectively. The 'sowing' and 'reaping' of verse 7 would then apply primarily to almsgiving, although Paul cannot resist giving the saying a moral 'twist' as he quotes it. It is obvious that the most faithful of Gentile Christians might 'lose heart' in doing such 'good works' when he saw how the Judaizers of the Jerusalem church rewarded them. Was Paul speaking as much to his own heart as to theirs? Were there times when even he almost 'lost heart' and wondered if he could ever

---

[1] See James Barr, *Semantics of Biblical Language* (London: SCM Press, 1983).

[2] This is not a popular viewpoint today, for to us it smacks of 'favouritism', but there is no question that it is biblical, and, in non-Christians lands, with impoverished Christian minorities, that it is very practical too. See Betz for this 'qualification' to the 'universalistic appeal'.

win over the stubborn, narrow-minded 'right wing' at Jerusalem by these deeds of love? We cannot say. All we know is that neither Paul nor the Gentile churches did in point of fact flag in this unselfish, loving service: the collection was taken, and brought to Jerusalem.

H. THE AUTOGRAPHED CONCLUSION (6:11–18)

The main part of the letter is now over. Paul takes the pen from his scribe (assuming that he has not written the whole letter himself) to write 'The Grace' in his own handwriting (cf. 2 Thes. 3:17), to assure them of the genuineness of the letter. But as he looks at the sprawling letters which he has written, he muses whimsically that they certainly make no fine outward show, and this becomes to him a parable of the whole of his life and ministry, and indeed of the Christian faith. As far as he is now concerned, there is nothing 'fine' in life but the cross of Christ; and he brushes the last vestiges of the Galatian quarrel from him in the knowledge of his own close relation to the crucified Messiah. On that note of peace the battle-scarred veteran ends the tortured letter.

'See how big letters I am using now that I am writing myself. It is those who want to "show off" and put a fine face on things who are trying to force you to get yourselves circumcised; it is only to avoid being persecuted for the sake of the cross of the Messiah. For not even those who do accept circumcision keep the law – and now they want you to get yourselves circumcised, so that they may have something to boast about in outward terms. May I never boast in anything at all, except in the cross of our Lord Jesus Christ, by which[1] the world has been crucified as far as I am concerned, and I as far as the world is concerned. To be circumcised means nothing; to be uncircumcised means nothing; the only thing that matters is to be created anew. Peace and mercy be upon all those who make this their rule of thumb, and upon God's Israel. In future let no-one bother me. I carry

[1] It is possible that in verse 14 we should follow the RSV margin with 'through whom', referring to Christ, rather than the text with 'by which'. The Greek is completely ambiguous.

round with me Christ's marks, stamped on my body. The grace of our Lord Jesus Christ be with your spirit, my fellow Christians. Amen.'

11. *Pēlikois grammasin, with what large letters,* probably refers to the sprawling untidy letters of one not a scribe by trade, and who was, perhaps, more used to writing Semitic letters than Greek. If the rest of the letter were 'professionally' written, then the contrast would be immediate. Most editors take *pēlikois* quite literally in the above sense of size. Other suggestions as to the meaning are given in BAGD under the words. It could refer to the style of writing, for instance. Those who see Paul's recurrent illness as ophthalmia will point to the large letters often written by the half-blind. But half-literate people also normally use large lettering, and nobody has yet accused Paul of falling into that category.[1]

12. The word *euprosōpēsai* (occurring only here in the New Testament) means *make a good showing.* For *en sarki, in the flesh,* to be taken closely with it, BAGD suggests 'before men'.[2] The Gentile would smile at the idea that circumcision could be considered by anyone to be *a good showing;* to him it was a barbarous and disfiguring custom, like the tattooing of a savage. But presumably Paul's point was that Judaism wanted 'ecclesiastical statistics'; so many circumcisions in a given year would certainly be something to boast about (Mt. 23:15). It is easy to smile at them: but 'baptismal statistics' can at times be just as dangerous if seen as a goal. Besides, Judaism honestly believed that mere outward circumcision achieved something; to them, it was the gateway to the covenant. Paul saw equally clearly that to accept circumcision meant that the whole 'sting' of the cross was gone. No longer was there an 'either/or' of law or grace: there was

[1]To suggest that Paul deliberately wrote this part of the letter in what we might call today 'capital letters', *i.e.* specially large letters, to draw attention to the importance of the content, would be to postulate a practice quite unknown in the ancient world. True, Cato wrote a history in 'large letters': but this was only to enable his young son to read it (Bruce). Of course, in one sense, all early manuscripts used 'capital letters', but they were of a standard size.

[2]'Outwardly' is probably a strong enough translation, unless we translate as 'in your physical condition', with reference to the physical results of circumcision.

only a 'both/and'. An eirenic age needs to remember Paul's explosion, and the theology that lay behind it. Of course, if Gentile Christians were to be circumcised, and if they kept the law, there would be no persecution, for there would be no rift with Judaism. Compare Peter's action in 2:12, 'fearing the circumcision party'.

13. The phrase *hoi peritemnomenoi, those who receive circumcision* (or perhaps just possibly 'the circumcisers' in the middle voice), is best taken to refer to the Jews whose habitual practice circumcision is, rather than the Gentiles who are now tempted to take the step. Admittedly this is a different sense from that of 5:3, where it must refer to the Gentile convert, but the different context here seems to warrant it. If it refers to Jews, it is employed in the sense of the more usual *peritomē*, 'circumcision', used as a synonym for the Jewish nation. This meaning would certainly suit Paul's rebuke. The Jews themselves have failed to keep the law (Rom. 2:21): why then try to involve Gentiles in the same failure by persuading them to accept the rite that binds to the law (Acts 15:10)?

Once again comes a play on words, this time on the verb *kauchāsthai*, to *glory*, or 'to boast'. The noun *kauchēma*, 'boast', Paul has used already in his warning in 6:4. Now he says that the only possible reason for the Hebrew proselytizing zeal (for which see Mt. 23:15) must be a desire to 'boast' in their outward condition of circumcision; for he has already shown that this outward rite cannot do any spiritual good.

14-15. As a counter to all this, we would expect Paul in reply to 'boast' in uncircumcision. But he cannot do that, for he, just as much as the Judaizers, is a circumcised Jew. Instead, he dismisses the whole subject at a far deeper level by saying that neither of these two outward states is now important, or even relevant. Paul could neither boast of being circumcised if he were a Jew, nor of being uncircumcised if he were a Gentile: the one thing that he can 'boast' about (or *glory . . . in*) is *the cross of our Lord Jesus Christ*, which has made all such distinctions meaningless. It completely breaks Paul's connection with the old 'outward world' (*the world has been crucified to me*), and gives both

Jew and Gentile alike a new perspective. The only thing that matters now is that Jew and Gentile alike should be *a new creation* in Christ, a new sort of humanity, with a new way of looking at everything, and therefore a new way of living.

The *kainē ktisis*, *new creation*, is an arresting thought of Paul's. Just as Genesis showed a creation marred and spoiled by sin, so later in prophet and apocalyptist arose the picture of a new universe, a new *ktisis* or *creation* of God (*e.g.* Is. 65:17, taken up by Rev. 21:1). Here, as 2 Corinthians 5:17, the word is probably to be translated 'creature' (as in AV), rather than 'creation'. That is to say, the reference is to the regenerating work of God in the individual Christian rather than to the total cosmic result thus secured.[1]

16. When Paul says *hosoi to kanoni touto stoichēsousin, all who walk by this rule*, or 'live their lives according to this principle', he is referring to the spiritual experience described immediately above. Such re-created people truly 'have the mind of Christ' (1 Cor. 2:16); they have God's way of looking at things. Paul has already used *stoicheō* of the Christian 'walk' in 5:25, where it is found in connection with *pneuma*, 'the Spirit'. With the dative as here, it usually has a more metaphorical sense, 'hold to', 'agree with', 'follow with', as in BAGD ('will hold to', in some MSS).

Upon the Israel of God: the second half of verse 16 poses a question of interpretation which hangs on the exact meaning of the introductory *kai*, 'and', left untranslated in the RSV. Does the world mean 'and', or 'that is to say' (NIV, 'even')? Obviously, the latter is the view of the RSV, but a strong case can be made for either view. If the world is to be translated 'and', then Paul's final prayer is for God's 'peace' and 'mercy' to be directed both towards those Gentiles who realize the unimportance of their uncircumcised state, and to Jews who likewise realize the unimportance of circumcision: the two groups are not identified. By so doing, these Israelites prove themselves to be *the Israel of God*, the 'righteous remnant'. To them, circumcision is a matter of the

---

[1] 2 Cor. 5:17 and Heb. 4:13 seem to have this sense of the word. Rom. 8:19–22, on the other hand, with its reference to the coming 'cosmic redemption' probably refers to the whole animate and inanimate creation ranged below humanity. BAGD quotes Cullmann to illustrate this view.

heart, not of the body (Rom. 2:29). These two groups would link closely with the two contrasting states described in verse 15 as *peritomē* and *akrobustia*, 'circumcision' and 'uncircumcision'. It would also be a fitting gesture of fellowship to 'orthodox' Jewish Christianity, lest they should think that they were included in Paul's attacks on the Judaizers. It would be a full recognition of the fact that Jew and Gentile alike are fellow-heirs of the grace of life; they have 'communion in the Messiah'; to quote a modern Jewish Christian. We may feel that it is an olive branch offered on the point of a bayonet; but it is a gesture of peace and reconciliation well fitting the closing verses of such a letter.

The other interpretation, adopted by the RSV, is bolder, but Paul is quite capable of it. This is to take *kai* as meaning 'even' (NIV), 'that is to say', or 'the equivalent of'. Linguistically, this is quite possible; the question must be solved theologically and exegetically. This would identify *all who walk by this rule* with *the Israel of God*. This is often put succinctly in the form of the statement 'the church is the new Israel'.[1] Put so bluntly, we may well wish to qualify the definition; but in broad outline, it seems to be what is propounded by Paul, and incontrovertible. In the first place, if *kai* does not mean 'even' but 'and', then Paul would be allowing two separate and distinct groups side by side in the kingdom of God; first, those who *walk by this rule* (the principle enunciated in verse 15), and, secondly, God's Israel. But those of old Israel who do not have this 'principle' are thereby automatically excluding themselves from the true Israel, God's Israel. This is the inevitable deduction from Paul's reasoning. In other words, while there is place for the believing Christian Jew in the kingdom of God, there is no place for the unbelieving, Jew or Gentile. Paul would go even further than that. He would say that the 'believing Jew' belongs to God's Israel, but that the Judaizer who does not *walk by this rule* does not belong. There cannot therefore be two groups within the church; there can only be one. That was why Paul was fighting at Antioch, for 'table fellowship' between Jewish and Gentile Christians.

Outside Galatians, in passages like Colossians 2:11 and (more

---

[1] See Betz for the various views on this point. However, it is not correct to say that, at the time, 'the borderline between Judaism and Christianity was not yet clearly drawn' (Betz).

strongly) Philippians 3:2–3, Paul seems to make the same identification even more clearly. But it is important to remember that,
while Paul says that Christians are the 'true Israel' in this sense,
he never says that Gentiles become Jews, nor that Jews become
Gentiles; that is an illegitimate deduction. What he does say is
that believing Jew and believing Gentile alike form the true
'Israel of God', the instrument of his purpose. It is interesting to
remember, in the context of verse 16, that 'Peace upon Israel' is
the great Old Testament blessing for God's people (Ps. 125:5), as
well as being one of the 'eighteen benedictions' of the early
Hebrew liturgy.

17. The phase *kopous parechetō*, *trouble me*, or 'cause me trouble'
(NIV), is very common in the colloquial Greek of the papyri. In all
such instances *kopous* has a bad sense, meaning 'trouble',
'annoyance', 'bother'. But Paul has used the corresponding verb
kopiaō already in 4:11 in the sense of 'labour', 'take pains'; there
the sense is good. Indeed, in several of his letters Paul uses this
word of the 'toil' characteristic of, and inseparable from, the life
of the true pastor and missionary. From such hard work, Paul
never asks to be freed; he has endured it gladly for this very
Galatian church, and his only fear is that it may have all been in
vain. What he does want to avoid is the endless harrying of the
Judaizers, with their stress on circumcision, their endless insistence on this sort of 'stigmata ', *marks* or 'signs', borne *en tō*
sōmati, *on my body*, or perhaps 'outwardly'.[1] To end all this
persecution once and for all, he will show the Judaizers that he
too bears 'distinguishing marks', but they are those that show
him to belong to Jesus Christ, not to Judaism. It may be that the
anxious queries of the wavering Galatians are also in his mind:
do they need to bear an outward sign, like circumcision, on their
bodies, to be certain of salvation? He wants to set their hearts at
rest, so that they too may be able to give a similar reply when
they are challenged by the Judaizers. The Galatian converts, like
Paul, bear *the marks of Jesus* already.

[1] Paul himself seems clearly to be thinking of these 'marks' as in opposition to circumcision, the main outward 'mark' of Judaism. For the wider possible meaning of 'stigmata',
see the Commentary on pp. 238f.

We have already seen the various uses of *bastazō* in this letter.[1] It always means 'to shoulder', 'to carry', with the idea that the object so moved is bulky or heavy. Therefore, whatever *the marks of Jesus* are, they are not something to be borne easily or lightly. Further, Paul bears them *en sōmati*, 'bodily', or 'outwardly'; therefore he cannot be referring simply to some spiritual state known only to himself.

But the heart of the problem lies in the question, What is the actual meaning of *ta stigmata tou Iēsou, the marks of Jesus*? Later Christian theology, somewhat naively, interpreted this as meaning that visible marks appeared on Paul's hands, feet, and side, corresponding to Christ's wounds, so close was his identification with his Lord. The experience of certain Christian mystics has been quoted as parallel. Without examining the question of whether such physical manifestations have actually occurred in later days, and without inquiring into the means by which they may have been produced (an enquiry which would seem to belong to the realm of abnormal religious psychology), we may safely say that such a literalistic interpretation would run counter to all Paul's thought.

The word *stigmata*, in non-biblical Greek, is used to describe the 'marks', or 'brands', that distinguish a slave as belonging to a particular master, rather as cattle or sheep are 'branded' today. Such 'brands' are often mentioned in Hellenistic 'placards' announcing the escape of runaway slaves, and many such documents have survived among the papyri. This is the most obvious meaning; and while the Jews do not seem to have had a similar custom in Old Testament days, the practice of 'ear marking' a voluntary slave is a close parallel (Ex. 21:6). The word *stigmata* is also freely used of 'ritual cicatrices' such as were common to many ancient and modern religions of more 'primitive' type. BAGD suggests 'tattooing' as a modern parallel. If Paul is using the word in this sense, then he is deliberately classifying Jewish circumcision with these other ritual gashes and marks. It is daring, but 5:12 shows that Paul was perfectly capable of such an identification. We could then paraphrase it: 'You want me to bear ritual cuts and gashes, do you? I do bear

---

[1]See the Commentary on 5:10 and 6:2 for the various nuances of this word *bastazo*.

such scars already, but they are those that mark me out as Christ's man.'

So much for the interpretation, which is clearly also that of the NEB, 'I bear the marks of Jesus branded on my body'. But what are these brands? Almost certainly, since they are outwardly visible (the wording *en tō sōmati, on my body*, involving this conclusion), they must be some of the scars borne by Paul as a result of his suffering for Christ's sake. Those who favour a South Galatian destination for the letter can point to the stoning at Lystra as a very relevant example (Acts 14:19), but 2 Corinthians 11 shows us many other experiences of Paul which must have left literal 'scars'. Stoning and flogging, whether by the scourge of the synagogue beadles, or the dreaded Roman lash, or the rods of Roman lictors, would leave unmistakable scars, reminders of suffering gladly endured for Christ's sake, that marked out their bearer as Christ's servant. Most of the relevant literature illustrating this possibility is quoted at the end of the excellent article in BAGD.

18. On this note of peace the letter will end, but, as his closing message, Paul adds, as often, 'The Grace', in a longer or shorter form. We are more familiar with the prayer in the fuller and longer form of 2 Corinthians 13:14, 'The grace of the Lord Jesus Christ and the love of God and the fellowship of the Holy Spirit be with you all.' This rich trinitarian formula is doubtless Paul's final development of the simple prayer that we have here, *The grace of our Lord Jesus Christ be with your spirit, brethren (i.e. fellow Christians*).[1] Yet we cannot say that the shorter form of the prayer is less rich theologically, though its richness may be less fully expressed. Rightly understood, all the theology of the trinitarian 'Grace' is here too,[2] for Christ is here, and central, as he must be in all expressions of the Christian faith.

[1] Betz points out the particular appropriateness of the use of this last word 'brethren' in Galatians, after all the heat of controversy. It is used in no other Pauline benediction.

[2] A similar variety and even amplification, if not development, in baptismal formulae may be traced within the Scriptures. The first disciples were baptized simply 'in the name of the Lord Jesus' (Acts 8:16). That was all that was necessary for Jews, who already had a belief in the one God, and who were already looking for the gift of the Spirit. Mt. 28:19 gives the full later 'trinitarian formula', doubtless very necessary in baptizing *ta ethnē*, 'the Gentiles', who had neither such knowledge of the one God nor expectations of the Spirit.

He is *Jesus*, the name corresponding to the 'Joshua' of the Old Testament, the 'saviour' of God's people (for so the name can be translated), who will lead them into the inheritance promised by God (Jos. 1:6). More, he is the *Christ*, the Messiah, the 'chosen one' of God's purpose, the fulfilment of all the hopes and aspirations of the Old Testament. His nature is fully expressed as *charis, grace* – the free undeserved love of God showered on humankind. Christ is grace personified; but he is more than that, for he is the very grace of God become incarnate. That is why we cannot speak of 'the grace of the Lord Jesus Christ' without at the same time thinking of 'the love of God', whether we state it explicitly in so many words or not. For the Christian, this link between Christ and God is safeguarded in Paul's shorter formula by calling Jesus *Lord*, the great title of God in Old Testament times. More, in many ancient witnesses, Christ is not only described at this point as *kyriou*, 'Lord', but *kyriou hēmōn*, 'our Lord'; here is the sense of 'belongingness' that we have found to be characteristic of all Pauline thought. Lastly, this blessing is to be *meta tou pneumatos hymōn, with your spirit*. To the Christian, in spite of the possibility of a purely general meaning, this will also here recall the Holy Spirit, the gift of the risen Christ, the one who is the common bond of our common life in Christ, by whom alone we are newborn as *adelphoi, brethren* or 'womb brothers and sisters' in Christ. To this prayer, Paul, with full meaning, sets his *Amen*,[1] common at the end of Hebrew blessings and prayers, from which it has passed into Christian usage (1 Cor. 14:16). But it is really an *Amen* to the uniqueness of Christ and the sufficiency of his cross for salvation, so that it is also an *Amen* to the whole letter, and indeed to Paul's whole theological position, since God himself has already set his *Amen* to Christ (2 Cor. 1:20).

---

[1]Betz, however, thinks that this (as, he thinks, in Romans, 1 Corinthians, *etc.*) was not from the hand of Paul but was added by the local church who received the letter, and was spoken by the congregation in response to it. In that case, the letter would have succeeded in its objective: the Galatians would have agreed and endorsed it whole-heartedly, and shown it in this way.